T0195925

GOD, DARWIN AND THE PROBLEM OF EVIL

James J. Garber

   www.trafford.com
North America & international
toll-free: 1 888 232 4444 (USA & Canada)
fax: 812 355 4082

"I wish to express my deep thanks to my wife, Rachel. for all the help she provided in reviewing and editing this book. I couldn't have done it without her.

Table of Contents

Preface

This book is the natural outgrowth of an earlier book, *Problem Gods: In Search of a Meaningful Deity*. Born and raised Catholic, attending sixteen years of Catholic schooling, I had accepted virtually all the tenets of the Roman Catholic Church as these doctrines had evolved over the centuries. During my formative years, it never occurred to me that any of these tenets needed to be questioned.

As a young boy my father, who was Jewish till the day he died, and I had our one and only theological discussion. We had a dog named, Skipper. He was prone to running away and one day we found him dead, having been struck by a car. My father was very attached to Skipper. I was too, but less so than my father and I knew from my Catholic indoctrination that only humans went to Heaven (or Hell) after dying. Animals didn't have an afterlife. After all I was an expert on theology for I had been a catechetical contestant in eight grade coming second to a young man who was to become a priest a few years later. At any rate, my father and I discussed the issue of canine immortality coming in short order to a theological deadlock; neither of us giving an inch. I maintained all fauna failed to have a life after death and my father maintaining an "obviously" heretical view.

When I was a senior in high school I must have read something on evolution and in due course I wrote a paper on this topic not realizing it was a concept not accepted by the Church hierarchy. Sister Henrita made only one comment the heretical aspect of evolution. Darwin's *The Origin of Species* had been around for a hundred years but our understanding of DNA was in its infancy. The year was 1953 and Watson and Crick were to publish their work on the structure of DNA that year which in time would give the world a much better understanding of how evolution works. So Sister Henrita gave me a decent grade on my paper and my theological life went on. The year incidentally was 1953 shortly before Watson and Crick were to become famous.

As a freshman in college, the next fall (still 1953), taking zoology we were required to read Gaylord Simpson's *The Meaning of Evolution* (published in 1949). This book made perfect sense and I thought very little about any controversy the topic created (no pun intended). The biblical (Gen. 1 & 2) version of creation just did not seem to be credible. It was too simple an explanation for all that has happened to Earth over the past 4.6 billion years. Making each biblical day much, much longer than 24 hours did make much sense. God, if so omniscient and could have easily inspired the Old Testament writers to scribble down at least some thousands or million of years instead of 'days'. God in its magnificence and goodness should have made things much clearer so as not to confuse so many people for so many centuries. None of the priests we had for religion said anything about evolution and our zoology professor who had a PhD seemed honest enough.

Over the years my wife, Rachel, our children and I went to church regularly. Some sermons were better than others. We discussed theology very little until the 'pill' came on the seen. Rachel and I belonged to the Christian Family Movement and met every other Sunday evening. We were all in the childbearing age and very often our discussion centered on birth control. Some of the couples, in time, left the Church over this issue. We never did but over the years Church dogma seemed less and less relevant.

Sometime in the 1970's I started reading Church history. This was a major turning point. My eyes were opened to the checkered moral, political and financial history of the Church. I was physician to Guest House, which was a residential treatment center for troubled priests most of whom were alcoholic though we did have several pedophiles early on. Then in 1975 our pastor, Father Thomas Adamson, was sent to Catholic University for one year and then transferred to the St.

Paul Archdioceses. Within a short time he was actively abusing young men, was defrocked in 1985. In 1988, he was convicted in civil court and the victims given a multi-million dollar settlement. He has never been criminally charged.

Too many things were going wrong with the Church. As Luther had been disenchanted after a visit to Rome, we also began asking questions. After completing a MA in Theology my first theology book, noted above, was published. During the theology program it occurred to me that the theistic God of Catholicism and the other Western religions was no longer fulfilling the need of our modern culture. Times and culture have changed. Science has forced a revision of the idea of God. IT had to be bigger and better than the God of Antiquity and the middle Ages. As they say, "Times are a changing" and how we view God must change as well. Everything evolves and our concept of God is evolving as well.

This book is not only about an evolving concept of God, but also of the world and our view of evil.

The cover shows an angle holding a chain. Angels are the helpers of God, and the chain represents the many ways in which we humans are bound down by many chains foisted upon us by God—the many evils that limit our lives and happiness.

Introduction

One morning we woke to the news that a fifteen year old high school boy had had axed his mother, father and two pre-teenage siblings to death. He then went to school with his normally blonde hair dyed black. Other than the black hair no other aberrant changes were evident. He had one other older bother who had left a few years before. His parents were considered to be "good Catholics" and he attended a local Catholic high school. Our son took one class with him and noted some minimal personality features that set him apart from the "usual' high school kid. This teenage axe killer was tried as an adult and is in prison today and will be imprisoned for the rest of his life. We have heard he has been treated for depression.

A few weeks later a young woman was shot to death by her former boy friend. She had, for reasons know only to her, had rejected him when he joined the army. Just recently a college student was trying to comfort a boyfriend who apparently was depressed and suicidal. For reason that may never be known he shot her and then himself.

There was a sixteen-year-old teen that was found to have some unusual yellow streaks on his retinae while at the ophthalmologist for a routine eye exam. No specific diagnosis was made. In due course, this teen became a physician. Several years later it was noted on an eye check that his visual acuity was 20/25. After internship and two years in the Navy he took an internal medicine residency and was offered a position on staff. After less than a year as an associate consultant, further evaluation of his eyes, a diagnosis of Stargardt's disease was made. This is an inherited autosomal recessive type of macular degeneration. He was told he would never become totally blind but the visual acuity would continue to diminish over the years. The clinic he was working at rescinded the staff appointment and he had some difficulty finding another position though finally did and practiced for forty years and is still working part time. He's had a fulfilling practice and a good life in spite of his visual handicap. He now legally blind. His beloved wife drives him wherever he needs or wants to go and takes care of most of his paperwork. His children and grandchildren tease him about his vision occasionally (well maybe more than occasionally)!

As you may have guessed, this is my personal story. This book is in part about the 'evil' that changed the course of my life as a physician, husband and father. But this 'evil' has not been all bad, by any means. Why did God afflict me with this evil? My vision has certainly impacted and continues to impact my life and the problem has forced me to adapt to my environment in many ways and definitely challenges me on a daily basis. In a very real way my eyes have been the stimulus for this book and my eyes have helped me to better understand God and the Problem of Evil.

Rochester is a very nice town. It is the home of the Mayo Clinic and has an IBM plant. There are doctors and engineers everywhere and it has a very low homicide and crime rate generally. Besides a tornado that hit in 1864 and a flood in 1878 not much evil has occurred here. It's a pretty comfortable place—maybe a little too comfortable.

When bad things happen to good people as Rabbi Kushner phrases it,[1] we start wondering why. It seems that today we hear of 'bad' happening almost ever day. There have been the shootings in Aurora, Colo., New Town, Conn, bombings in Boston, Mass., Oklahoma City, Jerusalem, Egypt, London, India and the many US outposts abroad. The memory of serin gas attacks in Tokyo, Syria; genocide in Rwanda along with the hundreds of suicide bombing all linger painfully in our memories. And of course, nearly everyone shutters at Hitler's Jewish holocaust. Stalin is said to have murdered 20,000,000 Russians during his reign. We in America have been touched and still are by 9/11. The list of evils in the world seems endless.

And though these recent and present physically and emotionally painful sores seem to gnaw away at our global awareness of evil, we need only reflect upon the relatively recent history of humankind to stir up lingering emotional lesions left by human horrors that have plagued us since *Homo sapiens* began walking upon this Earth. *Homo sapiens* is Latin for "wise person". Reflecting on these often humanly created horrors, we seem not so wise.

---

[1]   Kirshne, L., 2007, *When Bad Things Happen to Good People*, Kindle e-book.

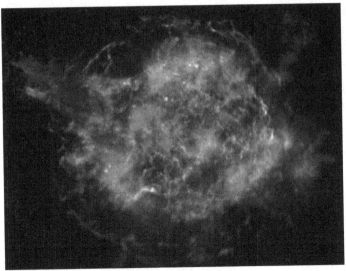

Figure 1. An early exploding supernova which Initiates the evolution of the ninety-two elements that make life possible on Earth.

Chapter 1

The Ever-Evolving Universe.

Undoubtedly *Homo sapiens* has faced evils from the dawn of human history, some 200,000 to 160,000 years ago. If we reach back to the origin of the Solar System 4.6 billion years ago, it is evident that the Earth has not always been a congenial place to live for humans or any beasts or blossoms. In the beginning, Earth was but a molten mass of primordial mud or more precisely basalt that flowed out thousands of volcanoes active at the time. Io, the largest of Jupiter's moons, has many volcanoes even today much as Earth did long ago. As the volcanic lava cooled it formed basalt and eventually the basalt became metamorphic rock such as quartzite and feldspar. These are made up of sodium, potassium, calcium, aluminum, silicon and oxygen. There was also ample iron and nickel in the Earth's crust. All the 'terrestrial' planets in our solar system, the four closest to the Sun i.e. Mercury, Venus, Earth and Mars, have a similar mineral content. The outer four planets, Jupiter,

Saturn, Uranus and Neptune have a rocky nucleus but are mostly composed of hydrogen and helium. Jupiter, if it had been a bit larger, would have been another sun.

The atmosphere of Earth initially was composed of mostly carbon dioxide and other noxious gases such as methane, ammonium, sulfur oxide along with some water. This atmosphere would have been lethal for humans. The atmosphere took about 400 million years to form and about a billion years or more to become 20% oxygen. The early unicellular organisms lived off of carbon dioxide (CO_2). For a long time Earth was not a very hospitable place.

About 3.5 billion years ago things began to change. Life slowly emerged. At first life forms were primitive one-cell organisms without a nucleus the so-called prokaryotes. What DNA they possessed floated around in the cytoplasm (cell fluid) unbounded by a nuclear membrane. In time eukaryotes evolved with their DNA bundled in a nucleus. These microscopic 'critters' called Archaea may have first formed around volcanic openings at the bottom of the oceans where temperatures around volcanic vents are above the boiling point (over 100º Celsius i.e. 212º Fahrenheit). These are called thermophiles (heat loving) and are still found at the bottom of the oceans.

Our Sun was a second-generation sun. The first suns (stars) that formed after the Big Bang were composed of hydrogen and helium. These two elements are gases and remain so until a first-generation sun runs out of most of its hydrogen and implodes. Without the atomic energy supplied by massive atomic hydrogen bombs that explode repetitively in any sun, the sun's formidable gravity will cause it to collapse into itself. This is what happens when a sun runs out of fuel i.e. hydrogen. A sun may 'live' for millions of years but eventually it flames out, forms a supernova (if massive enough) and collapses. This takes about twenty minutes to happen. In this process the gravitational energy forces the hydrogen and helium atoms to collide with each other, with tremendous force, resulting in the formation of larger elements such as lithium, carbon, nitrogen, oxygen, sodium, potassium, calcium and other heavier elements that are the constituents of living organisms of the sort we know on Earth. We are literally made of stardust.

Our Universe is 13.7 billion years old and the first generation star that imploded 4.6 billion years ago was the mother of our Sun and one might say the grandmother of our Earth. Thus, after life began to blossom, organisms evolved that relished CO_2. They loved it so much that the cyanobacteria, as they are called today, began gobbling up the carbon dioxide (CO_2) atmosphere so rapidly that in the space of a few million years the CO_2 was largely gone, leaving in its wake an atmosphere with 20% oxygen and under 2% CO_2. These cyanobacteria 'inhaled' CO_2 and 'breathed out' O_2. It took about billion years of earthly evolution to create the first life forms—a long, complex and very energetic process that finally provided a suitably friendly place for humans to breath their first healthy breath. Today all chloroform containing plants continue the same job of replenishing O_2 just as the Cyanobacteria did billions of years ago.

Evolution began with the Big Bang but it has continued ever since. Without this Darwinian process you and I wouldn't be here today. We would still be bacteria. It has taken a long time to go from unicellular to multicellular life forms and eventually to Homo sapiens. Table 1 shows this gradual evolutionary sequence.

Table 1: Geological Time Table. Most Recent Period at top.[2]

Eon	Era	Period	Extent, Million Years Ago
Phanerozoic	Cenozoic	Quaternary (Pleistocene/ Holocene)	2.588 - 0
		Neogene (Miocene/Pliocene)	23.03 - 2.588
		Paleogene (Paleocene/ Eocene/Oligocene)	66.0 - 23.03
	Mesozoic	Cretaceous	145.5 - 66.0
		Jurassic	201.3 - 145.0
		Triassic	252.17 - 201.3
	Paleozoic	Permian	298.9 - 252.17
		Carboniferous (Mississippian/ Pennsylvanian)	358.9 - 298.9
		Devonian	419.2 - 358.9
		Silurian	443.4 - 419.2
		Ordovician	485.4 - 443.4
		Cambrian	541.0 - 485.4
Proterozoic	Neoproterozoic	Ediacaran	635.0 - 541.0
		Cryogenian	850 - 635
		Tonian	1000 - 850
	Mesoproterozoic	Stenian	1200 - 1000
		Ectasian	1400 - 1200
		Calymmian	1600 - 1400
	Paleoproterozoic	Statherian	1800 - 1600
		Orosirian	2050 - 1800
		Rhyacian	2300 - 2050

In its 4.6 billion years circling the Sun, the Earth has been home to an immense number of species including the five kingdoms of life: animals, plants, fungi, eukaryotes and prokaryotes.

-3.6 billion years ago, simple cells (prokaryotes) first emerged

-3.4 billion years ago cyanobacteria began performing photosynthesis.

-2 billion years, complex cells (eukaryotes) evolved

-1 billion years, multicellular life developed.

-600 million years, simple animals appeared.

---

2   Wikipedia, Geological Periods.

-550 million years, bilaterians, animals with a front and a back began.
-500 million years, there were fish and proto-amphibians.
-475 million years, land plants.
-400 million years, insects and seed plants
-360 million years, amphibians.
-300 million years, reptiles.
-200 million years, mammals.
-150 million years, birds;
-130 million years, flowers.
-60 million years, the primates.
-20 million years, the family Hominidae (great apes).
-2.5 million years, the genus Homo (human predecessors; bipedal walkers).
-200,000 years, anatomically modern humans.

There have been adverse conditions and events throughout Earth's history. Up to twenty massive extinctions have occurred over the last 540 million years. The largest of these was some 250 million years ago. This was the Permian–Triassic (P–Tr) extinction event, referred to as the Great Dying. This event was at the boundary between the Permian and Triassic geologic periods, which included the Paleozoic and Mesozoic eras. Up to 96% of all marine species and 70% of terrestrial vertebrate species became extinct. It is the only known mass extinction of insects. Some 57% of all families and 83% of all genera became extinct. Because so much biodiversity was lost, the recovery of life on Earth took up to 10 million years.

The best-known extinction period was the Cretaceous–Paleogene (K–Pg) extinction event that occurred 64 million years ago during which three-quarters of plant and animal species on Earth were lost. This included all non-avian dinosaurs and extended over a relatively short period of time geologically speaking. This extinction is thought to have been triggered by an asteroid or meteorite strike on the Yucatan peninsula ([Chicxulub). The impact was so powerful that the dust raised caused an extended period of atmospheric diming of the Sun's rays. This led to cooling of the Earth with loss of vegetation necessary to maintain many life forms. The avian dinosaurs are warm-blooded and were able to survive and now are the birds that fill our skies. Many species of smaller mammals survived because they were also warm blooded and required less food to survive. The demise of the dinosaurs provided an ecological niche in which mammals could flourish and was the beginning of the rise of mammalian species. A number of terrestrial plants, including some ferns, were lost.

Among the species that disappeared were a number of crustaceans and corals. Turtles and lizards fared better. Reptiles other than the non-avian dinosaurs also made it through this period without any major extinctions. Crocodiles (*Crocodylus porosus*) have, of course, persisted over these several millions of years. Pterosaurs were flying reptiles that fell victim to the chilly K–Pg climate change. Many of these species had a wingspan of a few inches but the now extinct *Hatzegopteryx* was the largest flying animal known to science. Although no complete fossil of this 'bird' has been discovered, what few fossils paleontologists have discovered indicate the creature had a wingspan of at least ten meters. These were monstrous flying machines now long gone replaced by warm-blooded creatures better able to adapt to an ever-changing environment. Mammals with insulating fur and better nurturing instincts soon replaced the cold-blooded reptiles that bore but did not bother to rear their offspring. The early miniscule mammal over the next several millions of years

Comparative table of *Homo* species[3]

Species	Temporal range Mya	Habitat	Adult height	Adult mass	Cranial capacity (cm³)	Fossil record	Discovery / publication of name
H. habilis	2.1 – 1.5[37]	Africa	150 cm (4 ft 11 in)	33–55 kg (73–121 lb.)	510–660	Many	1960/1964
H. erectus	1.9 – 0.07[38]	Africa, Eurasia (Java, China, India, Caucasus)	180 cm (5 ft. 11 in)	60 kg (130 lbs.)	850 (early) – 1,100 (late)	Many[39]	1891/1892
H. rudolfensis membership in *Homo* uncertain	1.9	Kenya			700	2 sites	1972/1986
H. gautengensis also classified as H. habilis	1.9 – 0.6	South Africa	100 cm (3 ft. 3 in)			3 individuals[40]	2010/2010
H. ergaster also classified as H. erectus	1.8 – 1.3[41]	Eastern and Southern Africa			700–850	Many	1975
H. antecessor also classified as H. heidelbergensis	1.2 – 0.8	Spain	175 cm (5 ft 9 in)	90 kg (200 lb.)	1,000	2 sites	1997
H. cepranensis a single fossil, possibly H. erectus	0.9 – 0.35	Italy			1,000	1 skull cap	1994/2003
H. heidelbergensis	0.6 – 0.35[42]	Europe, Africa, China	180 cm (5 ft. 11 in)	90 kg (200 lb.)	1,100–1,400	Many	1908
H. neanderthalensis possibly a subspecies of H. sapiens	0.35 – 0.04[43]	Europe, Western Asia	170 cm (5 ft. 7 in)	55–70 kg (121–154 lb.) (heavily built)	1,200–1,900	Many	(1829)/1864

---

3   Homo species, Wikipedia.

7

H. rhodesiensis also classified as H. heidelbergensis	0.3 – 0.12	Zambia			1,300	Very few	1921
H. tsaichangensis possibly H. erectus	0.25 – 0.2	Taiwan				1 individual	pre-2008/2015
H. sapiens (modern humans)	0.2[44] – present	Worldwide	150 - 190 cm (4 ft. 7 in - 6 ft. 3 in)	50-100 kg (110–220 lb.)	950–1,800	(extant)	–/1758
H. floresiensis classification uncertain	0.10 – 0.012	Indonesia	100 cm (3 ft. 3 in)	25 kg (55 lbs.)	400	7 individuals	2003/2004
Denisova hominin possible H. sapiens subspecies or hybrid	0.04	Russia				1 site	2010
Red Deer Cave people possible H. sapiens subspecies or hybrid	0.0145-0.0115	China				Very few	2012

The primates (apes and humans) entered the evolutionary sequence around 22 million years ago. Gorillas, chimpanzees and bonobos came on the scene about 8 to 4 million years ago. Australopithicines followed the great apes with the earliest Homo genera including Homo neanderthalensis, Homo habilis and Homo erectus evolving about three to four million years ago.

Figure 2. Representation of Homo erectus female[4]
Attribution: By reconstruction by John Gurche; photographed by Tim Evanson [CC BY-SA 2.0 (http://creativecommons. org/licenses/by-sa/2.0)], via Wikimedia Commons

Precursors of *Homo sapiens*

Hominins were bipedal (walked on two feet) but not the first to walk on two feet. The australopithecines were the immediate forerunners of the Homo species that evolved into modern humans. The study of human evolution involves many scientific disciplines, including physical anthropology, primatology, archaeology, ethology, linguistics, evolutionary psychology, embryology and genetics.as we will see in later.

Genetic studies show that primates diverged from other mammals about 85 million years ago in the late Cretaceous period, and the earliest primate fossils appear

---

[4]   Smithsonian museum website.

in the Paleocene, around 55 million years ago. The family Hominidae diverged from the Gibbon family 15-20 million years ago, and one million years later, the orangutans came along. Bipedalism is the primary characteristic of the Hominins and the earliest bipedal Hominins were the *Sahelanthropus, Orrorin* and *Ardipithecus* (all extinct species). The gorilla and chimpanzee diverged from the hominids about 4-6 million years ago and either Sahelanthropus or Orrorin may be our last shared ancestors with these extant apes. The early bipedal species eventually evolved into the australopithecines and later the Homo species.

The earliest documented members of the genus *Homo* are *H. habilis*. These appeared around 2.3 million years ago. They are the earliest species to use stone tools. The brains of these early hominins were about the same size as that of a chimpanzee. During the next million years a process of encephalization (brain enlargement and specialization) began, and with the arrival of *Homo erectus* in the fossil record, cranial capacity had doubled to 850 cm^3. *Homo erectus* were the first of the hominins to leave Africa, and these species spread through Africa, Asia, and Europe between 1.8 and 1.3 million years ago. It is believed that these species were the first to use fire and complex tools (other than hand axes and scraping rocks). According to the Recent African ancestry theory, modern humans evolved in Africa possibly from Homo heidelbergehnsis Homo rhodesiensis or Homo antecessor and then migrated out of Africa some 50,000 to 100,000 years ago, replacing local populations of *Homo erectus, Homo denisova, Homo floresiensis* and *Homo neanderthalensis*.

Archaic *Homo sapiens*, the forerunner of anatomically modern humans, evolved between 400,000 and 250,000 years ago. Recent DNA evidence suggests that several haplotypes of Neanderthal origin are present among all non-African populations, and Neanderthals and other hominids, such as Denisova hominin may have contributed up to 6% of their genome to present-day humans, suggestive of a limited inter-breeding between these species.[5] Anatomically modern humans evolved from Archaic *Homo sapiens* in the Middle Paleolithic, about 200,000 years ago. The transition to behavioral modernity with the development of symbolic culture, language, and specialized lithic technology happened around 50,000 years ago according to many anthropologists although some suggest a gradual change in behavior over a longer time span.

Evolution of Homo sapiens, however, continues. We first made clothes around 72,000 years ago. Language developed 55,000 years ago about the time we slowly moved out of Africa making our way to the Middle East, India, China, Siberia, Australia and about 20,000 BCE to the Americas. We began cave art 45,000 BCE in Europe and Africa. Farming, and the domestication of animals developed about 7,000 BCE and the written word 4,000 BCE. Printing was developed early in China and then in Europe just 650 years ago in 1450 CE. And, of course, now we have electricity, the telephone, computers, and let us not forget IPods, IPads, the Kindle and Smart Phones! As it is said, the only constant is change and this is most evident in Darwinian evolution.

The Evolution of Religion and the Idea of God

Over the centuries there have been numerous adverse (evil) events but in spite of these, humankind has gradually emerged from the depths of prehistory to become an increasingly more sophisticated species. During our infancy as a species, humans lived in clans as small as twenty-five men, women and children. We were hunters and gathers. The men hunted and the women gathered fruits, nuts and grains along with having and caring for

---

[5] http://www.livescience.com/48399-when-neanderthals-humans-first-interbred.html

their children. Life was insecure. Drought, famine and territorial battles were common. The world was largely an unknown, frightening place. We did not know our origins or destiny. A primitive god arose in our consciousness to help explain the ways and woes of the world. The early religions were animistic; that is, most every worldly beings including animals, plants and even the wind, rain and other natural phenomena were infused with a soul that explained their behaviors.[6,7] The first gods were the Sun, Moon and seas. They held power over the winds, weather and waters. Hurricanes, earthquakes and epidemics were sent by the gods for idolatrous ideas counter to the will of the gods. The gods were ever vigilant and all knowing, always aware of offenses against them by mischievous mortals.

In time, these nature-based gods became more like humans (anthropomorphic) though Ra, the Egyptian supreme deity remained the Sun until Christianity and Islam spread throughout the Middle East. The Romans inherited this anthropomorphic theological system from the Greeks who in turn had borrowed the Sumerian, Babylonian and Assyrian deities that had been worshiped by these Mesopotamian cultures for centuries. The gods became much like we humans only bigger, stronger and frequently more vindictive, angry, jealous and lustful. The gods sometimes ornery, offensive outbursts helped explain the evil in the world. We have always needed reasons for the workings of the world around us and the evilness o f these gods helped us understand why we faced by so many continual evils.

The Jews had also been a polytheistic religion until the Babylonian Captivity (c. 582-c. 538). On returning to Jerusalem and their former homelands the Jews appear to have espoused a monotheistic theology with

---

6   Sir Edward Burnett Tylor, 2013, *Primitive culture: researches into the Development of Mythology, Philosophy, Religion, Language, art, and Custom*, Kindle e-book.

7   Ibid.

Yahweh as their one and only deity. As stated in the Ten Commandments:

1. I am the Lord your God who brought you out of slavery in Egypt.
2. You shall have no other gods but me.

The God of the Jewish Bible (Christian Old Testament) retained many of the vindictive, jealous, angry and even murderous traits of the pagan polytheistic gods. During the early Christian period, Marcion of Sinope (c. 80-c.160) was a bishop who rejected this anthropomorphic God of the Old Testament and, as a consequence, was excommunicated by the Roman Christian Church. He subsequently returned to Asia Minor and his bishopric. As the proto-Catholic Church evolved so did its God. Christ was not immediately recognized as equal in all respects to the Father. Although there are numerous New Testament citations used to support Christ's divinity, there are many scriptural scholars who claim that the notion of the Trinity and Christ as divine took time to become a tenet accepted by the early Church. Many Church Fathers such as Tertullian, Origen and Irenaeus wrote about the divinity of Christ. However, in the Fourth Century a tug-of-war developed between Arius (c. 256–336 CE) who was a presbyter in Alexandria, Egypt and Athanasius (296–373 CE) who was also a cleric in Alexandria. Arius was in a sense the first Unitarian, claiming that Christ was not co-equal with God the Father having been created after the Father and by the Father. As such, Christ was not consubstantial with the Father and, thus, not of the same nature or substance as the Father (homoousios). One way of phrasing this was that he was not the same as the Father but rather 'like' or 'similar' to the Father (homoiousios)[8]. This issue was first debated at the Nicaea Council in 325 CE. The Emperor Constantine

---

[8] The difference between *homoousios* and *homoiousios* is one iota which is the Greek letter "i". The saying that "there is not one iota of difference" is derived from the distinction between these two theological concepts.

chaired the council and, though not a theologian, for political reasons backed Athanasius. The topic came up again at the Council of Constantinople in 381 CE but was not resolved until the Councils of Ephesus (431 CE) and Chalcedon (451 CE). Arianism did not go away easily persisting into the seventh century only to reemerge with the Renaissance.

Isaac Newton was a closet Unitarian. He did not allow his theological writings to be published until after his death in 1727. Similarly, Joseph Priestley (1733-1804), along with Antoine Lavoisier (1743–1794), was the co-discoverer of oxygen and also a liberal minister who tried to fuse Enlightenment thought with traditional theism. His "modern" religious ideas ultimately forced him to flee England and settle in America. Unitarian thought continues today worldwide.

In the seventeenth Century, along with Priestley's attempts to unite rational thought with theism came deism. Whereas, the early gods were strongly anthropomorphic i.e. human-like, only bigger and more powerful, they functioned like humans with all our failing and faults.

With the Enlightenment several philosopher/theologians including John Locke (1632–1704), David Hume (1711-1776) and Voltaire (1694–1778) introduced the concept of God called Deism. Whereas the theistic God was both anthropomorphic (looked and acted like we humans IT was also metaphysical; that is, infinite, eternal, omnipotent, omniscient, omnibenevolent and an infinite transcendent supernatural spirit, the deist's God was not anthropomorphic, was transcendent i.e. above and beyond the reach of us humans and most importantly this God created the Universe and its laws but then stepped out of the way and let the Universe and all its inhabitants make their own way in the world. This God is not personal, providential and, thus, did not interfere with humans as they made their way through life. Prayer had no effect on the deistic God.

Today the majority of Abrahamic religions including Judaism, Christianity and Islam all see God as both anthropomorphic and metaphysical. Some religions, such as Hinduism, Buddhism and Jainism view God in a more deistic way. For these latter three religions God is less well defined and more difficult to imagine or intuit. More will be said about this later.*Anthropic Principle*

In astrophysics and cosmology, the anthropic principle (from the Greek, *anthropos*, human) is the philosophical consideration that observations of the physical Universe must be compatible with the conscious life that observes it. Some proponents of the anthropic principle reason that this explains why the Universe has the age and the fundamental physical constants necessary to accommodate conscious life. As a result, they believe it is unremarkable that the Universe's fundamental constants happen to fall within the narrow range thought to be compatible with life. The God most believe in whether deistic or theistic would have to create a world with exactly the laws we have. If He had not set the physical constants the way they are, then we wouldn't be here to argue about the Problem of Evil.

A more "modern" God has been proposed by some writers.[9] It has been said that today's science is tomorrow's God. The concept of God has always met many human needs both intellectual and emotional. The theistic God is very attractive to many people because this God though at times vindictive can also be caring, loving and provide help through prayer with solutions to our never ending human need for solace, comfort and material benefits.

Chapter 2
A World Full of Evil

We humans have been at war with one another as individuals, families, tribes, chieftains, states, and globally

---

[9]   Garber, James J., 2012, *Problem Gods: In Search of a Meaningful Deity, Bauu Institute and Pr4ss,* Boulder, Colo.

for untold eons. Many of these conflicts are in part or wholly rooted in controversies over gods or God, Allah or Yahweh, religions sects, the Bible, Qur'an and/or other 'holy' writings.

Hans Kung in his most recent book, Can We Save the Catholic Church?[10], claims that the number of men, women and children killed over the centuries, by the Catholic Church, in the name of God adds up to the staggering total of over 9,000,000. This includes heretical groups such as the Gnostics[11], Marcionists[12], Cathars[13], Huguenots[14], Anabaptists[15], Arians[16], Monophysites[17], Nestorians[18], Conversos[19], "Witches", Muslims and many others who were dogmatic dissidents over a host of theological tenets. The Crusades, Thirty Years War (1618-1648) all took their toll. During the Fourth Crusade thousands of Albagensians

---

[10] Kung, Hans, 2013, Can We Save the Catholic Church, Kindle Edition.

[11] Gnostics: a second century sect believed in a transcendent God, God's helper Sophia and the knowledge/presence of God within each person.

[12] Marcionists rejected the vindictive God of the Jewish Bible and dispensed with the entire Old Testament.

[13] Cathars were an ultra-aesthetic sect that rejected marriage and sexual intercourse viewing the body as evil. Cathar means the "pure ones".

[14] Huguenots: French Protestants.

[15] Anabaptists date from the sixteenth century. They don't believe in infant baptism. The name means "baptize over again" from the practice of re-baptizing members when they become adults even if baptized as children.

[16] Arianism dates from the third Century. Arius of Alexandria believed that Christ was not fully divine as was God the Father. Christ was inferior to the Father and was created by the Father.

[17] The Monophysites believed Christ had one nature and it was divine. He did not have a human nature. This aspect was just an illusion. Catholic dogma maintains that Christ's nature is at one and the same time wholly divine and wholly human.

[18] Nestorians believed that Christ had two separate natures one human and one divine.

[19] Conversos were Jewish converts to Christianity who sometimes remained practicing closet Jews.

and Walegensians[20], Jews and Eastern Christians were
killed without the crusaders ever setting foot on the Holy
Land. Most of this brutality was based on politics, greed
and blatant anti-Semitism. Thousands were tormented,
tortured and murdered in 1202 CE in the city of Zara
(present day Croatia) in order to enhance Venice's sea
trading potential. Pope Innocent III agreed to the sack of
Zara and surrounding areas in order to obtain financial
aid from the Venetians for the crusade. The Catholic
Church, in 1486, published a manual of acceptable torture
methods, the Malleus Malleficarum. This manual was
developed specifically for the Inquisition and especially
in the interrogation and torture of alleged witches. Today
these brutal methods make water-boarding look relatively
benign.

The list of global atrocities continues to grow today.
Sunnis kill Shias, Muslims kill Christians, Protestants kill
Catholics, and Sikhs kill Hindus (and all these in reverse).
A Russian once told me jest that Capitalism represented
man's inhumanity to man; Communism on the other hand,
he said, was just the reverse! Might this apply to all the
various sects, religions, political parties etc. around the
world today?

All of the above are human-induced evils. There
are, of course, untold evil events that arise out of all the
natural "imperfections" found in the workings of our
world including hurricanes, tropical storms, earthquakes,
tsunamis, fires, wind, rain, floods, mud slides, sink holes,
volcanic eruptions, avalanches, blizzards, hailstorms,
droughts, heat waves, tornadoes, cyclones and more. The

---

[20]   The Albagensians and Waldensians were Bible oriented Christians
who lived in southern France in the twelfth and thirteenth centuries.
They may have been the doctrinal descendants of the Bible-believing
Paulicians (who believed Christ was 'adopted' by the Father). They
were pre-Protestant schismatics that rebelled against the immorality,
corruption and the unscriptural doctrines of the Roman Catholic
Church.

suffering inflicted on humankind by these natural disasters over the centuries is immense and not entirely known.

Recently a woman tearfully informed me that her two-year-old daughter had died of Drave Syndrome. I knew that her child had been born with uncontrolled epileptic seizures. I researched this a bit and discovered this syndrome was an inherited disease with a limited prognosis. The child died because her DNA was disturbed by a quirk of nature and left her parents and two siblings asking the unanswerable question: "Why". We all see such sadness almost daily. Often we query plaintively, "God why did you let this happen? The list of "evils" in the world is truly endless both in time and type. "If forgers and malefactors are put to death by the secular power, there is much more reason for excommunicating and even putting to death one convicted of heresy." —Thomas Aquinas, Summa Theologica

Figure 3. Medieval Breaking Wheel
As the wheel is turned the victim's body
is crushed and bones broke

There were atrocities perpetrated by Christians for a host of reasons including the suppression of pagans from the 2nd Century C.E. forward. As Christianity spread into

Europe and Africa religious intolerance invaded as well. The Crusades, anti-Semitism, the Counter Reformation, the Inquisition with its hanging and burning of withes, and warlocks as well as suppression of women and theologians all followed. And of course, we must include the millions of native peoples who lost their lives to the sword and disease during the conquest of America by Catholic conquistadors. Many of these souls were simply victims of greed, egoism, power politics and/or unbridled hatred. The 'books' of these native people were burnt *en masse* and their language and rather sophisticated culture were, as a consequence, not revealed until the twentieth century. Catholic priests viewed these writings as heretical and ordered them destroyed.

In the early Church, many of those who were put to death were members of the early competing Christian sects noted above. When Constantine sanctioned Christianity, many pagans were persecuted as they had persecuted Christians before 312 CE. The number of Christians killed during the Roman persecutions is estimated to be below 100,000, which is much, much lower than the millions of Christians, Jews and Muslims killed by Catholics, Protestants and Muslims over the next two millennia.

Charlemagne in 782 CE beheaded 4500 Saxons, who were unwilling to convert to Catholicism. The peasants of Stewing (Germany) who were unwilling to pay suffocating Church taxes were put to death. In 1234 CE between 5,000 and 11,000 men, women and children were slain. In the Battle of Belgrad 80,000 Turks were slaughtered in 1456. During the 16th and 17th century tens of thousands of Gaelic Irish fell victim to Anglican English troops.

The Crusades

The Crusades extended over a period of two hundred years (1095-1291). The First Crusade began in 1095 initiated by pope Urban II. Thousands of Turks were killed in Hungary on the march to Jerusalem. Forty capital cities and 200 castles were ravished with an unknown number slain. It is claimed that the women were not raped though most were.

The Christians "did no other harm to the women found in the enemy's tents save that they ran their lances through their bellies," —Christian chronicler Fulcher of Chartres. Subsequent to crusader intrusions, famine led to "the already slain corpses of the enemies being eaten by the Christians", reported chronicler Albert Aquensis.

When Jerusalem was conquered in 1099 more than 60,000 Jewish and Muslim men, women and children were murdered and raped. The carnage was so horrific it was said that blood was literally running in the streets of Jerusalem. The Archbishop of Tyre, an eye-witness, wrote:

"It was impossible to look upon the vast numbers of the slain without horror; everywhere lay fragments of human bodies, and the very ground was covered with the blood of the slain. It is reported that within the Temple enclosure alone about ten thousand infidels perished."

In the Battle of Askalon, August 12, 1099 CE, 200,000 'heathens' were slaughtered "in the name of Our Lord Jesus Christ."

During the Fourth crusade beginning in 1204 CE, Constantinople was sacked, and thousands, many of whom were Christians, were slain, plundered and raped. During all the Crusades from 1195 CE until the fall of Akkon in 1291, 20 million victims in the Holy Land and Arab/Turkish areas may have died.[21]

Heretics

The Manichaean heretics who were crypto-Christians or Gnostic, originated in in Persia (present day Iran), believed in an evil, material force and an opposing good, spiritual force that battled one another for supremacy.

---

[21] All figures taken from contemporary Christian Chroniclers.

Between 372 CE and 444 CE they were exterminated by the thousands (the exact number is uncertain). Augustine of Hippo had been a Manichean but later sanctioned their extermination.

The Fourth or Albagensians Crusade was intended to eliminate other Christians and not regain the Holy Land. Among those targeted were the Albagensians, who viewed themselves as good Christians, but they were unable to accept the heavy taxes and the prohibition of birth control imposed by the Vatican.

This Crusade was initiated in 1209 by Pope Innocent III (said to be greatest single mass murderer prior to Hitler). Beziers (present day France) was the first city to be attacked by the crusaders in1209. It was virtually destroyed and all its inhabitants were slain. Victims included Catholics, who refused to turn over their heretical neighbors and friends. There were between twenty and seventy thousand fatalities. Several other cities were invaded with thousands of additional victims. Over the next twenty years of war nearly all Cathars (probably half the population of Languedoc (today southern France) were exterminated. After the war ended (1229) the Inquisition, which was established in 1232, began the search for all heretics in Western Europe. The majority of these were burned at the stake.

There were an estimated one million victims. The number of Inquisitional deaths is unknown. The Spanish Inquisitor Torquemada allegedly was responsible for 10,220 burnings at the stake. Other scholars have found evidence that 125,000 people were investigated by the Spanish Inquisition of which 1.8% or 2250 were executed. Bernard Gui was also a medieval inquisitor. He tried 930 people out of which 42 were executed (4.5%). Another famous Inquisitor, Jacques Fournier tried 114 cases of which 5 were executed (4.3%). Using numbers that are known, scholars have been able to surmise that approximately 2,000 people died in the Medieval

Inquisition (1231-1400 AD). Figures as high as nine million have been cited but most scholars agree that such a number is improbable.

There have been a number of famous cases that have caught the attention of historians:

- John Huss (1369 –1415)), a critic of papal infallibility and indulgences, was burned at the stake in 1415. He had been promised safe passage to the Council of Constance but was, nonetheless, imprisoned, tried and executed
- Giordano Bruno (1543-1600 was a Dominican monk, who was incarcerated for seven years and then burned at the stake in 1600. It is believed that he was considered a heretic for supporting Copernicus' heliocentric view of the solar system. Alfonso Ingegno states that Bruno's philosophy, called into question the truth-value of the whole of Christianity. Bruno suggested that we can now recognize that universal laws control the 'perpetual becoming' (evolution?) of all things. In our infinite Universe, A. M. Paterson[22] says that, while we no longer have a copy of t he official papal condemnation of Bruno, his heresies included "the doctrine of the infinite universe and the innumerable worlds" and his beliefs "on the movement of the earth" were the main tents that led to his death.
- Michael Servetus (509–1553) was a Spanish physician, theologian and polymath who denied the Trinity. He fled the Spanish Inquisition and seeking asylum in Geneva, John Calvin had him arrested and ultimately burned at the stake. He was one of the first Catholic Christians put to death by a Protestant leader

---

[22]   Paterson, A.M., 1979, *The Infinite Words of Giordano Bruno*, p. 168.

Witch hunts

From the beginning of Christianity to 1484 several thousand "witches" and "warlocks" died at the hands of faithful followers of Christ. Witches and warlocks were said to be slaves of the devil. Some were believed to be sexual partners with the devil. Many of these under torture admitted to twenty years or more as handmaids of Satan. Over the centuries it has been claimed by many that Eve had intercourse with the satanic serpent of Paradise.

During the witchhunts(1484-1750), according to modern scholars, several hundred thousand (about 80% female) were burned at the stake or hanged for their demonic connections. Evil that occurred in the lives of many people had to be blamed on someone other than God. Satan was a handy source for much suffering that medieval Christians endured. All sorts of evil events were attributed to the devil and witches. Men often claimed witches caused that erectile dysfunction. Hail storms, crop failures, sickness and death of cattle, horse and other livestock were similarly blamed on witches and warlocks. One witch claimed the devil asked her to pour a cup of water in to a small hole in the ground. This was followed only minutes later by a devastating hail storm.

God, in allowing the devil to perpetrate evil, added to the Problem of Evil i.e. why does God allow Satan to create evil? God, according to theological tradition, had driven angels into Hell because they had rebelled against God, possibly because they were jealous of God's favoring Homo sapiens. But why would God open the gates of Hell, making it possible for Satan and his underlings to invade Earth in order to foist evil onto humankind? This part of the Problem of Evil will be discussed below.

Some sources claim nine million people died accused of doing the devil's deeds, however, more realistic scholarly estimates range from 60,000 to 100,000 dying as witches and warlock. The torture used to obtain confessions from witches is beyond the imagination of most 21st Century people. These included[23]:

The Rack was an instrument of torture often used in the Middle Ages, and a popular means of extricating confession. The victim was tied across a board by their ankles and wrists, pulling the upper and lower body in opposite directions until dislocations of every joint occurred. The Stocks involved placing the victim's hands and head in the stocks, while they are kneeling on the stock. Then two pieces of timber are clamped together over and under, their feet. The soles of their feet are greased with lard, a blazing brazier is applied to the feet, and the feet are blistered and then fried. At intervals a board is interposed between the fire and their feet and removed if they disobeyed the command to confess guilt for what they are charged by the inquisitor.

Water Torture: The victims nostrils were pinched shut, and eight quarts of fluid (water, boiling water or vinegar) were poured down the victims throat through a funnel. Other techniques included forcing a cloth down the throat, while pouring water, which made a swallowing reflex pushing it further down into the stomach producing all the agonies of suffocation by drowning until the victim lost consciousness.

---

[23] http://www.bibliotecapleyades.net/vatican/esp_vatican29.htm#The%20Tortures

Figure 4   **Figure 5**   **Figure 6**

Heretic's Fork   Head Crusher   The Brinks

- The Heretics Fork: This instrument consisted of two little forks one set against the other, with the four prongs plunged into the flesh, under the chin and above the chest, with hands secured firmly behind their backs. A small collar supported the instrument in such a manner that the victims were usually forced to hold their head erect, thus preventing any movement.
- The Pear: The pear was a torture method used on females. This device was inserted into the vagina, or mouth of the victim and then expanded to the maximum width of the victim's vagina or mouth. The

openings would then become severely lacerated, ripping the tissue, flesh and membranes until the victim died.

- **The Brinks:** The Branks, also sometimes called Dame's Bridle, or Scold's Bridle is comprised of a metal facial mask and spiked mouth depressor that was implemented on housewives up until the early 19th century. Many clergymen supported the husband's right to handle his wife and to use "salutary restraints in every case of misbehavior" without the intervention of what some court records of 1824 referred to as "vexation persecutors".

- **The Breaking Wheel:** The wheel was one of the most popular and insidious methods of torture and execution practiced. The giant spiked wheel was able to break bodies as it rolled forward, causing the most agonizing and drawn-out death. Other forms include the "braided" wheel, where the victim would be tied to the execution dock or platform. Their limbs were spread and tied to stakes or iron rings on the ground. Slices of wood were placed under the main joints, wrists, ankles, knees, hips, and elbows. The executioner would then smash every joint with the iron-tyred edge of the wheel, however the executioner would avoid fatal blows to give the victim a painful death."

- **The Strappado** was one of the most common torture techniques. All one needed to set up a strappado was a sturdy rafter and a rope. The victim's wrists were bound behind his or her back. The heretic would placed on a platform several feet off the ground and with the rope pulled over a cross beam well over their head, the platform was pulled away and the person would fall toward the ground, dislocating their shoulders.

There were multiple other torture techniques used including breast grabbing" in women that might involve actually tearing the breast off the chest. The Garrote was slow strangulation, as in hanging by the neck, sometimes used to kill the heretic after being run through the Breaking wheel after which many of their bones were broken. The Iron Maiden or Virgin of Nuremberg was a tomb-sized container with folding doors. The object was to inflict punishment, then death. On the inside of the doors were vicious spikes. As the prisoner was shut inside he or she would be pierced along the sides of the body. The talons were not designed to kill outright but slowly and painfully. The list of such tortures goes on and on. It is amazing, as well as very disturbing, that we humans are so sadistically ingenious when we put our minds to making our fellow human beings suffer.

Religious Wars[24]

The figures below include the deaths of civilians from diseases, famine, etc., as well as deaths of soldiers in battle and possible massacres and genocide.

- In the 15th Century there was Crusades against the Hussites who were followers of John Huss. Huss was a pre-Reformation religious activist who opposed the autocratic policies of the pope. This war left thousands dead In1538, Pope Paul III initiated a Crusade against heretical England and declared all Anglicans apostates. At the time, war against England was not militarily feasible.

- In France about 20,000 Huguenots were killed in 1572 on the order of Pope Pius V. Up to the 17th century 200,000 Huguenots fled France.

- During the seventeenth century Gaspard de Coligny, a Protestant leader, was slain, after which a Catholic mob mutilated his body, "cutting off his head, his hands, and his genitals... and then dumped him into the river then, deciding that it was not worthy of being food for the fish, they hauled his body out and dragged what was left... to the gallows of 'to be meat and carrion for maggots and crows'."

- Also during the 17th century Catholics sacked the city of Magdeburg, Germany during which roughly 30,000 Protestants were killed. In one church fifty women were found beheaded with infants still sucking at the breasts of their lifeless mothers.

- At the time of the Thirty Years War (1618-1648) when German Catholics fought German Protestant at least 40% of population died during this war.

- Anti-Semitism: As early as the 4th and 5th centuries synagogues were burned by Christians. The number of Jews slaughtered is unknown.

- The very first synagogue was destroyed in the year 388 on order of Bishop Innocentius of Dertona in Northern Italy. Council of Toledo 694 sanctioned the enslavement of Jews, confiscation of their property, and forcible baptism of their children.

- The Bishop of Limoges, France, in 1010 had the cities' Jews, who would not convert to Christianity, expelled or killed.

- During the First Crusade (1095-1099) "thousands" of Jews were slaughtered, possibly as many as 12.000 in all: In addition, many additional Jews were killed in Worms (1096) and Mainz, (1100), as well as at Trier, Regensburg, Prague and other cities. (All locations were in Germany except Metz, (France) and Prague (Czechoslovakia).

- The Second Crusade beginning in 1147 led to the deaths of several hundred Jews in France.
- During the Third Crusade several English Jewish communities were sacked between 1189 and 1190 with the loss of hundreds of lives.
- In Fulda, Germany, during 1235, 34 Jewish men and women were slain. In 1257 and 1267 Jewish communities in London and Canterbury were plundered.
- Allegedly 10,000 Jews were killed in 1290 in Bohemia (then Poland). All Jews were exiled from England in 1292. The year 1337 saw a Jew-killing craze involving 51 towns in Bavaria, Austria and Poland. Deggendorf, Germany, was not exempt from anti-Semitism during this period.
- In 1348 all Jews living in Basel, Switzerland and Strasbourg, France, were burned at the stake. This included about two thousand individuals.
- In more than 350 towns in Germany all Jews were murdered, mostly burned alive. In this one-year more Jews were killed than Christians had been in 200 years of ancient Roman persecution of Christians.
- In the year 1389, Prague saw 3,000 Jews put to death simply because they were Jews.
- Seville was the site of 4,000 Jewish murders all sanctioned by Archbishop Martinez. An additional 25,000 were sold into slavery. Their identification was made easy by the brightly colored "badges of shame" that all Jews above the age of ten had been forced to wear after the Fourth Lateran Council (1215).
- In the year Columbus set sailed to the New World, more than 150,000 Jews were expelled from Spain, many

died on their way to accepting countries such as Poland.
Many Spanish ate pork to prove they were not Jewish;
a custom that persist today in Spain. Most Spanish use
both parents name in order to demonstrate that neither
parent was Jewish. This is another custom that remains
in Spain even today.

- In Chmielnitzki, Poland about 200,000 Jews were slain.
  (1648).
- This brutal anti-Semitism goes on and on, century after
  century, right up to the present day.
- Auschwitz is the most infamous of all the Holocaust
  camps. Millions were murdered there and much has
  been written about the horrors of this camp.[25]

Native Populations

Native Populations: Beginning with Columbus'
discovery of the New World, which was intended to
bring to Spain untold tons of gold ingots to relieve its
financial difficulties. The Spanish also wanted to foster the
expansion of Christianity. Within hours of landfall on the
first inhabited island he encountered, Columbus seized and
carried off six native people who, he said ought to be good
servants and would easily be made Christians. He could do
this because they belonged to no religion but now belonged
to Spain. Columbus considered the natives idolatrous
slaves, who were less than human. Theologians were to
debate the natives' spiritual status for several centuries.

Columbus was dedicated to war if the natives failed
to conform to Christianity and the authority of Spain.
Likewise, John Winthrop, first governor of Massachusetts
Bay Colony, vowed to carry the Gospel into those parts of
the world and to raise a barrier between the kingdom of

---

[25] Harding, Thomas, 2013, *Hans and Rudolf: The True Story of the German Jew Who Tracked Down and Caught the Kommandant of Auschwitz*, Kindle e-Book.

God and the Anti-Christ. Witchhunts though less vigorous than in Europe were to follow as well. On average two thirds of the native population were killed by imported smallpox before violence began. The surviving Indians fell victim to rape, murder, enslavement and death at the hands of Spanish or English soldiers. There were uncounted victims that fell victim to Spanish swords.

The population of the Caribbean islands in 1492 was about eight million, however, by 1496 it had declined by a third to a half of this figure. Eventually all the indigenous people were exterminated. In less than the normal lifetime of a single human being, an entire culture of millions of people, thousands of years resident in their homeland, had were gone. This, indeed, was genocide though little is made of this massacre today vis-à-vis the Nazi holocaust.

Following this slaughter the Spanish turned their attention to the mainland of Mexico and Central America. The exquisite Aztec city of Tenochtitlan (Mexico city) was next. Cortez, Pizarro, De Soto and hundreds of other Spanish conquistadors sacked southern and Mesoamerica in the name of Christ. De Soto also sacked Florida.

Estimates of the dead run as high as 60,000,000. A significant percentage of the natives that died did so of smallpox and other European disease such as measles (rubeola). Cortez killed hundreds of thousands of Aztec soldiers. He also employed natives to fight Montezuma, many of whom died of sickness as well as the sword.

Among the number of natives killed in Massachusetts, there were many brutally killed for minor offenses in spite of the kind acts provided the Puritans the winter of their first year in New England. We are reminded of this every Thanksgiving. In Massachusetts, the colonists who were themselves refugees from religiously intolerant England, murdered natives during the "Pequot War". This war extended from 1634 to 1638 and involved the Narragansett and Mohegan tribes. Some seven hundred native were killed or sold into slavery during this war. As so often happens, the suppressed become the suppressors.

As usual, men, women and children were slain proclaiming, "the Lord was pleased to smite our Enemies in the hinder Parts, and to give us their land for an inheritance" quoting Deuteronomy:

13:"And when the Lord thy God hath delivered it into thine hands, thou shalt smite every male thereof with the edge of the sword

14: But the women, and the little ones, and the cattle, and all that is in the city, even all the spoil thereof, shalt thou take unto thyself; and thou shalt eat the spoil of thine enemies, which the Lord thy God hath given thee." (Deut. 20:13-14)

In this way they continued until the extermination of the Pequot was near. The surviving handful of Indians "were parceled out to live in servitude. John Endicott and his pastor wrote to the governor asking for 'a share' of the captives, specifically 'a young woman or girl and a boy if you think this is good'."

EXECUTION OF THE THIRTY-EIGHT SIOUX INDIANS
AT MANKATO, MINNESOTA, DECEMBER 26, 1862.

Figure 7. Hanging of Thirty-eight Dakota Indians in 1862.

Other tribes were to endure the same suffering. Similar scenarios played out in most areas of America—some early and some later. In Minnesota during the Indian uprising of 1862 some nine hundred pioneers and two hundred Dakota Indians were killed. This country's largest single group hanging in its history followed this. Thirty-eight Native Americans were hanged simultaneously in Mankato, Minn. (my home town) on December 26, 1862. For many years there was a stone monument in the center of Mankato memorializing these deaths. Only recently has this been removed and replaced by a life-sized sculpture of a buffalo. No one currently knows what has happened to the monument, which was about the size of a large cemetery marker. The local county museum no longer displays a model of the gallows used in the hangings. In a single massacre in "King Philip's War" of 1675 some 600 Indians were killed. Reverend Cotton Mather[26], pastor of the second church in Boston and a well-known writer at the time, saw no issue with the Christians who perpetrated this unfortunate deed.

Before the arrival of the English, the western Arenac people in New Hampshire and Vermont had numbered 12,000. Less than half a century later about 250 remained alive. The Pocumtuck people had numbered more than 18,000; fifty years later they were down to 920. And so it has evolved for all the tribes of North and South America. These deaths were due to human actions. As noted above smallpox and other epidemics introduced by European soldiers and settlers were responsible for an untold loss of life. The introduction of alcohol caused countless emotional and physical ills with subsequent deaths the carnage from drug and alcohol are still with us today. The natives

---

[26] Cotton Mather (1663-1728) a Harvard graduate with an honorary doctorate from the University of Glasgow, was a socially and politically influential New England Puritan minister, prolific author and pamphleteer. He is often remembered for his role in the Salem witch trials.

provided some payback from the suffering and death tobacco and syphilis have brought to us non-natives.

Some authors estimate that more than one hundred fifty million Indians (of both Americas) were lost between 1500 and 1900. Two thirds may have been due to smallpox and other epidemics, which leave fifty million killed directly by violence, ill treatment and slavery. And let us not forget the deaths in Hawaii, Alaska the Middle East, the Orient and Africa that have and continue to occur. It has been one hundred and fifty years since slavery was abolished in the United States, yet residuals of racial bigotry are still with us.

In all the Americas such natural and human evils continue to the present day. We have seen the appalling number of inhumane acts carried out by Christians over the centuries.

Table 4. Deaths caused by non-Christians over the centuries:
184-205CE – Yellow Scarves Rebellion (Taoists) – China – 7 million
1300s-1521CE – Human Sacrifices (Aztecs) – Mexico – 1 million
1855-1877CE – Panthay Rebellion (Muslims) – China – 12 million
1932-1933CE – Holodomor (communist atheists) – Ukraine – 10 million
1941-1945 CE– Nazi Genocides (statist atheists) – Germany – 11 million
1959-1962CE – Great Leap Forward famine (Communist atheists) – China – 43 million
1971CE – Bangladesh Atrocities (Islamists) – East Pakistan – 3 million
1975-1979CE – Khmer Rouge Repression (communist atheists) – Cambodia – 3 million
September 11, 2001 – Terrorist attacks (Muslim Jihadists) – USA – 3000

Terrorism

The most "news worthy" international and national evil in recent years is terrorism. This has been especially evident since September 11, 2001 when nearly 3,000 people died when two commercial airline jets were intentionally flown into the Twin Trade Towers in Manhattan. This is an evil that will be long remembered. Terrorism may be classified in several ways and these various terroristic types can be expanded on depending on ones view of evil. Obviously Al-qaeda sees terrorism differently today than the Catholic hierarchy's understanding has been over the centuries or John Calvin's definition of terrorism when Michael Servetus was burned at the stake in 1553.

Terrorism categories:

- State or non-state government sponsored terrorism.
- Religiously motivated terrorism.
- Racially or other bigotry inspired (such as homophobes).
- Anti-government terrorists.
- Individual terrorists, such as serial, mentally ill or sexual killers.

There have been terrorists that only kill killers or prostitutes or women they have raped. Many killings are family related. How many of these murders are stimulated by mental health issues is unknown.

The following is an incomplete chronological list of terroristic attacks since 1800 that were carried out in several countries and includes various national, racial and religious terrorists.

1800–1899

- United States: In 1865–1877: Over 3000 Freedmen and their allies were killed by the Ku Klux Klan and well-organized campaigns of violence by other local whites in a campaign of terrorist violence that weakened the reconstructionist governments in the American South and helped re-establish legitimized segregation.[1][2]
- France: December 9, 1893 French anarchist Augusta Vaillant bombs the French Chamber of Deputies injuring 20 deputies

1900–1949

- Ottoman Empire 1903: Members of the anarchistic group, Gemidzhii, carried out the Salonica.

- United States 1910: Los Angeles Times bombing by a member of the International Association of Bridge and Structural Iron Workers Union killed 21 people and injured an additional 100.
- United States 1920: Wall Street bombing killed 38 people and wounded 300 others.
- United States 1921: The Tulsa race riot killed 39 people and injured over 800.
- Romania 1921: 100 soldiers and police officers were killed by a bomb thrown at the Bolgrad Palace by Bessarabian separatists.
- Bulgaria 1925: A group from the Bulgarian Communist Party blew up the roof of St. Nedelya Church in an assault during a funeral service, killing 150 people and injuring 500.
- British mandate for Palestine 1937–1948: The Irgun are responsible for numerous attacks in British-mandated Palestine. The Irgun were a Jewish paramilitary outfit.
- Sweden 1940: Politically motivated bombing targeted at the communist newspaper Norrskensflamman (Northern Flame) by various perpetrators. Five persons were killed, two of whom were children, along with five others injured.
- United States 1940: Time bomb is left at the British Pavilion at the 1939 New York World's Fair, 2 policeman are killed.
- United States 1940–1956: George Metesky, the "Mad Bomber", placed over 30 bombs in New York City in public places such as Grand Central Station and The Paramount Theater, injuring ten during this period in protest against the local electric utility. He also sent many threatening letters.
- Romania 1947: Three Romanian terrorists kill an aircrew member aboard a Romanian airline. This is attributed as the first hijacking that resulted in a fatality.

- Syria1949: 12 killed and dozens injured in the Menarsha synagogue attack, Damascus.
- Philipines1949: 13 people are killed as a Philippine airliner explodes in flight travelling from Daet to Manila. A time bomb had detonated 30 minutes after departure near Alabat Island.

1950–1969
- Israel 1954: an Israeli civilian passenger bus was attacked by unknown assailants at the Scorpions Pass in the Negev, resulting in the deaths of eleven passengers.
- United States 1955: A bomb aboard United Airlines Flight 629 explodes killing all 44 on board, seen as a copycat incident to Canadian Pacific Air Lines Flight 108.
- Cyprus 1956: One man was killed and six others injured when a bomb exploded in Nicosia.
- Lebanon 1958: Three people were killed in a bomb blast in Beirut. The bombing also injured ten more and on the day that United Nations General Assembly was pondering ways to end violence in the Middle East.
- Cuba 1960: The French freighter La Coubre explodes, killing between 75 and 100 people with 200 injured. The government suspects sabotage.
- United States 1962: Continental Airlines Flight 11 explodes and crashes near Unionville, Missouri, killing all 45 on board (the only initial survivor succumbed to injuries later in hospital) after it was determined to be a suicide committed as insurance fraud.
- Canada 1963–1970: Front de libération du Québec committed frequent bombings, targeting English businesses and banks, as well as McGill University. The whole bombing campaign resulted in 8 known deaths and numerous injuries.
- South Vietnam 1965: Two simultaneous explosions took place near a restaurant in the 1965 Saigon bombing

during the Vietnam War. The attack killed 42 people and 80 were wounded.

- Greece 1967: A bomb exploded on board Cyprus Airways Flight 284 near Rhodes killing all 66 people on the aircraft.
- Israel 1968: Three bombs were detonated in Tel Aviv, killing 1 person and injuring 51 people.
- Italy 1969: Piazza Fontana bombing, Milano, killing 17 people and wounding 88.

1970–present

- Switzerland: A bomb explodes in the rear of Swissair Flight 330, causing it to crash near Zürich, killing 38 passengers and all nine crew members. A Palestinian terrorist group carried out the attack.
- Israel: Avivim school bus attacks by Palestinian PLO members, killing 9 children and three adults and crippling 19 children.
- Italy: Reggio riots, a bomb attack caused six deaths and 66 injured on the train Palermo-Turin, near the Gioia Tauro railway station.
- United States: The Army Mathematics Research Center on the University of Wisconsin–Madison campus was blown up resulting in one death
- Israel: Two bombs explode in Tel Aviv at the central bus station killing one person and injuring 24.
- United States, 1970-1972: The Jewish Defense League was linked with a bomb explosion outside of Aeroflot's New York City office, and a detonation outside of Soviet cultural offices in Washington. Also a JDL member allegedly fired a rifle into the Soviet Union's mission office at the United Nations. Two JDL members were convicted of bomb possession and burglary in a conspiracy to blow up the Long Island residence of the Soviet Mission to the UN.

In addition to these many murderous incidents there have been thousands more over the years. The mass murder of 1.7 million people in the Killing Fields of Cambodia will remain in our imaginations for years to come. Most everyone is aware of the recent school shootings in Colorado, Connecticut. and elsewhere. There is Columbine, Oklahoma City, Aurora and New Town and the list continues to grow. Pictures of the Boston marathon bombings are etched in our memories never to fade. The amputees who are now adjusting to their new way of life speak to us courageously from the evening news. It seems that almost every day we hear of more tragedies. Civil war in Syria, Somalia, Uganda become less and less 'civil' and more and more horrific. The terror continues in Iraq and Afghanistan running apace with no solutions in sight. Between 2003 and 2010 there were 1760 suicide bombing in Iraq. Since the withdrawal of US military there has been no change in the rate of suicide bombings. Egypt's unrest has resurfaced and continues unabated. Will all this evil ever end or are we humans doomed by our very nature to hate and hurt until Earth is swallowed up by our dying Sun some three billion years from now if we manage not to do ourselves in before then.

Table 5. Deaths Caused by Christians:
1562-1598 – French Wars of Religion–4 million
1095-1291 – Crusades to the Holy Land – Middle East, Spain, Africa – 1.5 million (This does include all sides of the conflict)
1184-c. 1860 – Various Christian Inquisitions – Europe – 17,500
1184-c. 1860 – Various Christian Inquisitions – Europe – 17,500
Pagan religious services became punishable by death in 356. Between 315CE and 6th century thousands of pagan believers died

As a point of comparison, there were eight hundred executions per year during the early post-Reformation period in England, where the Inquisition never opera ted (according to Sir James Stephens' "History of English Criminal Law"). In a BBC study, which aired in a documentary called "The Myth of the Spanish Inquisition" (June 9th, 1995), they estimated 3000 to 5000 people died during the Inquisition's 350-year history rather than the tens of thousands sometimes claimed.

According to the World Christian Encyclopedia 2nd Ed. Vol. I, page 11 (a Protestant source) the number of martyrs from 33-2000 CE there were 64.4 million martyrs Of those martyrs, 11.8 million were Roman Catholic and 3.7 million were Protestants. The overwhelming majority were Eastern/Oriental Orthodox martyrs. Of the 64.4 million martyrs, 55.9 million were killed by Secular governments, 9.1 million killed by Muslims, 7.4 million killed by Ethno-religionists (animists), 4.9 million killed by Roman Catholics, 2.9 million killed by Quasi-Christians/Other Christians, 0.6 million killed by Eastern Orthodox.

The evil that nature imposes on humans is extensive, continuous and pervasive. We all have experienced the emotional and physical suffering associated with bad weather, tornadoes, earthquakes, tsunamis and/or hurricanes. Sometimes a house fire or tornado cannot only leave us homeless but even lifeless. These natural evils may be a little more understandable since most would agree that such natural disasters seem to be part of nature. We live in an imperfect world. Weather, winds, rockslides, wild fires and a host of other evil events are accepted as part of nature. Most of us wouldn't expect the world to be without these happenings although one might make a case for a "perfect" would if God were "perfect" in every way.

Natural evils include floods, fires, tornadoes (cyclones), hurricanes, typhoons, earthquakes, tsunamis, droughts, famines, epidemics etc. are major evil disasters. There other 'lesser' events such as sink holes and mud slides.

These are all beyond the power of men to control and can injury or kill a few to thousands. Some of these come from outer space such as meteorites, comets or asteroids. The asteroid strike at Chicxulub in the Mexican Yucattan wiped out the majority of non-avian dinosaurs. The tsunami that flowed over parts of Japan in 2010 killed many and caused radioactive emissions to fly out of uranium powered electrical plant. An epidemic of Yesinia pasties (bubonic plague) wiped out 30% of the European population in 1348-50. We hear of such tragedies on a regular basis. Over and above these 'evil' events blizzards, sandstorms, cloudbursts and hailstorms cause inconveniences for many and death for some.

One may rightly ask why God would allow these 'evils' to happen. If (theistic) God is as great and good as portrayed God should be able to make a world that is free of such catastrophes. As all-good, all-powerful an all-knowing God should be good enough to desire the very best, even infinite good, for humankind. He must be so perceptive that He could foresee and then devise a method of preventing all disasters and powerful enough (infinitely powerful) to impose some saving system to avoid any and all natural evils long before they could threaten any of us seven billion humans.

In addition to momentous physical mayhem there are epidemics and other serious infectious that have taken millions of lives over the centuries. These are less of an evil today with the availability of antibiotics and immunizations but by no means totally controlled. Malaria, tuberculosis and even polio remain major medical problems worldwide. It would seem relatively easy for God to create all humans with immunity to all infectious diseases and their causes such as Yersinia pestis//bubonic plague and HIV/AIDS/ human immunodeficiency virus. Similarly, children who are born with any one of a host of genetic disorders, such as Down's syndrome, Fragile X disease[27] or Cystic Fibrosis face difficult lives with DNA modification still a thing of the future. An all-benevolent God should make DNA so that it never is altered and always codes for perfect creatures.

Unfortunately, in the real world in which we live and God is believed to have created, DNA, like so many of earthly things is not perfect nor is DNA perfectly stable. DNA, even if 'perfect' when in the father's sperm or mother's ova may be altered (mutate) for a variety of reasons. Radiation from any source, such as outer space, local uranium such as in a electric power plant or an atomic bomb may alter the sequence of DNA nucleosides[28] thus changing one or more genes contained in the DNA that goes on to produce a new little baby. This may lead to major congenital abnormalities including mental retardation or serious physical changes in arms, legs or other organs. Other toxic substances to which the fetus may be expose while in the womb, such as alcohol, cigarettes or medicines can also harm the newborn infants. Thalidomide, a sedative and anti-nausea pill taken while the mother was pregnant accounted for thousands of babies who were born with abnormal arms and/or legs.

---

[27] Fragile X syndrome a mental deficiency disorder characterized by one short 'leg' on the X chromosome seen mostly in boys.

[28] There are four nucleosides: alanine, thymidine, guanine, cytosine (Attic) and three off which codes for a specific amino acid. Amino acids are the building blocks for proteins, which are the main molecule that make the body work properly. If there is a mutation (change) in the DNA the ATGC arrangements are disturbed and this is what is referred to as a genetic abnormality. Down syndrome, for example, is due to a duplication of the 22rd chromosome so instead of two there are three 22nd chromosomes which induces all the features of Down's syndrome including reduced intelligence, characteristic facial appearance etc.

Stargardt's disease, the visual limitation I have is due to an autosomal recessive disorder. Most of us have 23 sets of chromosomes (DNA packets). Every gene has two alleles (coding packets). This means that for me to have Stargardt's disease I must receive one allele for Stargardt's from each parent.

We very frequently hear of children who die within a few months or years while sleeping in their cribs. Sudden infant death (SID) is a shockingly painful event for the child's parents and family. Why would an all-good and all powerful God allow such a thing to happen? It seems incomprehensible to many believing people that such terrible tragedies should happen. The child is perfectly innocent and the parents usually loving and caring people.[29]

Moral Evils versus Natural Evils

Moral evils, that is, behaviors by our fellow human beings (or for that matter by ourselves) that produce unhappy outcomes for others or ourselves, are possibly more bothersome and in a certain sense more evil because they are the result of a voluntary decision and subsequent action by an independent being with freewill who is capable of making rational, practical and premeditated decisions about the consequences of their (or our) behaviors.

The physical laws of nature are fixed (by God?) and immutable. They are in effect at all times. Gravity always acts on two massive bodies. $F = MmG/r^2$ This is what Isaac Newton told us over two ----hundred years ago in 1666. When two bodies (M and m) come close to each other they are attracted to each other by a gravitational force (F) that depends on their relative masses, M and m, multiplied by the gravitational constant ($G = 6.67384 \times 10^{-11}$ m^3 kg^{-1} s^{-2}) divided by the distance between the two objects squared (r^2). Such are the laws of nature that affect us at all times. Generally these are good and helpful but if we happen to fall off a cliff it can be very evil.

All of the above statistics and formulas may be too much information but the point to remember is that gravity

---

[29]   SIDS is associated with parents smoking in the home.

is always working. It is acting on all bodies at all times.[30] So the laws of nature whether they relates to gravity, the speed of light, the charge or mass of a proton, electron or neutron or any of a thousand laws that keep our Universe running. So it is a little easier to accept nature's foibles for they aren't really imperfections; they are jut nature doing its thing.

One might, however, ask (and some scholars do) why our world with all its laws couldn't be a little more kindly toward us fragile human beings if God is so perfectly good, powerful and smart.

Part II

Chapter 3

Solutions to the Problem of Evil

The Greater Good Response to the Problem of Evil

The 'Greater Good' solution argues that some greater good will come out of an evil act or event. The proponents of this solution claim that God cannot bring about some greater good without permitting a specific moral or natural evil. An example of the 'Greater Good' argument might be one that is often mentioned in regards to the Mayo Clinic that is located in Rochester, Minn. The Mayo Clinic is the one of the largest and best-known medical clinics in America. It provides high-quality medical care for thousands of patients ever day and is the largest employer in Rochester providing jobs for nearly 40,000 people. In 1864, a tornado struck the city and the Franciscan nuns who were working here at the time, asked Dr. William Worrall Mayo, to come to Rochester to care for the injured victims of the tornado. In due course his sons Drs. William James Mayo and Charles Horace Mayo joined him in 1883

---

[30] Relativity and quantum theory do influence space and time so that this is true in most situations for us Earth-bound beings.

and 1888. The Mayo Clinic celebrated its 150th anniversary in 2014. Many consider the foundation of the Mayo Clinic as a greater good that arose out of a natural evil.

The Freewill Response for the Problem of Evil

Related to the greater good response is the freewill argument that appeals to human moral freedom. The freewill defense asserts that the existence of beings with freewill is of great moral value, because with freewill comes the ability to make morally significant choices. This entails the possibility of making both good and bad moral decisions, but to have freewill allows humans to perform good acts for individuals and society as a whole. This far outweighs the evil that may ensue. God, therefore, is justified in creating a world that allows freewill. A world with free beings and no evil would be even better, however, this would require that human's function as automatons and thus they would not be truly human. It is logically impossible for God to prevent evil without curtailing human nature. It is the old square circle conundrum.

In addition, according to many religions, Heaven, a most wondrous place, awaits those who use their freewill to do good deeds and follow God's commands. Meriting Heaven through morally good acts is a greater good, outweighing the evil that may result from evil acts free humans might perform.

Critics of the freewill argument suggest that such evils as murder, rape, pedophilia and the like, far out weigh the benefits of human freewill. One option would be for God, who is infinitely resourceful, to create humans with freewill but also make their capacity to evaluate potential outcomes of their actions so astute that they would never err in their decision-making. Is this possible even for a theistic God with all His knowledge and power or would this be equivalent to making all humans divine? Some, like Spinoza, believe that we are modes of God as noted above. However, if we are part of the essence God already, why don't we function like 'little gods'? After all, the Bible says we are made in His 'image and likeness'. (Genesis 1:26).

God could limit evil by making moral actions especially pleasurable, so that they would be irresistible for us. He could also punish immoral actions immediately and make it obvious that moral rectitude is in our best interest; or He could allow us to make bad moral decisions, but intervene to prevent the harmful consequences of these acts. Such an approach would mean that freewill has less or no real value. In a sense, we wouldn't really be free. The debate depends how we define freewill and determinism, humanity and automatons. These concepts are not always easy to separate.

Genetics and environment play important roles in how ethical an individual my ultimately turn out to be. There is mounting evidence that a child's environment during his or her formative years will influence their moral decision-making ability. As an example, serial killers tend to come from abusive homes though obviously not all abused children end up serial killers. It is likely that genetics influences their adult moral behaviors. There are some factors in most criminal's early life that impact their relationships as adults. How much these factors determine moral behaviors and mitigate responsibility for evil deeds is uncertain. So the question remains, just how free is human freewill?

The Individual versus Society

Humans, since prehistory, have been struggling to survive. This pits two human elements against each other: individual needs and societal needs. Much of what we base moral decisions on relate to our perceived individual needs and wants. If we are starving and find some food, will we eat all the food ourselves or offer some to others. If we are scavenging for food all by ourselves and a starving total stranger wanders by, we are less likely to share the food. We might even steal what food he has hunted down or gathered up. On the other hand, if we have a spouse or children, it is more likely that we will share the food with them.

This phenomenon is labeled "kin selection". Kin selection is the evolutionary strategy that favors the reproductive success of an organism's relatives even at some cost to the organism's own survival. Kin altruism is behavior that drives kin selection.[31] This is an evolutionary response that maintains and improves our survival as well as that of genetically related individuals. Darwin mentions this in *The Origin of Species*. Kin selection and altruism favor survival of those closely related to the person performing helpful acts. Some frame this in terms of protecting and maintaining the genetic profile of ones family. In Richard Dawkins' terminology it's the "selfish gene" at work. [32]

The other side of this equation is that of societal needs. Our personal needs and that of our kin come first. However, we all (unless we are anchorites that live alone in some desert cave) live in a society and that society helps us live well and happily. Society provides jobs, resources, community, comfort and a host of other very helpful services. As a result, we need to support the society in which we live.

Societies have needs just as individuals do. Often times these needs come into conflict and that is why society develops laws, cultural mores. There are some things we can and cannot do. Generally we can't drive on the left side of the road unless we live in the UK or Japan. We stop at red and go on green lights. We own a house and other people can't come in unless invited. As the Declaration of Independence says we have a right to life, liberty and the pursuit of happiness. Actually Thomas Jefferson took this from John Locke who actually wrote life, liberty and

---

[31] Wikipedia.

[32] Dawkins, Richard, 1976, *The Selfish Gene,* Kindle eBook.

property. So we all have to give a little so we can live happy, healthy and peaceful lives.

When our individual needs and wants bump up against other's needs and wants compromises need to be made and that is what society is all about, but in the end we, or most of us, can live productive and peaceful lives. It is through this give and take that *Homo sapiens* has survived and improved as a species over the last 200,000 years or so. This is Darwin's natural selection at work.

Freewill and Natural Evils

Another argument against the freewill defense is that it fails to address natural evils, such as earthquakes, hurricanes and epidemics, etc. Advocates of the freewill response may offer a different explanation for these natural evils. As an example, Alvin Plantinga has famously suggested that natural evils are caused by the free choices of supernatural beings such as demons or Satan. Others have argued that natural evils are the result of our biblical 'parents', who corrupted the perfect world created by God when Adam and Eve sinned. Others say that natural laws are prerequisites for the existence of intelligent free beings and these natural laws are necessary to run the world. Others claim that natural evils provide us with knowledge of evil, which in turn makes our free choices more significant and valuable. It has also been suggested that natural evils are a means of divine punishment for immoral acts that humans have committed, and so natural evil is thus justified as God's retribution for our voluntary misdeeds.

It seems, nonetheless, that a theistic God ought to be able to create this world, along with its most intelligent beings, so that they would function in a perfectly rational way. This would include Adam and Eve who would not have disobeyed God over one piece of fruit, and thus would not have reduced an ideal world to this imperfect planet, Earth, some 6004 years ago, at least according to Genesis 1 & 2 and Bishop James Usher.[33]

Irenaeus' Theodicy:[34] The Soul-Making Defense

Irenaeus (d. 202 CE) was an early Church Father and bishop of what is present day Lyon, France. His solution to the Problem of Evil is referred to as the "soul-making" defense. Essential to the soul-making theodicy is the claim that evil and suffering are necessary for spiritual growth. For any one of us to grow spiritually and morally we must suffer in order to better understand what suffering is all about and how it affects all of us. Evils teach us how to help our family, friends and even strangers. We will become more virtuous as a result of such suffering. In a way this is another form of the greater good theodicy. The greater good in this instance, however, is spiritual growth.

Irenaeus' approach to the Problem of Evil was expanded upon some eighteen hundred years later by the influential philosopher of religion, John Hick (1922-2012). A perceived inadequacy of this theodicy, according to Hicks is that personal evils do not always promote positive growth and can have a negative effect on the human spirit. Recall the serial killers abused as children. A second issue concerns the distribution of evils suffered. Were it true that God permits evil in order to facilitate spiritual growth, then we would expect evil to disproportionately befall those in poor spiritual health. This does not seem to be the case, since decadent people may enjoy affluent and happy lives, which protects them from evil, whereas many pious and morally good, often suffer excess worldly evils when they

---

[33]   Bishop James Usher (1581 –1656). In 1650, after studying the genealogy of Christ as presented in the Bible, declared the Earth had been created in 4004 BCE and thus was under 6000 years old at the time.

[34]   Theodicy is a term coined by Leibniz (see below) and literally means God's justice. A theodicy is an argument justifying God's choice to allow evil in the world.

seemingly are already spiritually sound people. There is an accepted biased view that the rich are less ethical than the poor while, in fact, studies show that economically stressed groups are more often involved in crimes. At least, they are more often convicted of crimes. It does not appear that this level of criminal behavior is always due to bias on the part of courts or that the rich are able to obtain better legal advice, though this certainly happens. The fact is that the poor more often commit crimes because they are simply more in need of funds to stay afloat on a day to cay basis. If soul-making is promoted by suffering why are so many poor in our prisons?

A third issue associated with Irenaeus' 'soul-making' theodicy is that the qualities developed through experiencing evil are useful because they help humankind evolve to a higher level. In favor of a modified soul-making argument it may be said that the desired moral qualities are intrinsically valuable. In support of this view there is empirical verification. As will be discussed later, evil is essential to the evolutionary process. If there had been no suffering over the 4.6 billion years Earth has been around, we would not have evolved to the level we are at today. We are better humans and live in a more advanced society because of the difficulties we have faced over the centuries. Human growth and improvement in more than spiritual ways has occurred because we have overcome many challenges. In this sense, Irenaeus was right but it is not just soul-making that has been affected; it is the soul, the body, the mind and society as a whole that have grown and improved over the tens of thousands of years humans have been on Earth.

The belief in an afterlife has also been cited as justifying evil. Christian theologian Randy Alcon in *Heaven, The Purity Principle*, (2011), argues that the joys of Heaven will compensate for our sufferings on Earth, and writes:

"Without this eternal perspective, we assume that people who die young, who have handicaps, who suffer poor health, who don't get married or have children or who don't do this or that will miss out on the best life has to offer. But this assumption [that there is no afterlife] has a fatal flaw. It presumes that our present Earth, bodies, culture, relationships and lives are all there is…[but] Heaven will bring far more than compensation for our present sufferings."[35]

The Bible, ancient and modern religious authorities, human desires and the vast majority of humankind all maintain that there is a Heaven to look forward to if we are morally good and Hell for those who are morally bad. Most all of us want to live forever. We want a peaceful, trouble free life that goes on eternally. We want to be loved by all our friends, family and most especially by God forever. No matter how much we want such a life and no matter how many people believe in an afterlife, the fact is that there is no certainty that there is such a place. There is no empirical evidence to support such a concept.

There have been many people who claim to have died and then come back to life on Earth. Recently, Alex Malarkey who had written a best selling book along with his father, Kevin Malarkey, *The Boy Who Came Back From Heaven,* in 2010, just recently (Jan. 16, 2015) admitted he made this up after he was seriously injured in an accident. He was in a coma for two months following which he had difficulty speaking and walking and thought the story would get him some needed attention and sympathy. We simply have no way of verifying any of these "death and back to life" stories.[36]

If there is no afterlife then, of course, Randy Alcon's Problem of Evil argument is without merit.

---

[35] Alcon, Randy, 2009, *If God Is Good: Faith in the Midst of Suffering and Evil*, Kindle e-book, p. 243.

[36] http://www.washingtonpost.com/blogs/style-blog/wp/2015/01/15/boy-who-came-back-from-heaven-going-back-to-publisher/.

The Soul-Body Dualism Problem

Alcorn's, *The Purity Principle*,[37] is an epilogue to his, *if God Is Good*. In this book Alcorn presents a somewhat novel view of Heaven that is based on an updated interpretation of the Bible. He paints a most blissful view of life in Heaven. It is not a boring place floating in the clouds with everyone lounging around playing the harp. Rather, it is an earthly place, in which everyone enjoys the pleasure of God i.e. His beatific vision, while involved in a multitude of enjoyable activities. Alcon makes this a life after death that fully compensates for any sufferings endured during life on Earth.

This compensatory Heaven is based on Alcon's interpretation of the Bible, which he himself admits may seem heretical to some Christians. Unfortunately, there is no empirical certitude that such a heavenly place exists or that it is as Alcon describes it. Philosopher Stephen Maiden has called this the "Heaven Swamps Everything" theodicy, and argues that such an description of afterlife is invalid because it combines compensation and justification for all evils suffered and committed. He observes that this reasoning...may stem from imagining an ecstatic or forgiving state of mind on the part of the blissful. In Heaven no one bears grudges, even the most horrific earthly suffering is as nothing compared to infinite bliss, all past wrongs are forgiven. But "are forgiven" doesn't mean, "Were justified"; the blissful person's disinclination to dwell on his or her earthly suffering doesn't imply that a perfect being, i.e. God, is justified in permitting such earthly suffering. In addition, Alcon's view of Heaven is anthropomorphic. If we humans live on in Heaven as spirits, as is the usual religious view of our afterlife, then we aren't in a given place, we can't enjoy activities anything like the activities we enjoy on Earth. We can't sit

---

[37] Alcorn, R.,] L., 2009, *The Purity Principle,: God's Safeguards for Life's Dangerous Trails* (LifeChange Books) | Kindle eBook

around and look at God while enjoying His presence. As spirits we are not able to "sit around", "look" at anything (we aren't in space-time and spirits don't have eyes). We can't be involved in activities. Activities imply complex natures. Spirits are 'simple', that is, they don't have parts. Theologians tell us that anything that has parts, such as eyes, arms, hearts, brains and atoms/molecules, are mutable and thus corruptible. Such beings come to an end at some point in time. In other words, they die. But once we, as humans, die and our soul (spirit) goes to Heaven, we no longer are corruptible and will persist for all eternity. As spirits we can't even think because this involves brain activity and we no longer have a brain.

As young Christians we were taught that the soul acts through the brain and the other parts of our body. This implies that there is a 'soul-body' connection—a dualistic union. This implies there are two spheres that make up the world, which includes us humans. One is immaterial and one material. The soul is spiritual and immaterial. The body is material. They each belong to two entirely different spheres. The soul is 'simple'; it has no working part and thus is incorruptible and eternal. The body has trillions of working parts (cells, tissues and organs) and is thus corruptible. Anything with parts can come apart. Spirits are not corporeal or material and thus cannot exist in space or time. By definition only material things reside in space-time. Since these two 'spheres', the material and immaterial are limited to their separate spheres or realms. How is it that they can connect with one another? How is it that the soul can influence the body and in turn, how can the body relay information, images and feelings back to the soul? As currently defined the soul and body can't 'talk' to each other.

This is the body-soul dualism with which Rene Descartes (1596-1650) struggled five hundred years ago. He and many philosophers/theologians have anguished over this issue without resolution ever since.

Stephen J. Gould (1941–2002) of Harvard attempted to resolve this enigma by simply saying there is no resolution to this dualism. Religion and science reside in two entirely different 'magistaria' as he calls their two spheres, and these spheres or magistaria are 'non-overlapping'. We can never discuss religion and science (the spiritual and material) in the same way at the same time. They are "non-overlapping magisterial" (NOMA). They live in separate worlds never to be united.

Descartes tried to overcome this dualistic impasse by suggesting that the human soul resides in the pineal body—a small organelle situated in the center of the brain. Unfortunately, the pineal is material and is situated in space and time. The soul on the other hand is 'spiritual' and cannot be located anywhere in space and time. In addition, the soul has no way of communicating with anything material. We have been told by (in my case) priests, nuns and many others) that God, angels and even devils can interact with us. In essence we were led to believe that spirits can do anything from create the material world, keep the world going, stand by our side (as guardian angels), hear and respond to our prayers, and hover over us with caring kindness. The problem with these images is that spirits, as defined, are incapable of doing any of these things. To be able to connect with us, they have to be able to talk, touch, and comfort us. As material beings we have no means of experiencing such behaviors and spirits have no way of relaying such behaviors to us without being in some way material beings. However, if material, they cannot be eternal, all-knowing, all-powerful etc. as is God said to be and to a lesser extend are other spirits said to be. We've been told that spirits basically can do anything in some magical way. This is a comforting concept but logically impossible. God can't make square circles and He can't, as a spirit, create or connect with material beings. This too is logically impossible. Likewise, angels cannot dance on the head of a pin; they have no feet with which to dance.

We humans love myths. They explain things otherwise inexplicable. They help guide our lives, provide moral principals, and make the world a little more meaningful but they are after all fictional stories that comfort and guide us but are many times simply myths and not real. Most of us in the western world no longer believe in polytheistic gods. Science has clearly established that the Universe arose out of a 'Big Bang 13.8 billion year ago and that it was 4.6 billion years ago that Earth evolved and another billion years or so before life to emerged. Not everyone believes these scientific facts but the reality is that there was no Great Flood that wiped out all but Noah's family. The world wasn't created in six days and the first day of creation didn't begin at nine o'clock Sunday morning, October 23, 4004 BCE. The problem with this day and date, is that there was no time before creation and if James Usher were correct, then the calendar should have begun on day one and the calendar should be reset to reflect the number of days and years since then. So since Usher proclaimed this in 1650 then our calendar today would read 6019 (4004 + 2015) and Christ would have been born in the year 4004 although the exact year of Christ's birth is uncertain. It probably was 4 BCE. And, of course, there have been adjustments before and since Christ's birth. Julius Caesar made changes some forty years earlier and Pope Gregory XIII skipping ten days in 1582 to get the calendar on track.

The fact is that the Universe began with the Big Bang about 13.8 billion years ago and that may be as close as we can come to the time of creation. The point is that as science advances we need fewer myths to help us understand the world in which we live. It's difficult to give up ancient ideas even when they have become outdated. We like the comfort of simple, easily grasped stories that have been with us for millennia. It is so much easier to believe in a magically made Universe that popped into existence from nothing with a few divine words or the gentle waving of God's hand. The fact is that a spirit, even if divine, can't speak any words or wave His hand because He has no lips or hands by definition.

To understand the Big Bang is not easy. First of all how did the Bid Bang get started in the first place? Somebody or something had to set it in motion, right? So we need a first mover or first cause, as Aristotle suggested, or gods or a God as religions over the centuries have posited. And if this was a God was an anthropomorphic God, a deist God, a theistic God or some other kind of deity. In my *Problem Gods: In Search of a Meaningful Deity* I offered a deity more in line with todays science, including relativity and quantum theory.

The prevailing scientific model of how the Universe developed over time from the instant in which the Universe is thought to have begun rapidly expanding from a singularity is as of 2013, estimated to have begun 13.798 ± 0.037 billion years ago. It is convenient to divide the evolution of the Universe so far into three phases.

0 to 10^{-43} second after the Big Bang started, the four physical forces as we now know them (weak, strong, electromagnetic and gravitation) were but one force, and the nascent Universe was unimaginably hot. There was only intense energy and no matter, i.e. no atoms. In time as the Universe cooled the energy was converted into matter including quarks and antiquarks, electrons, protons and neutrons. After about 379,000 years the electrons and protons combined into atoms (mostly hydrogen). $E=mc^2$ is the formula Einstein developed showing the amount of matter that can be created out of a given amount of energy.

There was a period of rapid expansion of the Universe called the inflationary period. The Universe expanded very rapidly. Residual radiation produced during this time continued through space largely unimpeded. This relic radiation is known as the cosmic microwave background radiation and it is one of the ways we know of the Big

Bang. Eventually the Universe ended up composed of 75% hydrogen and 25% helium.

In time gravity causes hydrogen and helium to collect into large masses of matter that we now know as suns or stars. The gravitational force of a sun is huge and this causes the hydrogen to 'ignite' via atomic energy. There are literally millions of hydrogen bombs in each sun that produce the light and heat that comes from our Sun and all stars. The first stars and all stars thereafter were and are composed of these many hydrogen bombs exploding in all suns/stars. Over time these stars and suns run out of fuel, i.e. hydrogen and implode. In a matter of minutes, if massive enough, they collapse forming a supernova and then explode. During this brief implosion of the supernova, hydrogen and helium are crunched together with such force that they form larger atoms including lithium, carbon, oxygen, sodium, potassium, calcium, iron and even silver and gold. Many other new atoms are formed this way leaving stardust scattered in space. Then the sun making process begins all over again.

Our Sun is a second-generation descendant of a supernova. But now this new Sun of ours contains all the ingredients for life including us humans. This happened about 4.6 billion years ago as noted earlier. It took another billion years or so before life began to emerge on Earth and since then evolution given all the billions of species that have or are living on Earth today. We are literally made of stardust.

There is much more to this process that began with the Big Bang but we need not go into to this now. The basic point is that this is all very complex and not completely understood even today. It is reasonable that a large percentage of humans prefer the Genesis version of creation. It is not such a brain busting process to comprehend and it is the physicists who love to play with such mathematical and physical complexities.

Karma, Previous Lives and the Problem of Evil

The eastern religious concept of karma holds that good acts result in pleasure and bad acts in suffering. The doctrine of karma is part of the theology of Buddhism, Hinduism and other eastern religions. The theology of karma holds that there is suffering in the world, but there is no undeserved suffering, and thus no evil that is undeserved. The obvious objection to this approach is that some people suffer misfortune that is undeserved. This objection is answered by coupling karma with reincarnation, so that such suffering is the result of immoral behaviors in a previous life. This view eliminates any divine responsibility for the evil that is justified punishment for individual human immoral freewill behaviors.

Buddhism holds that all humans must gain nirvana by performing good deeds (good karma). Nirvana is the ultimate state obtained after death and it is achieved after ample good karma is built up during ones life or series of lives after repeated incarnations. If there is not enough good karma and too much bad karma then following death a person is doomed to be reincarnated as a lower level being. Instead of being a human once again a person may be a dog, a bird or even such low life as a worm. But if the he or she is able at this lower level to perform enough good deeds he or she might be reincarnated at a higher level and possibly after several reincarnations may make it back to being a human and finally with proper karma achieve nirvana for all eternity.

Nirvana is not like the Heaven of Christianity but rather is seen as a transcendental, "deathless" realm, in which there is no time and no "re-death." By following the Noble Eightfold Path, which culminates in the practice of *hyena* the mind is brought to rest and all three desires of passion, hatred and delusions are extinguished.

Generally, there are six realms of samsara. These
include: several Gods, the Asuras, Hungry Ghosts, Hell
Beings, as well as, Animals and Humans. In essence
nirvana is a quiet peace of mind unfettered by turmoil
and worldly cares. In Buddhism the suffering and evils
of life are explained as part of a process of cleansing
oneself of those aspects of one's being that prevent us from
entering into nirvana—the final ultimate peaceful state of
mind. This quietude is thought to be worth all the hassle
of reincarnations. In the end, this is one solution to the
Problem of Evil. The Buddhist God, however, is not like the
theistic God of Christianity. He is much less well defined
and thus not so difficult to exonerate from creating such an
evil world.

Human Limitations Regarding our Knowledge of God and the Problem of Evil

Another so-called 'skeptical theistic' argument holds
that due to humans' limited knowledge we cannot expect
to understand God or His ultimate plan. When a parent
takes an infant to the doctor for a routine vaccination
to prevent childhood diseases, it's because the parent
cares for and loves that child. The infant, however, will be
unable to appreciate the need for a needle stick and cries
in response to the pain. It is argued that just as an infant
cannot possibly understand the motives of the parent due
to its cognitive limitations, so too are adults unable to
comprehend God's reasoning. Given this view, the difficulty
or impossibility of finding a plausible explanation for evil in
a world created by a theistic God is to be expected.

Related to this argument is the concept of God as a
transcendent being. As transcendent, God lives in a realm
beyond our own. His nature is beyond not only the physical
world in which we live but also the spiritual, intellectual
world in which we live. God as such is totally beyond our

comprehension, imagination, and sensory world and thus this limits us to understanding only the world around us.

A related argument is that good and evil are strictly beyond human comprehension. Since our concepts of good and evil as instilled in us by God are only intended to facilitate ethical behavior in our relations with other humans, we should have no expectation that these ethical concepts are accurate beyond what is needed to fulfill this societal ethical function and therefore these perceptions cannot presume to be sufficient to determine whether what we call evil really is truly evil in the greater scheme of things. Evil for one person may be viewed as good by another. Though many believe in absolute ethical standards, this is a view that is hard to support empirically. If ethics are culturally and genetically based then they tend to change over time. If ethics is based on Darwinian natural selective advantages and these selective advantages are continually evolving as our environment evolves, then ethical standards must also change and evolve. This makes our understanding of the world along with good and evil just that much more enigmatic. As is said, the only constant is change.

With our inability to identify God's reasons for permitting evil, there remains a question as to why we have not been given clear and unambiguous assurances by God that He has good reasons for allowing evil, which would be within our ability to understand. Here discussion of the Problem of Evil moves to the atheistic argument of the Problem of evil. Does God really exist? Is what we call evil just an integral part of a purely materialistic world?

Denial of the Existence of God and the Problem of Evil

The atheistic view of the Problem of Evil can be simply stated as follows:

1. If the theistic God were all-good, all-knowing and all-powerful, then He would be capable of preventing all earthly evils.
2. There are earthly evils.
3. Therefore, there can be no theistic God.

This syllogism has been discussed before. It is simple and clear-cut but only applies to a theistic God. Any deity defined as less than infinite in all respects, can be accepted, as a being that allows evil without logical inconsistency. We can have a non-theistic God and evil existing together.

Such a God is, of course, unacceptable to followers of the three Abrahamic religions who are all theists. If theists are true to their various theologies, they must espouse a God that is capable of everything that is not logically self-contradictory, like creating a "round square". There has been some dogmatic decline for many Jews, Christians, and Muslims in recent decades and as a result theism is not as strongly held and pervasive as it once was and there is less of a problem with worldly evil for many believers. Still nearly 90 percent of Americans believe in God and the majority hold to the classical theistic God of the past 2000 years. As many as forty-five percent of Americans still believe in the Biblical account of creation. These classic theological tenets meet many emotional and spiritual needs and in spite of recent scientific advances resist changing their views of creation and God.

Evil as the Absence of Good

The privation of good (*privatio boni*) is a theological doctrine that holds evil, unlike good, to be insubstantial; so that thinking of evil as a positive or real thing, something that exists, is untenable. Rather, evil is considered to be the absence or lack ("privation") of good. This notion of evil is attributed to Augustine of Hippo (354-430), who wrote:

"And in the Universe, even that which is called evil, when it is regulated and put in its own place, only enhances our admiration of the good; for we enjoy and value the good more when we compare it with the evil. For the Almighty God, who, as even the heathen acknowledges, has supreme power over all things, being Himself supremely good, would never permit the existence of anything evil among His works, if He were not so omnipotent and good that He can bring good even out of evil. For what is that which we call evil but the absence of good? In the bodies of animals, disease and wounds mean nothing but the absence of health; for when a cure is effected, that does not mean that the evils which were present—namely, the diseases and wounds—go away from the body and dwell elsewhere: they altogether cease to exist; for the wound or disease is not a substance, but a defect in the fleshly substance—the flesh itself being a substance, and therefore something good, of which those evils—that is, privations of the good which we call health—are accidents. In the same way, what is called vices in the soul are nothing but privations of natural good. And when they are cured, they are not transferred elsewhere: when they cease to exist in the healthy soul, they cannot exist anywhere else."[38]

Using this metaphysical scheme it is evident that there is no evil in existence; all that God created is good. This evil is nothingness, just as death is the absence of life. When a person no longer receives life, he or she dies. Darkness is the absence of light: when there is no light, there is darkness. Light is an existing thing, but darkness is nonexistent. Wealth is an existing thing, but poverty is nonexistent. Thomas Aquinas maintains a similar view of

---

[38] Augustine. Quoting Epictetus, *The Enchiridion: What is Called Evil in the Universe is But the Absence of Good.*

evil as the absence of good. In the *Summa Theologica* he writes:

"Article 1. Whether good can be the cause of evil?

Objection 1. It would seem that good can not be the cause of evil. For it is said (Matthew 7:18): "A good tree cannot bring forth evil fruit."

Objection 2. Further, one contrary cannot be the cause of another. But evil is the contrary to good. Therefore good cannot be the cause of evil.

Objection 3. Further, a deficient effect can proceed only from a deficient cause. But evil is a deficient effect. Therefore its cause, if it has one, is deficient. But everything deficient is an evil. Therefore the cause of evil can only be evil.

Objection 4. Further, Dionysius[39] says (Div. Nom. iv) that evil has no cause. Therefore good is not the cause of evil. On the contrary, Augustine says (*Contra Julian.* i, 9): "There is no possible source of evil except good."

I answer that: It must be said that every evil in some way has a cause. For evil is the absence of the good which is natural and due to a thing. But that anything fail from its natural and due disposition can come only from some cause drawing it out of its proper disposition. For a heavy thing is not moved upwards except by some impelling force; nor does an agent fail in its action except from some impediment. But only good can be a cause; because nothing can be a cause except inasmuch as it is a being, and every being, as such, is good."

Both Augustine and Aquinas, as is their custom, are metaphysicians and as such can only use reason to reach their conclusions. All their works are speculative, such as Aquinas' five proofs for the existence of God. Even Aquinas" cosmological proof is not based on empirical evidence. The same applies to his approach to the Problem of Evil.

---

[39] This is probably Dionysius the Areopagite, a judge who is mentioned in the Acts of the Apostles, (Acts 17:34).

As an example, when Aquinas speaks of disease as the absence of good health, he fails to account for the modern medical definition of disease. Obesity accounts for many of our current health problems. Obesity results from excessive eating, genetics and lack of exercise as well as the scourge of 'fast food' restaurants and their French fired potatoes or 'chips' as they say in the UK. The lack of exercise may be a negative situation but too many calories, eating improper foods, desire for such foods and societal attitudes regarding foods cannot all be considered the absence of proper eating and proper life styles.

There are even better examples in infectious diseases. These conditions are caused by the presence of bacteria, viruses and other microbes. Even cancer of the uterine cervix is due to the papilloma virus. The cause of virtually all cancers can be traced to genetic modifications of normal cells leading to cellular overgrowth. Cancer is not just due to the absence of 'good' normal cells. Abnormal 'bad' cells are ultimately the cause of cancer. To use Aquinas' philosophical term, they have a 'being' of their own. These are 'bad beings' instead of 'good' beings present that cause diseases. There is, indeed, in Aristotle words, a substantial or essential reality to these disease processes. Actual beings that are bad are evident in many situations. Not all beings are good, thus, God has made beings that end up bad. Not all created things are forever good. Beings can be transformed from good to bad. God at best has allowed bad beings to evolve.

The presence of evil is certainly evident in moral evil. Moral evil occurs when a human being with freewill makes a definite decision to commit an evil deed. We all are guilty at sometime or another of performing acts that we know cause unhappiness or suffering in the lives of others. We often excuse these acts as necessary for our own good.

As we listen to the news each day there is evil reported worldwide. Thousands of excuses are given for evil acts whether small or large. It is difficult for most of us to understand why a father would kill his three daughters or why a mother would drown her child. Such evils may relate to mental illness, nonetheless, these acts are tragic happenings that a 'good and loving' God it seems should not allow.

There is nothing intrinsically evil about natural evils such as hurricanes, mudslides, earthquakes and tsunamis. A lightning strike is simply a natural phenomenon. It is a natural occurrence associated with winds that cause voltage differences in the atmosphere. But when lighting touches off a wild fire, lives and property may be lost. This is an evil but not due to the absence of 'good' weather. There are real, very real happenings that occur. Rain is good in drought areas but rainstorms may be associated with lightening or floods. These are all existential happenings. They are not just the absence of 'good' weather.

At any rate, with the help of modern empirical science the 'absence of good' solution fails to solve the Problem of Evil in spite of the efforts of two of the greatest theologians of Christianity: Augustine and Aquinas.

Taoism and the Problem of Evil

A related view, which draws on the Taoist concept of yin-yang, allows both evil and good to have positive reality, but maintains they are complementary opposites, where the existence of one is dependent on the other. Compassion, a valuable virtue, can only exist if there is suffering; bravery only exists if we sometimes face danger; self-sacrifice is called for only where others are in need. This is sometimes called the "contrast" argument. Perhaps the most important criticism of this view is that, even granting its success in dealing with the Problem of Evil, it does nothing to undermine the argument that evil is the absence of goodness, and so this response, similar to the soul-making argument is only superficially successful.

In addition, we are still faced with the question of why God allows evil. One might say that evil contrasted with virtue helps us to grow ethically. This is again the 'soul making' argument covered earlier. Undoubtedly this is true, but why doesn't God skip the 'middle man' i.e. evil, and create a world without evil? Couldn't we be born with pervasive virtue? The world would be so much better. We wouldn't have to earn our stripes, so to speak, and the world might be a much more pleasant place. Otherwise, God is made out to be a demanding taskmaster and not all good and all kind.

Taoism like Stoicism has the one plus in that it offers us a positive attitudinal approach to evil. There are many things we can do nothing about. Stoicism suggests we accept things we cannot change but to work 'hard as Hell' to change the things we can. Taoism offers a similar approach to life. It emphasizes living in harmony with the Tao. The Tao is the absolute principle underlying the Universe, combining within itself the principles of yin and yang and signifying the way, or code of behavior that is in harmony with the natural order. In other words, accept and live in harmony with the natural order. For Christians and many other religions, this means to live harmoniously with God and the laws of nature as He has designed them.

As we shall see later that Darwinian theory supports such an approach to the Problem of Evil but it also requires a God that is not truly theistic. The Taoist approach is in accord with the thesis of this book: we as a species can only evolve to a higher lever by facing and dealing with our ever-changing environment.

Evil as illusory

It is possible to hold that evils such as diseases and earthquakes are mere evil illusions, and that we are mistaken about the existence of actual evil. This approach is favored by some religious groups, such as Hindus and Buddhists, as well as, Christian Scientists.

In the Hindu tradition the Problem of Evil is considered to be the Problem of Injustice. As such, God is omnipotent, omniscient, and, yet injustice is found throughout the world. How is this possible?

God cannot be charged with injustice, it is clamed, because He considers the virtues and vices in each of our lives, that is the karma or behaviors performed by each individual in a prior life(s). Metempsychosis or reincarnation is a key element of Hinduism and Buddhism as seen above. If a person experiences pleasure or pain in this life, it is due to virtuous or vicious actions done in a past life. Since reincarnation paradoxically has no beginning (as claim the proponents of this approach) then the opponents of this system cannot argue that there is no karma effect in a person's previous life. Those that favor karma as the answer to evil maintain that there was no "previous birth" at the very beginning of creation, because the creation cycles are 'beginningless', that is, they go back eternally into the past. These cycles are like God who is also 'beginningless'. He extends eternally from the past and will continue eternally into the future. For us humans who are creatures of beginnings and endings, this concept is beyond our comprehension. Thus, the Hindu resolution for the problem of Injustice is that the existence of injustice in the world is only apparent and not real, for we merely reap the results of our moral actions sown in a past life, which is compatible with the justice of an omniscient and omnipotent God. I find this solution difficult to follow. At any rate it seems they are saying that evil is illusory because it is the price we pay for immoral acts performed in a previous life and so the evil we experience today is simply the just due we deserve for past evil acts. I find it hard to believe that natural evils can be viewed as illusory. A tornado is as real as something gets. Emotional evils may be illusory in the sense that we can at times reduce emotional suffering by thinking differently about our feelings as the Stoics suggested 2500 years ago.

At a higher level of existence, Hinduism holds, there is no evil or good since these are dependent on temporal circumstances. Hence, a person who has realized her true nature, is beyond such dualistic notions. This may be circular reasoning or simply a tautology. Either way the argument that evil is illusory is at best very difficult to follow.

Another approach to this argument is that the Problem of Evil is present but does not exist *per se* i.e. in and of itself, since souls in the Buddhist's view are eternal and not directly created by God. In Dvaita (dualistic) philosophy,[40] souls exist eternally and are not creations of God *ex nihilo* (out of nothing), and thus are not products of nature as are bodies, wealth, power, and suffering. In effect, Hinduism identifies *avidya* (ignorance) as the cause of evil, and this ignorance is uncaused. Suffering from natural causes is explained as a natural karmic result of previous births not due to God's actions. Moreover, even within the realm of ignorance, good and evil are an individual's deeds, and God dispenses the proper consequences, i.e. punishment that naturally flows from an individual's actions. God does have the power to mitigate suffering if He so chooses: He is simply dealing out what is just punishment for the person's actions, past and present.

God experiences every pain, suffers every indignity, dies every death, and experiences the illusion of being part of each separate individual. The idea that God suffers along with every human is a tenet of modern day Process Theology.

---

[40] Dvaita philosophy stresses a strict distinction between God, the Supreme-Soul, and our individual souls. According to Dvaita, the individual souls of beings are not 'created' by God but do, nonetheless, depend on Him for their existence. Because God did not create individual souls, he is not responsible for the evil they do.

Buddhism and Evil

Buddhism rejects the authority of the *Vedas* and of the other writings of Hinduism. The Buddhists on the other hand explain the nature of evil through the process of 'constant becoming'. Evil is the perpetuation of the illusion of evil by the chain of 'dependent origination'. The ignorance that Buddha spoke of involves the failure to understand that the world is impermanent, devoid of a self and in a constant state of becoming (evolving?) which accounts for suffering.

The Buddha proclaimed that the whole of existence is suffering:

"The Noble Truth of Suffering (*dukkha*) is this: Birth is suffering; aging is suffering; sickness is suffering; death is suffering; sorrow and lamentation, pain, grief, and despair are suffering; association with the unpleasant is suffering; dissociation from the pleasant is suffering; not to get what one wants is suffering, in brief, the five aggregates of attachment are suffering". (*Samyutta Nikaya* 56,11).

There are, according to Buddha, three fundamental defilements of the mind that combine and interact leading to suffering: greed (*raga*), aversion (*dvesha*) and ignorance (*avidya*). These arise out of a desire to experience existence in a personal way, but personhood is nothing but an illusion. The desire to perpetuate the illusion of personal existence produces suffering, so its extreme solution must be the abolition of personhood. There is no suffering if there is no person left to experience it.

Buddha proclaimed four spiritually noble truths. These are the truth of suffering, the truth of arising, the truth of cessation, and the truth of the path. It is the truth of suffering that relates to the Problem of Evil but arising, cessation and the path all seem to contribute to evil. They are all difficult processes. Life is difficult. But why need life be so difficult? The answer offered in this present book is evolution, which maybe what Buddha was talking about

2500 years ago though he had no vision of Darwinian natural selection and DNA. Buddha did, however understands that challenges drive us toward a better life. This is much the same as the 'soul-making' of Iranaeus and the evolution of Darwin.

Evil as a Test of Our Faith

In the Book of Job, we read about a man that was good and faithful to God but as is the case in many OT parables, Job is tested by God who allows the devil to devastate Job monetarily, physically and emotionally. He loses all his cattle, crops, family and health. All these evils are allowed by God as a test of his faith in God. Job passes the test with flying colors and God then returns all his goods and gives him a new family. (Job 1.1-2.7 & 42.7-42.16). Also in Job14:1 the OT reads:

"Man that is born of a woman is of few days, and these full of trouble."

It is an obvious fact that all of us suffer to some degree or another on a daily basis. Either the weather isn't quite to our liking or we worry about money or our job or health. And the list goes on and on. We have many happy minutes, hours or days as well but some experience a life full of emotional and/or physical pain so that for many only suicide seems to offer any relief.

At this moment of writing, a good friend is in the hospital undergoing treatment for acute myelogenous leukemia. This is a very serious "blood cancer" with a limited prognosis. He is faced with the question, "Why is this happening to me." He's 58 and has been generally healthy, but now he may be dying with this devastating disorder; a disease that took his wife just a few years ago.[41] Is God allowing this to test his faith? He is understandably very depressed over all this and is searching for the

---

[41]   Since writing this, our friend is now in total recovery from his leukemia one year after treatment.

reasons, "why me, why now, why my wife?" He is a good person, very caring and compassionate—a modern day Job; so why, why, why?

If God is all-good, all-knowing and all-powerful, He knows that this man is faithful and God fearing. No divine test should be necessary. God, with His infinite nature, knows all past and present happenings. He knows what my friend will do always and everywhere. So why would God choose to enlist such a despicable demon as Satan to do these dirty deeds to Job, my friend and the billions of human beings throughout the ages and all over the Earth?

We might pose the same questions as well for the suffering that all sentient animals endure daily.

Denial of God's Omnibenevolence and the Problem of Evil

Dystheism is the belief that God is not wholly good. Pantheists and panentheists,[42] who are dystheistic may also avoid the Problem of Evil by defining God as other than theistic, i.e. God as not fully metaphysical nor entirely anthropomorphic. Pantheism holds God and the Universe are one. They are, if one can use the term in reference to God, coextensive. Panentheism, on the other hand, considers God as 'extending' beyond our Universe. God in this view is bigger than our known Universe. God includes our Universe but much more. Again, as pointed out above, a spirit by definition is not limited by space

---

[42] Panentheism (from Greek πάν (pân) "all"; ἐν (en) "in"; and θεός (theós) "God"; "all-in-God") is a belief system which believes the divine being whether monotheistic, polytheistic, or an eternal cosmic animating force, penetrates every part of nature and timelessly extends beyond all of nature. Panentheism is differentiated from pantheism by claiming the God is synonymous or co-extensive with the Universe but does not extend beyond the known Universe. Unlike pantheism, panentheism is the belief that God is greater than the Universe and though God includes the Universe, He also extends infinitely beyond it. From the Google dictionary.

71

and time and, thus, God as a spirit, cannot be viewed as extending anywhere in space or time. Just as God is eternal and thus not of or in time, He is 'spaceless', and cannot exist in or be of space. Nonetheless, theists see God as residing throughout the Universe and infinitely beyond it and existing eternally in time. Any 'spiritual' being, by definition simply cannot do these things. If you redefine God as partially spiritual and partially material then you would have to redefine 'spirit' and 'matter'. If 'spirit' is a little bit material, such a spirit cannot be immortal because anything that is even partially material is mutable and cannot be immortal. In addition, if 'spirit' has some material elements then we are faced with the age-old problem of Descartes' dualism. How do you connect a spirit that is 'spaceless' to a material element that exist only in space? They 'live', so to speak, in two entirely different realms.

The dystheistic God, as opposed to the theistic God, is not 'all-everything' including not all-good, not all knowing and not all-powerful. Dystheism, thus, eliminates the Problem of Evil but leaves us with a God that isn't capable of doing all the things that traditional religions and most humans want in a God such as create the world, care for us, answer all our prayers and personally attends to our every need. A metaphysical God can be all-good, etc.; an anthropomorphic God can be fatherly and all-caring, etc. but cannot be all-everything. A metaphysical/anthropomorphic God is self-contradictory by definition. He is a round circle.

Thus, the dystheistic God may have a logically consistent nature but cannot be omnibenevolent and thus this type of God solves the Problem of Evil but this leaves us with a God who is limited in what He can do and thus fails to satisfy the needs of the majority of believers worldwide.

Chapter 4
A Historical View of the Problem of Evil

In ancient Mesopotamia the Problem of Evil was based on polytheistic religious thought. There were multiple anthropomorphic gods. Their behaviors, like the behaviors of us humans, were often chaotic, self-centered, and emotional. These multiple gods were constantly battling for control. Their interests lay not with mere earthlings but with power over other gods, womanizing and punishing all those who fail to honor and obey them. There was no Problem of Evil because the ancient gods were not theistic. They were not all-everything. They could err. They were like us humans, given to failings of reason, the passions and behaviors that the theistic God is not, b y definition, allowed to display.

In Ancient Egypt, it is thought the problem took at least two forms, as found in the extant manuscript, *Dialogue of a Man*. In this treatise a man accuses his soul of wanting to desert him, and of dragging him towards death before his time. He says that life is too heavy for him to bear, that his heart would come to rest in the West (i.e. the afterlife), his name would survive, but his body would be protected. He urges his soul to be patient and wait for a son to be born to provide the offerings he needs in the afterlife. His soul describes the sadness death brings and responds to the man's complaints about his lack of worth; his being cut off from humanity; and the attractiveness of death; exhorting him to embrace life. His soul promises to stay with him.[43] This man appears to be extremely depressed and pulled down by the worries of the world. He seems not to be suicidal according the translator of the papyrus.

Egyptian gods are seen as being far removed from ordinary humans. The Egyptian gods are portrayed as distant and anthropomorphic and are not responsible for creation and thus not responsible for human acts, good or

---

[43] Egyptian religion, Wikipedia.

bad. Also, these gods were not theistic. As non-creators and not infinite, they could not be blamed for evil, moral or natural.

Chapter 5 The Bible

The Hebrew Bible

A verse in the Book of Isaiah is translated in the King James Bible as:

"I form the light, and create darkness: I make peace, and create evil: I the LORD do all these things" (Isaiah, 45:7).

The Hebrew word for evil is *rag'/*רַע, a word that occurs 663 times in the Jewish Bible. Evil is a generic term for something considered bad in either a physical or moral sense. The King James Bible translates the Hebrew (*ra'/*רַע) as evil 442 times and includes other words for evil including wickedness, hurt, trouble, and affliction.

The Book of Job is one of the most widely known formulations in Western thought that questions why suffering exists. Originally written in Hebrew as an epic poem, the story as we have seen above, centers on Job, a perfectly just and righteous person. He makes no serious errors in life and strives to do nothing wrong; as a result he is very materially successful. A character described only as the 'Accuser' (Satan) challenges God, claiming that Job is only righteous because God has rewarded him with a good life. The Accuser proposes that if God were to allow everything Job loves to be destroyed, Job would then cease to be righteous. God allows the Accuser to destroy Job's wealth and children, and to inflict him with sickness and boils. Job discusses his condition with three friends. His three friends insist that God never allows bad things to happen to good people, and assert that Job must have done something to deserve his punishment. Job responds that this is not true and that he would be willing to defend himself against these accusations. A fourth friend, Elihu, arrives and criticizes all of them. Elihu states that God is perfectly just and good. God then responds to Job in a speech delivered from "out of a whirlwind", explaining the Universe from God's perspective, stating that the workings of the world are beyond human understanding. In the end, God says that the three friends were incorrect, and that Job was incorrect for assuming he could question God. God more than restores Job's prior health, wealth, and gives him a new family, as though he has been awakened from a nightmare into a new spirituality. The Book of Job offers two answers: suffering is a test, and you will be rewarded later for passing it. God is thus not held accountable by human standards of morality. Ecclesiastes sees suffering as beyond human abilities to comprehend.

An oral tradition exists in Judaism that God determined the time of the Messiah's coming by erecting a great set of scales. On one side, God places the captive Messiah with the souls of dead laymen. On the other side of the scale, God places sorrow, tears, and the souls of righteous martyrs. God then declares that the Messiah will appear on Earth when the scales are balanced. According to this tradition, then, evil is necessary in the bringing of the world's redemption, as sufferings reside on the scales. The Talmud states that every bad thing is for the ultimate good, and a person should praise God for bad things just as he praises God for good things.

Tzimtzum in Kabbalistic thought holds that God has withdrawn Himself so that creation can occur, but this withdrawal means that all of creation lacks full exposure to God's all-good nature. In essence the burden of evil falls back on humankind as their just due.

These explanations of Jewish thought regarding the Problem of Evil include several elements, some of which we have discussed earlier. First of all, God is beyond our comprehension. What He wills is not always within our limited understanding. Second, He can be questioned but a satisfactory answer is not always forthcoming. Thirdly, God can test us in order to affirm our ultimate willingness to follow His commands and fourthly, God will reward us if we respond well to the test.

These ideas from the Book of Job are typical of the OT. These are ancient ideas but modern thought and experience belie such views. As mentioned before, God is incomprehensible, but as all-good and powerful He is capable of making decisions that are understandable even for the human mind. Also, we all have experienced situations or known people who suffered great misfortunes without being compensated for such trials even when they are demonstrably good people. And of course, God, if all-knowing, already knows that Job is a good, God fearing man. No tests are needed for God who knows all things.

The Old Testament versus the New Testament

The Jewish view of the Problem of Evil varies some from other views but it maintains that God has good reasons for allowing evil, not all of which are humanly knowable. At one point God seems less than infinitely divine. He has a certain anthropomorphic aspect and even a deistic bent. Of course the OT portrays God as more humanlike than God the Father of the NT. He is more emotional, jealous, and avaricious. Jesus Christ, whom Christians believe is the second person of the Trinity, is depicted in the NT as much more loving, understanding, and less demanding than the OT God, even though Christ is considered consubstantial with the other two persons of the Trinity. As consubstantial Christ is fully divine and equal in all respects to God the Father and the Holy Spirit. The OT and NT Gods are, thus, quite different. This probably represents a cultural difference in how God was viewed in antiquity versus the Middle Ages. The OT God took on a more stern and severe aspect, which may have reflected the hardships the Jews suffered in Egypt and Canaan. They were basically slaves in Egypt and nomads without a home while wandering in the desert. The face of God has always reflected the cultural face of those who defined their God or gods. When the polytheism of the Near East and ancient Greece was transformed into the monotheism of Judaism, Christianity and Islam, this Abrahamic God took on many of the characteristics of the early gods all rolled into one God. Christ was the good God who was also fully human and even gave up his life in order to save all humankind. This was a theological first. Never before was God so kindly. This, too, was most likely due to cultural influences.

The OT is replete with evil, most of which we would view as unjust today. The following is an incomplete list of OT mandated evils:

- Kill People Who Don't Listen to Priests.

"Anyone arrogant enough to reject the verdict of the judge or of the priest who represents the LORD your God must be put to death. Such evil must be purged from Israel. (Deuteronomy 17:12 NLT).

- Kill Witches. "You should not let a sorceress live." (Exodus 22:17 NAB).

- Kill Homosexuals.

"If a man lies with a male as with a women, both of them shall be put to death for their abominable deed; they have forfeited their lives." (Leviticus 20:13 NAB).

- Kill Fortune tellers:

"A man or a woman who acts as a medium or fortuneteller shall be put to death by stoning; they have no one but themselves to blame for their death." (Leviticus 20:2 NAB).

- Death for hitting one's parent.

"Whoever strikes his father or mother shall be put to death." (Exodus 21:15 NAB).

- Death for Cursing Parents.

1) If one curses his father or mother, his lamp will go out at the coming of darkness. (Proverbs 20:20, NAB).

2) All who curse their father or mother must be put to death. They are guilty of a capital offense. (Leviticus 20:9 NLT).

- Death for Adultery.

"If a man commits adultery with another man's wife, both the man and the woman must be put t death." (Leviticus 20:10 NLT).

- Death for Fornication.

"A priest's daughter who loses her honor by committing fornication and thereby dishonors her father also, shall be burned to death." (Leviticus 21:9 NAB).

- Death to Followers of Other Religions: "Whoever sacrifices to any god, except the Lord alone, shall be doomed. (Exodus 22:19 NAB).
- Kill Nonbelievers: "They entered into a covenant to seek the Lord, the God of their fathers, with all their heart and soul; and everyone who would not seek the Lord, the God of Israel, was to be put to death, whether small or great, whether man or woman. (2 Chronicles 15:12-13 NAB).
- Kill False Prophets: "If a man still prophesies, his parents, father and mother, shall say to him, You shall not live, because you have spoken a lie in the name of the Lord. When he prophesies, his parents, father and mother, shall thrust him through." (Zachariah 13:3 NAB).
- Kill the entire town if one person worships another god. "Suppose you hear in one of the towns the LORD your God is giving you that some worthless rabble among you `have led their fellow citizens astray by encouraging them to worship foreign gods. In such cases, you must examine the facts carefully. If you find it is true and can prove that such a detestable act has occurred among you, you must attack that town and completely destroy all its inhabitants, as well as all the livestock. Then you must pile all the plunder in the middle of the street and burn it. Put the entire town

to the torch as a burnt offering to the LORD your God. That town must remain a ruin forever; it may never be rebuilt. Keep none of the plunder that has been set apart for destruction. Then the LORD will turn from His fierce anger and be merciful to you. He will have compassion on you and make you a great nation, just as He solemnly promised your ancestors. The LORD your God will be merciful only if you obey him and keep all the commands I am giving you today, doing what is pleasing to him." (Deuteronomy 13:13-19 NLT).

- Kill Women Who Are Not Virgins On Their Wedding Night:

"But if this charge is true (that she wasn't a virgin on her wedding night), and evidence of the girl's virginity is not found, they shall bring the girl to the entrance of her fathers house and there her townsman shall stone her to death, because she committed a crime against Israel by her unchasteness in her father's house. Thus shall you purge the evil from your midst." (Deuteronomy 22:20-21 NAB).

- Kill Followers of OtherReligions.

If your own full brother, or your son or daughter, or your beloved wife, or your intimate friend, entices you secretly to serve other gods, whom you and your fathers have not known, gods of any other nations, near at hand or far away, from one end of the earth to the other: do not yield to him or listen to him, nor look with pity upon him, to spare or shield him, but kill him. Your hand shall be the first raised to slay him; the rest of the people shall join in with you. You shall stone him to death, because he sought to lead you astray from the Lord, your God, who brought you out of the land of Egypt, that place of slavery. And all Israel, hearing of this, shall fear and never do such evil as this in your midst." (Deuteronomy 13:7-12 NAB).

The list goes on and on. The percentage of woman that are not virgins when married the first time is about 97 percentage in America today. Of those who are very religious when they marry about 80% are not virgins.[44] If we all followed the OT dictates, the vast majority of newly weds would have to be eliminated. I am assuming that this command includes men who are not virgins on their wedding night as well.

The NT has many cruel comments as well, many just as evil and harsh.[45] A few NT evils as found in Matthew's gospel are the following:

- "Those who bear bad fruit will be cut down and burned with unquenchable fire." Matt.3:10, 12."
- "Jesus strongly approves of the law and the prophets. He hasn't the slightest objection to the cruelties of the Old Testament." 5:17. "Jesus recommends that to avoid sin we cut off our hands and pluck out our eyes. This advice is given immediately after he says that anyone who looks with lust at any women commits adultery." Matt. 5:29-30. I would assume this includes most men that are not gay.
- "Jesus says that most people will go to hell." Mat. 7:13-14.
- "Those who fail to bear good fruit will be hewn down, and cast into the fire." Matt. 7:19.
- "The children of the kingdom [the Jews] shall be cast out into outer darkness: there shall be weeping and gnashing of teeth." Matt.8:12.
- "Jesus sends some devils into a herd of pigs, causing them to run off a cliff and drown in the water below." Matt. 8:32.
- "Cities that neither receive the disciples nor hear their words will be destroyed. God. It will be worse for them than for Sodom and Gomorrah. And you know what God supposedly did to those poor folks." Matt. 10:14-15.
- "Jesus says that we should fear God who is willing and able to destroy both soul and body in hell." Matt. 10:28.

---

44   http://waitingtillmarriage.org/4-cool-statistics-about-abstinence-in-the-usa/.

45   http://skepticsannotatedbible.com/mt/cr_list.html.

- "Jesus says that he has come to destroy families by making family members hate each one another. He has come not to send peace, but a sword." Matt.10:34-36.
- "Jesus condemns entire cities to dreadful deaths and to the eternal torment of Hell because they didn't care for his preaching. Matt. 11:20-24.
- "Jesus will send his angels to gather up all that offend and they shall cast them into a furnace of fire: there shall be wailing and gnashing of teeth." Matt. 13:41-42, 50.

These NT quotes are examples of the sort of evils that are attributed to Christ. The tenor of these quotes seem to me to be as harsh and vindictive as those in the OT but they are offset somewhat by the many kindly acts performed by Jesus as recorded in the NT. Of course, the NT was written mostly in the first century CE, the culture of this century was different than the culture when the OT was composed. If one accepts these statements as written, they do portray a world full of evil with vindictive punishments by God for these several immoral, impious and hateful acts perpetrated by humans at the time. The Problem of Evil is not dealt with to any extent because God is obliged to punish evil beings that perform evil deeds. No mention is made of natural evils.

Chapter 6
The Growing Authority of the Catholic Church

Many early Christians were socially and economically disadvantaged. Having a caring, compassionate God in Jesus Christ brought comfort into their emotional and spiritual lives. Over time, however, the Roman Catholic Church became more Roman and less catholic. The Church, especially after Constantine's conversion to Christianity in 312 CE, evolved into an institutionalized, authoritarian, political and financially oriented religious organization. Helena and her son, Constantine flowered the Church with cathedrals, wealth and authority. If one looks at the Church hierarchy as Martin Luther did in 1511, just before the Reformation, the hierarchy appeared worldly, money hungry and sexually immoral. During the High Middle Ages the Church took on the character of a super power, often battling with the nascent countries of Europe for political control of society. The most famous case was in 1077 when the Holy Roman Emperor, Henry II, was literally brought to his knees in the snows of Canossa in Northern Italy by Pope Gregory VII. This was a complex political battle that led to Henry's excommunication and ultimately his acquiescence to Pope Gregory.

At one point the Vatican proclaimed itself the supreme political power over all of Western Europe and this authoritarian posturing persisted for several centuries, even up to 1870 when Italy reclaimed virtually all of the land in Northern Italy that the Vatican had held since the Middle Ages as its Papal States. The Vatican retained only one square mile of land near Rome as the present-day Vatican.

Much of the Church's political machinations were determined by the political situation in Europe during the Middle Ages. The countries in Western Europe at the time were poorly organized and the Church helped to stabilize the geo-political structure somewhat. However, once power is gained it is hard to abandon.

Politics has played a role in the Church's view of God since the Second Century when it began a doctrinal struggle with the various 'heresies' of the early Christian

Church. Theologically, Proto-orthodox Christianity[46] was in various doctrinal conflicts with the Gnostics, Manicheans and other early sects. By the time of the Council of Nicaea in 325 CE, Christ was declared divine and this doctrine was confirmed in several subsequent councils including the Councils of Constantinople (381), Ephesus (431), and Chalcedon (451). The face of God was changing from the OT God of the Jews to the NT Trinity with Christ as equal to God the Father.

The Divinity of Christ

Christ never declared himself divine. He was referred to in the NT several times as the "Son of Man" and the "Son of God", but these titles and especially the latter one did not imply divinity. It meant simply that he was "A Godly Man". Constantine, who knew no theology, appointed himself head of the Council of Nicaea for political reasons and supported Athanasius of Alexandria (c. 296–373), against Arius (c. 250-339). Arius believed that Christ was not fully consubstantial with God the Father. He was only semi-divine, was not eternal from all past time because the Father had created him in time. As human, Christ was of space-time in contrast to God the Father who existed outside of space-time. Athanasius believed that Christ was the second person of the Trinity and as such was consubstantial with the Father and the Holy Spirit. Consubstantial means that Christ possessed the same substance, essence or being as the other two persons of the Trinity. In a sense it would be like three persons having the same soul. The term hypostasis is often applied in

---

[46]   Proto-orthodox Christianity is a term, coined by New Testament scholar Bart D. Ehrman, used to describe the early Christian movement that was the precursor of Christian orthodoxy. Ehrman argues that this group, which became prominent by the end of the third century, ultimately stifled its opposition, and in the end emerged as the Roman Catholic Church that held sway until the Protestant Reformation.

such theological situations. This term has also been used in describing Christ as having one soul but two aspects, one human and one divine. Christ since the Council of Chalcedon has been said to be, at one and the same time, fully human and fully divine but possessed of but one soul.

There have been several divine trinities spoken of throughout history including in Babylonia, Assyria and Egypt. It is likely that Christianity borrowed this concept from earlier religions. The first trinities portrayed the gods as father, mother and child. This format has been applied to the Triune God of Christianity with the Father, Son and the Holy Spirit, the last as a feminine figure.

The Catholic Church early on began minimizing the role of women in the Church even though there were women priests, such as Mary Magdalene, Phoebe, Petronella, and others when Christ was alive and for a time after his death. Pope Celsius I in 494 CE wrote a letter to the bishops of three regions of southern Italy complaining of women presiding at the liturgy. As men dominated the Church, God the Father became more like the OT God. Christ, however, for the most part did maintain his compassionate image as depicted in the NT but the Holy Spirit lost His feminine features

The authoritarian God of the OT was resurrected early in the history of the Catholic Church. The pope assumed the title of *Vicarius Filii Dei* (Vicar i.e. Representative of the Son of God). This title was first used in the forged medieval document, *The Donation of Constantine,* which identified the pope as the successor to the apostle Peter and thus the pope as successor to Peter as 'Vicar of Christ'. Its interpretation of the pope's position has been disputed over the past four centuries. *The Donation of Constantine* was a forged Roman imperial decree attributed to Constantine by which the emperor supposedly transferred authority over Rome and the western part of the Roman Empire to the Pope. This document was probably composed in the eighth century. It was used, especially in the thirteenth century, to support claims of political supremacy by the papacy over the Papal Estates. At the time, these included most of northern Italy. The intent of the title 'Vicar of Christ' was to strengthen the authority of the pope. *The Donation of Constantine* indicated that the Emperor Constantine not only gave the land to the Church but that the pope, as the Vicar of Christ, was the recipient of all divine commands and that he was next only to Christ in interpreting such divine commands. In essence, what the pope proclaimed came directly from Jesus Christ and the pope's word was thus infallible, not to be questioned by any mere human. This, in effect, *The Donation* legitimatized, among other things, the many murders perpetrated on "heretics" in Antiquity and during the Middle Ages.

The compassionate Christ of the NT had now evolved into the Son of the OT God. God through Christ was once again a vindictive, jealous, authoritarian and hateful God who not only allowed evil in the world but also, in fact, performed evil through the pope, the Vicar of Christ. Of course, this scenario only made the Problem of Evil more of a problem.

During the reign of Pope Pius XII he wrote two encyclicals: the *Mystici Corporis Christi* (The Mystical Body of Christ, 1943) and, *Humani generis* (The Origins of Humans, 1950), both strengthened the authority of the pope as the Vicar of Christ, the one and only interpreter of God's word.

The Church over the past centuries has continued to strengthen its theological position. It no longer burns "heretics' at the stake but does continue to suppress and excommunicate voices that speak out against various policies of the Church. Pierre Teilhard de Chardin (1881--1955), a Jesuit and noted paleontologist, was exiled to the Far East for his views on Darwin's Theory of Evolution. Gustavo Gutiérrez (b. 1928) was reprimanded for his Liberation Theology that the Church felt smacked of Marxism. In just the past few years the Leadership

Conference of Women Religious has been investigated for its views on theological issues that the Church believes to be less than orthodox.

The authoritarianism of the Church continues though without burnings at the stake. Nonetheless, these are injustices that are mediated by the Church in the name of God making Him responsible for evil and leaving unresolved the Problem of Evil.

The Gnostic Response to the Problem of Evil

Gnosticism refers to several early (Christian?) sects that competed with the Proto-Catholic Church. They saw the world as evil because it was created by an imperfect demiurge, Sophia[47]. The Gnostic God was transcendent, that is, totally above and beyond the reach of humans. God, as transcendent, can have no interaction, contact or intercourse of any sort with material beings. As we have seen, a spirit is by definition, devoid of any material elements. Because of this limitation God had to create a creator who was capable of interactions with material beings and for the Gnostics this was Sophia. However, since Sophia is not a god in the fullest sense, she is imperfect and as a result made an imperfect world—a world full of suffering and evil. The Problem of Evil in the world is therefore not directly due to an all-knowing, all-good and all-powerful God. Evil is due to this imperfect demiurge that God made. Does this solve the Problem of Evil? I think not, it just adds one step to the process of the Problem of Evil because God created Sophia and therefor is ultimately the cause of evil.

As noted above, our body precludes any intellectual or physical awareness of God. God must, as transcendent, be

---

[47] Demiurge: In Gnosticism and other theological systems, a heavenly being, subordinate to the Supreme Being that is considered to be the creator and controller of the material world and antagonistic to all that is purely spiritual.

beyond our understanding. I suppose our soul as spiritual could conceivably perceive God since one spirit ought to be able to connect with another spirit such as God and angels, however, this takes us into the mind-body dichotomy that has plagued us for centuries. Since psychologists maintain that all human knowledge comes through the five senses, there has to be some interaction between the soul and body, so far even our best psycho-physiological thinkers have not solved this mind-body dualism problem.

Theologians tell us that the soul mediates its functions though the body. Our sensations, emotions, imagination and consciousness are all combined functions of both our body and soul. This is said to occur through the mind-body connection in the pineal gland of the brain. Without the body a person cannot collect information through the five senses. Once sensed this data is then delivered to the soul where it is processed, and then returned to the body especially the brain but also other parts of the body so that we can use this information in activating the nerves, muscles, enzymes, hormones etc. to respond to the information obtained from the five senses. This is accomplished by stimulating behaviors that are beneficial to all of us. The body collects data via the senses, feeds it to the soul which in turn analyzes it; decides how the body should respond to this data in such a way that is most helpful in maintaining life, keeping us secure, allowing us to propagate, and interact with others in socially beneficial ways so that we and those around us live better more productive lives. This to and fro interaction between body, mind and back to the body allows for freewill decisions and behaviors that help all of us.

The problem with this system is, how does the physical, sensory input get transferred to the soul? The spiritual and physical realms are entirely separate. Descartes tells us the soul is situated in the pineal gland, a structure in the middle of the brain. But how can a spirit like our soul be anywhere? It is not a 'space-time' entity. Likewise the soul cannot function in space-time. Our brain and body are apace-time limited biological entities. We do everything sequentially. We are mutable, that is changeable, and live in an ever-changing world. We can't be out of step with the cosmos. The microcosm has to be in tune with the macrocosm.

Our soul has to be timeless or it cannot be eternal as it must be eternal in order for any of us humans to live eternally in Heaven (or for those unfortunate souls in Hell). Physical beings cannot, by definition, live forever. Physicality implies change or mutability and this means an end to our physical existence at some time in the future. The soul cannot be located in the pineal gland. It can't be situated anywhere in space or time by definition.

This mind-body relationship problem involves a logical issue just as our interaction with God faces a spirit-matter boundary that is insurmountable. The physical is tied to space and time; the spiritual is not of space and time. So how can these two entities connect with each other?

We cannot ask God to make a square circle. The very nature of square and circle makes such a geometric figure impossible even for God. The two concepts are mutually exclusive. The same applies to the mind-body problem. If a spirit could interact with a physical body, then it could not be eternal, be capable of viewing the beatific vision (seeing God in Heaven) or live forever. As a corollary, if a body could connect with a spirit such as our soul, then it could not exist in space and time and it could not possess the five senses and live in our physical Universe. We couldn't be born, walk, talk, eat, sleep and love our spouse, children, friends and colleagues. Love is an emotion and emotions are of the body not the soul. We couldn't shake hands or hug one another. To have a soul and body interact in any way would be like having a square circle. As a consequence of these limitations, the whole idea of a soul (spirit) working with a body (matter) is logically impossible in spite of what we have been told since early childhood.

The omnipotence of God raises questions as to the extent of God's infinite powers. Some solutions for the Problem of Evil suggest that God's omnipotence allows Him to do anything and everything that is not logically impossible. This would exclude such actions as allowing evil. God's very nature prohibits this. It is easy to say that God can do anything, but theologians tell us this is only true if the actions required are not self-contradictory.

Now I recognize the above arguments against a soul-body pairing are hard to grasp and even harder to accept. Most of us have been told from childhood that we are made up of a body and a soul and that God is a pure spirit as are angels, devils and ghosts. It is a difficult task to undo all this past teaching and adopt a new paradigm that does not admit of a soul. We know we have a body. That is quite evident when we stub our toe. These ideas of soul, spirit and God meet deep-seated emotional needs. They bring us answers to ancient questions that we have not otherwise been able to solve. These spiritual answers are, however, magical, mystical solutions that are based on the Bible, ancient authorities and the teachings of parents, pastors and other people we believe are trustworthy. Such solutions, nonetheless, do not meet the demands of reason and logic. There is absolutely no empirical, scientific evidence for the existence of spirits or souls. Until definite evidence is gathered to support the notion of spirits and souls, they cannot be considered anything more than myths just as the ancient gods of Greece and Rome are now viewed as myths.

We've been told since early childhood that we can't have everything we want. The fact is that we want an eternal life. Few of us want to die. We want a fatherly God that we can pray to and from whom we receive the many gifts that make life easier. We want someone that can make all our daily anxieties, sufferings and evils go away. Life is so difficult and we would like all these pains and sorrows to just disappear and leave us living a leisurely, comfortable life. Unfortunately, our world doesn't work that way. We humans have created myths, theologies and spiritual beings to make all of life seem better. To toss out our religious and magical beliefs that have provided emotional comfort for us for so many years is neigh impossible but if we are to be true to God, the world in which we live, and ourselves, this is a rational necessity.

Manichaeism

Mani or Manichaeus (c. 216–276 BCE) taught a dualistic theology that involved two equal deities, the one good and the other bad. These two divine beings are in an ongoing spiritual struggle. The good god rules over a world of light, and the bad god rules over a material world of darkness. The god of light fought to bring light into our world and the god of darkness wrestled to maintain cosmic darkness. Our human world under this scheme was created in darkness. Since the beginning, darkness has been gradually transformed from a world of matter and darkness to a world of spirit and light. We seemingly are slowly evolving into a spiritual world—a spiritual, non-material world that is without evil. It would be a stretch to make this into a Darwinian evolutionary system though Teillard de Chardin in his *Phenomenon of Man* suggests that such a process is ongoing in the cosmos and will eventually reach to the *Omega Point* when we will be one in Christ.

Manichaeism was widespread throughout the Aramaic speaking regions in antiquity. It reached its peak between the third and seventh centuries CE, and at its height was one of the most widespread religions in the world. Manichaean churches and scriptures existed as far East as China and as far West as the Roman Empire. It was briefly the main rival of Christianity in the struggle to replace classical polytheistic paganism. Manichaeism survived longer in the East than in the West, and it appears to have finally faded out after the fourteenth century in southern China.

Manichaeism is considered a dualistic moral philosophy in which a moral course of action involves a clear black and white choice between good and evil. Augustine of Hippo (354-430) was a Manichaean before converting to Christianity. Following this change of heart, he was a fierce opponent of this sect.

Mani's system is based on Mesopotamian theology. It has the advantage of solving the Problem of Evil by allowing for a bad god that is responsible for all evil and a good god that remains pristine and not responsible for any evil. The catch, of course, is that the good god is not a theistic god and doesn't coincide with the Abrahamic God of the OT or NT. We have to revise our concept of God to use this solution to the Problem of Evil. This would be difficult for the reasons noted above. The God of Judaism, Christianity and Islam has been around a long time. We are bonded to Him and He satisfies many human needs.

Tertullian and the Problem of Evil

Tertullian (c.160 – c. 225 CE) was a Christian theologian from Carthage (Roman Empire in North African). As a Christian apologist and a polemicist he wrote against early Christian heresies. Tertullian has been called "the Father of Latin Christianity" and "the founder of Western theology." He influenced the Church's nascent doctrines in many ways.

Though a conservative, he did originate and advance many doctrines of the early Church. He is perhaps best known for being the oldest extant Latin writer to use the word "Trinity" and gave the earliest formal description of Trinitarian theology. He coined the phrase, "three Persons, one Substance" which was to provide the doctrinal basis for what has become the most important of all Christian tenets. As with so many Christian beliefs, the Trinity was not specifically defined in the NT and only gradually evolved over the first several centuries of Christianity.

Tertullian opposed the teachings of Mani and wrote against Manichaeism because it ran counter to his view of the Trinity. There was but one God with three equal or consubstantial persons: Father, Son and Holy Spirit. The Trinity created problems for those who believed that all three Persons were all-good, all-powerful and all-knowing. The three persons of the Trinity were not three Gods, rather they were three "persons in one God" and this God was a theistic God. This has been discussed above.

Tertullian's solution to the Problem of Evil runs as follows:[48] Evil exists, not because God ordained all evil acts as a necessary part of creation, but God, by His own authority, gave humans two gifts. The first is the gift of freewill; the second gift is the ability to use the freewill as we see fit. Because God gave us freewill, He withholds His power to prevent evil that God knows will occur when humans freely and recklessly employ these gifts.

Tertullian's defense of God in allowing evil in the world is based on the "freewill" defense and is found in his, *The Five Books Against Marcion*, Book 2.

Tertullian makes the following key points regarding the Problem of Evil:

* God's purpose was to be known by humans and this is the '*first goodness*' as he labels it. Knowledge and the enjoyment of God are good. This purpose led God to create the Universe and make humans with the ability to pursue 'the knowledge of Himself', which Tertullian explores in detail (ii.4 and ii.6*)*.
* Tertullian believed humans were created in the image and likeness of God and this means that 'man was constituted by God [to be] the free, master of his or her own will and power', which allows humans to know

---

[48]   http://evangelicalarminians.org/tertullian-on-the-problem-of-evil-and-free-will/. An interview with John Frame when asked about God's relationship to evil.

God and to oversee creation (ii.5 and ii.6). This might be interpreted to mean humans are involved in their evolution and the evolution of the world as a whole.

- God gave 93man freedom of will and mastery over himsel' and 'He from His very authority in creation permitted these gifts to be enjoyed' (ii.7**)**.
- This gift of freewill allows humans to choose freely because 'man is free, with a will either for obedience or resistance' (ii.5 and ii.6).
- It is this freewill that is the basis for responsibility for 'the reward neither of good nor of evil could be paid to the man who should be found to have been either good or evil through necessity and not choice' (ii.6). The last part of this statement, which is hard to follow seems to make humans as free and responsible for their good or bad choices and the rewards or punishments that follow. What do you think?
- This freewill given to humans enables them to be "rational beings, capable of intelligence and knowledge, yet still being restrained within the bounds of rational liberty' and 'subject to Him who had subjected all things unto Him" (ii.4). In other words freewill allows humans to be rational beings, which is superior to being non-rational automatons.
- Since humans have 'unshackled power over their will' it must be concluded that they and not God are responsible for the evil that occurs (ii.5 and ii.6 and ii.9). Nothing evil could possibly have come forth from God.
- Evil exists because God has 'afforded room for a conflict' between humans and the devil which started at the time of the Fall of Adam and Eve. In this conflict humans are able to conquer the devil and crush this enemy with the same freedom of his will as had made him succumb to him (the devil)'. Humans must choose which side they will take in this conflict, just as they had to choose in the beginning, thus proving that the

fault of the Fall and subsequent evil was *all our own, not God's, and* so gain his (human) salvation by a victory' (over the devil). (ii.8 and ii.10).

- The victory is achieved by Christ and received by humans through faith in Christ

He enjoins those who are justified by faith in Christ and not justified by the law as the Jews claim. Peace in God the Father is through the Son.

Tertullian's view anticipates Calvin and Luther. Faith plays a major role in Tertullian's solution to the Problem of Evil. If freewill and faith are not the answer to the Problem of Evil and God does indeed determine all events, then reconciling a good God with the occurrence of evil is, as one Calvinist admits, 'more difficult'. The question, though, is whether God merely permits evil, or whether, in addition, He actually brings evil about in some way. I think the latter is true. Scripture often says that God brings about sinful decisions of human beings. This is a harsh teaching of Scripture, and on one level it makes the Problem of Evil more difficult. The early Church, however, had no such problem affirming that God does not cause evil. He only permits it because He allows us to exercise freewill, which is necessary for us to be truly human and not just automatons, i.e. we have freewill.

The issue still remains that if God is all-good, etc. then He ought to be able to make us so reasonable that we would always choose good rather than bad. Give us enough grace or smarts and we would be free, fully human and morally good. Right?

Tertullian wrote his Trinitarian treatise after becoming a Montanist. Montanism was a religious system characterized by ecstatic prophecy. Montanus (c. 135 –177 CE) made predictions about the future often while in a frenzied state of mind much like charismatic Pentecostals do today. The early Church was not opposed to prophecies but Tertullian's style and ultimately his Montanistic theology ran up against the Church's more conservative views in the second century. Montanism recognized female bishops and presbyters (priest). Women and girls were forbidden to wear ornaments, such as necklaces and bracelets, and virgins were required to wear veils. There was an emphasis on ethical standards and asceticism. Montanists prohibited remarriage following divorce or the death of a spouse. They also emphasized keeping strict fasts and added new fasts to those mandated by the Catholic Church.

Although many Church Fathers were ultimately canonized by the Catholic Church, Tertullian never was and, in fact, he was excommunicated as a result of his Montanistic views.

Augustine of Hippo and the Problem of Evil

Augustine was the first theologian to propose the concept of an Original Sin. It is a very special kind of sin according to Augustine. First of all, Adam and Eve alone committed this first sin.[49] Secondly, we are all tainted by Original Sin. None of the billions of people that came after Adam and Eve committed any sins while *in utero* yet everyone, according to Augustine, claims that anyone who dies without having this sin cleansed from their soul by baptism, will never enter Heaven. Thirdly, in the past, Catholic theologians taught that these unbaptized babies would go to Limbo. This was a pleasant enough place; nothing like Purgatory or Hell, but since these babies could not get into Heaven they would be denied the Beatific Vision of God, which is, according to Christian theology, the essential joy of Heaven. Fourthly, in recent years there has been debates about infants who are not baptized before they die, especially if they die *in utero*. Some theologians say that if the mother "wishes that the baby be baptized"

---

[49] Of course, Satan and the other devils had sinned against God before Adam and Eve's Original Sin.

in utero, this would satisfy the sacramental requirement for baptism and if aborted before birth would go straight to Heaven. Cardinal Joseph Aloisius Ratzinger; (later Pope Benedict XVI) when head of the Congregation of the Doctrine of Faith stated in 1984 that he rejected the claim that children who die unbaptized cannot attain salvation. Subsequently, in 2005, as pope, he sanctioned a commission statement that Limbo was not a firm doctrine of the Church only a hypothesis and that we needed to rely on the infinite wisdom and goodness of God to provide for such unbaptized babies and adults. The 1992 Catechism of the Catholic Church states that, "God has bound salvation to the sacrament of Baptism".

The best one can say now is that Original Sin in infants is still not a totally resolved issues. This issue has evolved over the centuries and remains part of the Problem of Evil.

Can we imagine that a theistic God would allow a totally innocent child, who has never sinned, be stained by the sin of Adam and Eve and end up in Limbo or even Hell for this? And, of course, we are dealing with mythological parents, Adam and Eve, who never existed in the first place. We humans evolved through a complex series of random mutations, natural selection and a lineage of prehistoric species to get to where we are today. Theologians often create problems that don't help solve the Problem of Evil. Such machinations only make things worse for us Earth bound humans who are limited by a less than divine intellect! I often wonder what happened to all the babies in Limbo when the Catholic Church closed the doors to Limbo!

Augustine claims that natural evil, as found in disasters such as earthquake, is caused by fallen angels i.e. devils, whereas moral evil (evil caused by the freewill of human beings) is a result of humans having become estranged from God, and as a result, choose to deviate from God's designated path. Augustine argues that God could not have created evil, since the world was created as good, and that all notions of evil are simply a deprivation or privation of goodness. Evil cannot be a separate and unique positive action or thing. For example, blindness is not a separate entity, but is merely a lack or privation of sight. Thus the Augustinian theodicy claims that evil, including all suffering, is the absence of good because God did not create evil; it is we humans who chose to deviate from the path of perfect goodness.

This, however, raises a number of questions involving genetics. If evil is merely a consequence of our choosing to deviate from God's desired path, then genetic dispositions to evil must surely be in God's plan and thus cannot be blamed on human choice. Some people have genetic profiles that are associated with criminal behavior. In addition, as mentioned at the beginning of this book, I have Stargardt's Disease, an autosomal recessive (inherited) disorder that is purely genetic in origin. It has resulted in the gradual loss of much of my vision. It is a type of macular degeneration that has progressed over the years. I am fortunate in the sense that, though my central vision is gone, I will always have some peripheral vision. This disorder has had a significant impact on my life and one could call it an evil. However, it is not my fault that I have Stargardt's Disease. I did nothing to deserve this disorder. It just happened that each of my parents had the allele (gene) for this problem and there is a 25 percent chance that any of their offspring would end up with the disease. My brother was not affected. The occurrence of Stargardt's Disease in this situation is simply the luck of the draw. Nor are my parents to blame for giving me this disease. It just happened. There was no freewill decision on their part. There is no moral evil; it is simply a natural evil. God must be blamed for it because He set up the genetic laws that led to my Stargardt's.

In addition, this disorder is not just the absence of good eyesight. There are two alleles that cause the disease. There are definite changes in my ocular fundi (back of the eyes) that are present. This disease or evil is caused by something definitely bad! There are bad genes and bad yellow scars on my retinae. I have pictures of the back of my eyes and they look awful. Augustine's argument from the 'absence of good' just doesn't hold up in light of modern science.

Erasmus, Luther and the Problem of Evil[50]

The difference between Desiderius Erasmus (1466–1536) and Luther regarding the Problem of Evil boils down to the question of freewill. Erasmus had generally avoided involving himself in theological disputes, however, he was urged by many of his contemporaries, particularly by his good friend Thomas More, as well as Pope Clement VII, to apply his skill and learning to Luther's polemic regarding the Problem of Evil. Luther had become increasingly more aggressive in his attacks on the Roman Catholic Church. The debate between Erasmus and Luther came down to differences regarding the doctrines of divine justice, divine omniscience and omnipotence. While Luther and many of his fellow reformers emphasized the control and power that God held over creation, Erasmus stressed the justice and liberality of God regarding humankind.

Luther and other reformers proposed that humans were stripped of freewill by sin and that divine predestination ruled all activity within the mortal realm. Luther held believed God was completely omniscient and omnipotent; that anything which happened had to be the result of God's explicit will, and that God's foreknowledge of events brought events into being.

Foreknowledge and Predestination

Erasmus argued that foreknowledge did not equal predestination. Instead, Erasmus compared God to an astronomer who knows that a solar eclipse is going to

---

50 Erasmus and the Problem of Evil, Wikipedia.

occur. The astronomer's foreknowledge does nothing to cause the eclipse—rather his knowledge of what is to come proceeds from an intimate familiarity with the workings of the cosmos. Erasmus held that, as the creator of both the cosmos and humankind, God was so intimately familiar with his creations that He was capable of perfectly predicting events which were to occur, even if they were contrary to God's explicit will. He cited biblical examples of God offering prophetic warnings of impending disasters, which were contingent on human repentance, as in the case of the prophet Jonah and the people of Nineveh:

"Get up and go to the great city of Nineveh. Announce my judgment against it because I have seen how wicked its people are." (Jonah 1).

God has foreknowledge of what evil the people of Nineveh are capable of and sends Jonah to warn them of what consequences they face if such evil deeds are carried out. The foreknowledge of God, thus, does not make God the cause of human moral evil. However, as creator of all humans, one might still make God responsible for moral evil. As theistic, God should be able to make them morally good. This takes us back to Paradise, Adam and Eve who was superior human beings and still committed the Original Sin and as a consequence we are all tainted from the moment of our conception. Couldn't He have made our original parents just a little better so that the devil could not have hoodwinked them so easily? The theistic God of Christianity and Islam is certainly smart enough and powerful enough to manage this it would seem.

Erasmus, Freewill and the Problem of Evil

If humans had no freewill, Erasmus argued, then God's commandments and warnings would be in vain; and if sinful acts (and the calamities which followed them) were in fact the result of human predestination, then that would make God a cruel tyrant who punished His creatures for

99

sins He had determined they would commit. Erasmus, on the contrary, insisted that God had endowed humankind with freewill, valuing freewill as essential to human nature, and rewarded or punished them according to their own choices whether good or evil. Erasmus argued that Scripture either implicitly or explicitly supported this view, and that divine grace was the means by which humans became aware of God, as well as, being the force which sustained and motivated humans as they freely sought to follow God's laws.

Erasmus ultimately concluded that God was capable of interfering in many things (human nature included) but chose not to do so; thus God could be said to be responsible for many things because He allowed them to occur (or not occur), without having been actively involved in them, i.e. freewill choices.

Luther's response to Erasmus came in his, *On the Bondage of the Will* (1525) which Luther himself later considered one of his best pieces of theological writing. A year later, Erasmus replied to this work with the first part of his two-volume *Hyperaspistes*, but this was a longer and more complex work, which received comparatively little popular recognition.

In sum, despite his own criticisms of the Roman Catholic Church, Erasmus believed that the Church needed reform from within but that Luther had gone too far. Erasmus had asserted that all humans possess freewill, and that the doctrine of even single predestination was not in accord with the teachings contained within the Bible. He argued against the belief that God's foreknowledge of events was the cause of events, including moral acts, and held that the doctrines of repentance, baptism and conversion depends on the existence of freewill. He likewise contended that grace simply helps humans come to the knowledge of God and supports them as they use their freewill to choose between good and evil; choices which lead to salvation through the atonement provided by Jesus Christ.

Luther in response maintained that sin prevents human beings from working out their own salvation and that they are completely incapable on their own of moving towards God. As such, there is no freewill for humanity because any will they might have is overwhelmed by the influence of sin. Central to Luther's analysis is his belief concerning the power and complete sovereignty of God.

Luther concluded that Satan dominates unredeemed human beings. Satan, as the prince of the mortal world, never lets go of those he has conquered unless he is overpowered by the stronger divine power. When God redeems a person, He redeems the entire person, including the will, which then is liberated to serve God. No one can achieve salvation or redemption through their own choices—people do not choose between good and evil, because they are naturally dominated by satanic evil, and salvation is simply the product of God unilaterally changing a person's heart and turning them toward good deeds. Were this not so, Luther contends, God would not be omnipotent and would lack total sovereignty over all His creatures. Luther held that arguing otherwise is insulting to the glory of God. As a result, Luther concluded that Erasmus was not actually a Christian.

Luther's other theological doctrine of interest is his belief in *solo fide*, i.e. faith alone.
Romans 5:1 says,
"Therefore, having been justified by faith, we have peace with God through our Lord Jesus Christ."

This statement by Paul in his Letter to the Romans has long been used to support the concept that we cannot do good deeds in order to get to Heaven. Faith in Jesus Christ is the only necessary freewill act. Good deeds are laudable but because of God's supreme sovereignty, we cannot buy our way into Heaven with good deeds. Faith is the primary ticket to Heaven.

I have long believed that this view of Luther's was based on the harsh relationship he had especially with his father. Luther was very morally scrupulous, so much so that he found it impossible to believe that his sins could be removed by personal good deeds. Thus, only faith not deeds would allow him to gain Heaven and even then this was dependent on God's irresistible grace. We are elected or predestined, at least initially (single predestination) for Heaven or Hell for reasons known only to God, so Luther believed.

Luther recalls:

"(that) for the sake of stealing a nut, my mother once beat me until the blood flowed".

His father, Hans, also ruled his son with an iron fist, Martin later recalled, "my father once whipped me so hard I ran away - I hated him until he finally managed to win me back". Hans had high hopes for his first son and his heart was set on Martin becoming a lawyer, which would enable Luther to climb even higher up the social ladder. Hans was a copper smelter. Young Martin followed his father's wishes without protest. He was sent to the best schools in the area and then University at Erfurt. In 1505, Hans was devastated to learn that his son, without consulting him, had decided to embrace religion and had sought admission to the house of the Augustinian Hermits in Erfurt. This raised the extreme ire of Hans. Whether these family influences determined Luther's scrupulosity is, of course, uncertain. Whatever the source of his ultimate religious tendencies and theological thoughts, he was convinced after seeing the immorality of the Vatican hierarchy, that Church reform was absolutely necessary. In his treatise, *Concerning Christian Liberty,* he was most ingratiating toward Pope Leo X but was firm in pushing church reform. He maintained to the end that only faith in Christ could bring salvation. Nothing he could do, including good works, were of salvific benefits. Again, whether this belief related to a poor self image arising from his parent's stern reprimands will never known but Luther felt so insecure about salvation that he had to find a way to Heaven that relied heavily on God and very little on himself. Thus, he needed only to have faith in Christ.

Pelagianism and Semi-Pelagianism

The teachings of Pelagius are generally associated with the rejection of Original Sin and the practice of infant baptism. Pelagianists believe that Original Sin did not taint human nature and that human will is still capable of choosing good or evil without special divine aid, i.e. grace. Pelagius taught that the human will, as created by God, is sufficient to live a sinless life, although Pelagius believed that God's grace assisted every good deed. Pelagianism has come to be identified with the view, (whether Pelagius would agree or not, that human beings can earn salvation by their own efforts. This theological theory is named after Pelagius (354 – c. 420), although he denied, at some point in his life, many of the doctrines associated with his name today. In essence, Pelagius took away God's total sovereignty and this was not an acceptable orthodox Catholic view. God's sovereignty was a sacrosanct tenet. Giving too much freedom to humans limited God's power. On the other hand this orthodox stance complicates the Problem of Evil. Once again the responsibility for evil falls back on the 'shoulders' of God, (if you'll forgive the anthropomorphism which I try to avoid at all costs).

The writings of Pelagius are no longer extant but they were condemned at the Council of Carthage (418 CE) and the Council's records provide some idea of Pelagius' beliefs. Pelagianism stands in contrast to the official hamartiological[51] system of the Catholic Church that is based on the theology of Augustine of Hippo.

Semi-Pelagianism is a modified form of Pelagianism that was condemned by the Catholic Church at the Second

---

[51] Hamartiological: of the branch of Christian theology that studies sin.

Council of Orange in 529 CE. Semi-Pelagianism is an early Christian theological and soteriological[52] school of thought through which humanity and God are restored to a right relationship. Semi-Pelagianism varies from Pelagianism in that instead of humans as totally capable of effecting their own salvation, Semi-Pelagianism in its original form is a compromise between Pelagianism and the orthodox teaching of the Church Fathers. They taught that humans couldn't be saved without the freely given, grace of God whereas in Semi- Pelagianism, a distinction is made between the beginning of faith and the increase of faith. Semi-Pelagianism teaches that the latter half of salvation, is the growth of faith through the work of God, while the beginning of faith is an act of freewill, with grace supervening only after a person made some voluntary, non-grace based movement toward God. After this initial freewill act on the part of a person is started then God is said to shower grace upon the person who then is able to move on the final path to union with God. Because this system did not maintain God as the sovereign actor in salvation, Semi-Pelagianism was also labeled heretical by the Catholic Church.

The Roman Catholic Church condemns Semi-Pelagianism because it claims that the beginning of faith involves an act of freewill on the part of humans. In contrast, the Church maintains that the initiative must come from God, but requires 'free synergy' (collaboration) on the part of humans: "God has freely chosen to associate humans with the work of His grace. The fatherly action of God follows the initial actions by us humans. God's grace works in collaboration with what we have started. In the Catholic view God gives us grace and good works play a minimal role in salvation. No one can merit the initial grace of God. Moved by the Holy Spirit and by charity, we can then merit for ourselves and for others [in purgatory] the

---

[52] Soteriology is the study of salvation theology i.e. how we are saved and get to Heaven.

graces needed for our sanctification and increase of grace needed for the attainment of eternal life."[53]

Basically Semi-Pelagianism is heretical because God doesn't have control over the entire process of giving grace to a believer. In orthodox teachings, God must give the initial nudge towards the acquisition of grace following which humans can carry on the process of gathering grace. This is a truly fine line, but for some theologians it maintains God's sovereignty. Semi-Pelagianism takes away at least part of God's responsibility for evil and thus helps us a bit with the Problem of Evil.

In summary:

- Catholic view of salvation: It teaches that the initiative for good works comes from God, it requires free synergy (collaboration) on the part of humans. "God has freely chosen to associate humans with the work of His grace.

- Pelagianism: Humans initiate and maintain the road to salvation. Pelagians also believe that Original Sin did not taint human nature and that human freewill is still capable of choosing good or evil without special divine aid.

- Semi-Pelagianism teaches that after the initial freewill act of a believer, God then provides the grace for final salvation.

In a real sense, the Church's view of salvation only complicates the Problem of Evil for if God is always sovereign. He then retains all responsibility for moral evil that humans commit. Once again it is God who is responsible for evil in the world, including both human moral evil and natural evil. God has failed to give humans enough grace in order that they can follow through with morally good acts. In this system, though the person uses freewill after God's initial gift of grace, a more powerful, continuous injection of grace would then allow the person

---

[53] Quote from Wikipedia.

to avoid moral evil and act in a morally beneficial way. The notion of divine sovereignty makes the Freewill solution to the Problem of Evil untenable because human will is not truly free. God determines our will by providing or not providing the proper spiritual drive i.e. grace, toward ongoing moral behaviors.

There is another issue related to God's sovereignty. Since the Catholic Church and specifically the pope is the ultimate interpreter and propagator of God's messages, and since God is always sovereign then the Church can claim to be eternally infallible. The pope has claimed to be infallible in matters of faith and morals sine 1870 when the First Vatican Council proclaimed:

"The holy Roman Church possesses the supreme and full primacy and principality over the whole Catholic Church. She truly and humbly acknowledges that she received this from the Lord himself in blessed Peter, the prince and chief of the apostles, whose successor the Roman pontiff is, together with the fullness of power. And since before all others she has the duty of defending the truth of the faith, so if any questions arise concerning the faith, it is by her judgment that they must be settled."

The pope has functioned as infallible *de facto* for centuries before this statement. Although papal infallibility is said to apply only to matters of faith and morals, in fact, the Church has extended its interpretive powers to other intellectual areas. Examples include the condemnation of Galileo because he approved of the Copernican view of the Solar System, which is, we now know, a strictly scientific matter. If infallible, the Church should have known that the issue was not one of faith or morals. For this breech of heavenly "faith and morals" Galileo was sanctioned by the Inquisition, barely avoiding a death sentence by renouncing this heliocentric view of the heavens.

Giordano Bruno (1548 -1600 CE) was put to death for his view of the cosmos although he also held that the

Trinity, the divinity of Christ, the virginity of Mary, and Transubstantiation were not valid theological doctrines. Bruno also correctly proposed that the Sun was just another star moving in space, and claimed as well that the Universe contained an infinite number of inhabited worlds, i.e. planets orbiting other stars. Today he would have been excommunicated but not burnt at the stake. We might ask why killing someone for heresy was an infallibly correct decision in 1600 CE when it wouldn't be considered such today. Bruno was not so lucky as Martin Luther because Bruno was a Dominican friar who lived in Naples and had no protector as Luther had in Frederick the Wise of Saxony who kidnapped Luther and hid him in Wartburg castle for two years after he was condemned at the Diet of Worms in 1521.

We could also ask why the Church was infallibly correct when it denied Copernicus' heliocentric world in 1543 CE (*De revolutionists orbium coelestium*). He was denounced because this contradicted Genesis' version of creation and the motion of the Sun as portrayed in Joshua 10:13: "And the Sun stood still". One could say this wasn't a matter of faith, however, contradicting the Bible would be considered a matter of faith by most any believer including the pope.

The Inquisition was responsible for burning thousands at the stake as 'heretics' for their views on a host of doctrinal issues that weren't always related to matters of faith or morals. What the Church considered evil in the Middle Ages are now merely "errors" deserving only expulsion from the "true" Church. There are many "mistakes" the Church has made relating to matters of faith and morals over the centuries forcing the Church to reverse its views. This should never happen if it were truly infallible.

In addition, the Catholic Church has many times claimed that it has not changed since Christ founded the Church before his death and resurrection. As with all earthly things the Church has evolved over time. Not all its doctrines have been etched in stone since the first century.

Table 8

Doctrine	Date
1. Prayers for the dead: 300 CE.	
2. Making the sign of the cross: 300 CE.	
3. Veneration of angels & dead saints: 375 CE.	
4. Use of images in worship: 375 CE.	
5. The Mass as a daily celebration 394 CE.	
6. Beginning of the exaltation of Mary as "Mother of God" applied at Council of Ephesus 431 CE.	
7. Extreme Unction (Last Rites 526 CE.	
8. Doctrine of Purgatory-Gregory I. 593 CE..	
9. Prayers to Mary & dead saints 600 CE.	
10. Worship of cross, images & relics 786 CE.	
11. Canonization of dead saints 995 CE.	
12. Celibacy of priesthood 1079 CE.	
13. The Rosary 1090 CE.	
14. Indulgences 1190 CE.	
15. Transubstantiation-Innocent 1215 CE.	
16. Auricular Confession of sins to a priest 1215 CE.	
17. Adoration of the wafer (Host 1220 CE. 18. Pope Gregory IX establisheS the Inquisition to arrest, try, convict and execute heretics 1227 CE.	
19. Cup forbidden to the people at communion 1414 CE.	
20. Purgatory proclaimed as a dogma 1439 CE.	
21. The doctrine of the Seven Sacraments confirmed 1439 CE.	
22. Tradition declared of equal authority with Bible by Council of Trent 1545 CE.	
23. Apocryphal books added to Bible 1546 CE.	
24. Last execution by the Inquisition in Spain in 1826 CE.	
25. Immaculate Conception of Mary 1854 CE.	
26, Infallibility of the pope in matters of faith and morals, proclaimed by Vatican Council 1870 CE.	

| 27. Assumption of the Virgin Mary 1950 CE. |
| 28. Index of Forbidden Books ends 1966 CE. |
| 29. Galileo exonerated 1992 CE. |
| 30. Limbo eliminated 2005 CE. |

This table lists a number of doctrines that have been initiated and/or eliminated over the centuries. Although the Church insists that no matters of faith or morals have changed over time, there have been a number of dogmas altered. The most notable perhaps is the exoneration of Galileo in 1992. It is evident that the Catholic Church and many other sects punished or killed many people who held beliefs counter to those maintained by the sect. The many errors evident in the OT and NT speak to the pervasive errancy found in the Bible. The information contained in the Bible is based on faith alone. The OT and NT were written and revised between 3000 and 1500 years ago when mythology was an accepted literary form held by most people to be valid. Myths explained mysteries that were otherwise unsolvable. Today we have empirical scientific evidence for many of these ancient mysteries. Many evils were perpetrated because they were based on these myths. We know better today but many so-called heresies remain today and many people are punished in on way or another by the Catholic Church and other churches for not adhering to these long held doctrines such as creationism or the concept of the Trinity. These "heretics" are no longer killed for such beliefs but are punished in other ways such as excommunication. Nonetheless, Christians continue to kill Muslims and vice versa. One might call these 'dogmatic deaths 'and the Bible still sanction such killings as noted above.

The Catholic View of the Nature of Evil

The Catholic Church's view of evil is largely based on Aquinas, who is the official theologian of the Catholic

Church. Evil is, according to Aquinas, threefold, viz., metaphysical[54], moral, and physical, the consequence of moral evil is guilt and guilt promotes the perfection of the 'whole. The Universe would be less perfect if it contained no evil and evil's sequelae. Thus fire could not exist without the corruption of what it consumes; the lion must slay the fawn in order to live, and if there were no wrong deeds, there would be no place for patience and justice. God is said (as in Isaiah 45) to be the author of evil in the sense that the corruption of material objects in nature is ordained by God, as a means for carrying out the design of the Universe; and on the other hand, the evil which exists as a consequence of the breach of divine laws is in the same sense due to the divine will. The Universe would be less perfect if its laws could be broken with impunity. Thus evil, in one aspect, i.e. as the counter-balancing of sin, has the nature of good. But the evil of sin, though permitted by God, is in no sense due to Him. Denying divine omnipotence is not necessary in this solution of the Problem of Evil. God could have created another equally perfect Universe in which there would be no place for evil but he chose to create an evolutionary world that allows the Universe and all its creatures to progressively evolve into more perfect beings physically, emotionally and morally.

To understand the Catholic view of evil it is necessary to review Aquinas' notion of metaphysical evil and its solution. The dimension of evil that Aquinas focuses on is the metaphysical problem of evil that often promotes an anti-theistic view of God:

1) God is the creator of everything, and
2) Evil is a thing, therefore,
3) God creates evil.

This argument compels the theistic believer (someone who believes in an all-everything God) to address several

---

[54]   Author: Bill King, Quodlibet Journal: Number 2-3, Summer 2002. Volume 4

sticky issues. Not only does the theist have to give an account of what evil is, but he or she must address what the cause of evil is, and whether or not God is ultimately that cause.

In approaching Aquinas' response to the metaphysical Problem of Evil, first we must understand the notions of 'matter', 'form' and 'privation'. Aquinas maintains that evil is a privation, and that God cannot be the source of a privation. Usually, the typical kinds of responses to the Problem of Evil are said to be either a defense or a theodicy. A theodicy is a justification for the actions of God in allowing evil whereas a defense claims to show that the arguments against theism in approaching the Problem of Evil, is ineffective.

As the term good signifies 'perfect being', so the term evil signifies nothing else than 'privation of perfect being'. In its proper form, privation is predicated of that which is fitted by its nature to be possessed, and to be possessed at a certain time and in a certain manner. Evidently a thing is called evil if it lacks a certain perfection it ought to have. Thus, if a man lacks the sense of sight, this is an evil for him. But the same lack is not an evil for a stone, for the stone is not equipped by nature to have the faculty of sight.

Because Aquinas' approach to the Problem of Evil is based on Aristotle's metaphysics, which is, indeed, "very philosophical" I have chosen to include the details of Aquinas' proof in Appendix A at the end of the book as noted above.

Aquinas remains, even today, the Catholic Church's primary source of theology, I felt his approach to the Problem of Evil needed to be part of this book so I have include a short section here as an introduction to his argument on evil. In its simplest form evil is the privation or absence of some natural feature of a being's essence or 'substance' to use Aristotle's terminology. When the nature of a being is complete this is good but when some element of a beings nature is missing this is evil. This is the 'absence of good' argument against the Problem of Evil. God has created all that is good and He is not responsible if some good is absent. God has made everything for a reason. This is called a theological view of the world. Everything God has created is aimed at some end. Religions, for example, believe we are all ado of a specific reason, i.e. to go to Heaven and be joined to God. Anything that does not promote the achievement of this final goal is thus evil. If it promotes this end it is good. The thesis of this book does not based on a teleological approach to the Problem of Evil. God made us so that we are challenged on every side so that we can face these challenges (evils) and evolve to a higher level. Since the solution proposed here is based on evolutionary theory and since evolution is a probabilistic process. As random this implies that what God has created including the evolutionary forces that help us deal with change (evils) and make us ever-changing (evolving) creatures. We humans are here today because we have responded to environmental change utilizing individual, cultural and societal adaptations that have included a system of morality that, though continuously changing, helps us humans as a species to survive and improve over time. What we call evil forms part of the evolutionary pressures that force us to adapt and improve.

Thus, what Aristotle and Aquinas call privations or the absence of good are metaphysical concepts that relate to such Scholastic terminology as essences, form, and matter and how they are in some way deficient. On the other hand, what I call evil is not necessarily the privation or absence of good, rather, evil is the normal workings of nature. Our human nature includes freewill. Sometime we make mistakes. After all we are not perfectly good by our very nature. Evil follows such failings of our nature. Nature is run by laws. These laws may lead to earthquakes, tornadoes or floods. These are all natural occurrences. They are evils not because they are the absence of good but because they run afoul of our natural needs. This is not a result of the absence of goods.

The world is diverse. It is full of a diversity of living beings. The needs of these creatures vary and one beings needs will run headlong up against another being's needs. Lions eat deer. We eat cattle. Bacteria live off our body parts. On the other hand there are also beneficial interactions with other beings. The bacteria in our bowels help us digest food. Milk cows benefit from the care humans provide for them. Dogs, cats and other pets are maintained by humans and mutual good results. So at times our nature clicks with the nature of another species; sometimes they conflict with that species. We cannot just look at them metaphysical concept of ones nature or essence but rather view interactions from a practical, physical, or emotional standpoint.

Luther, Calvin, Zwingli and the Problem of Evil

Like all monotheists, Lutherans are faced with the dilemma created by evil and suffering.[55] Does God want to relieve suffering, but is unable to do so? In such a case, God is good but not all-powerful. Is God able to relieve suffering but unwilling or unconcerned to do so? Either way God is deficient. We have seen this dilemma before as did Luther and now is an issue for his followers today.

Luther believed that God created the Universe from nothing. This belief emphasizes God's omnipotence and sovereignty. This means that anything wrong with the Universe cannot be attributed to anyone except God. The material Universe, as created by God must be good, but many natural events that God has created, such as tornadoes and the like cause evil. So if God made all material things, why do so many of His creations produce evil? He is omnibenevolent and should not have made such

---

[55] Patheos, http://www.patheos.com/Library/Lutheran/Beliefs/ Suffering-and-the-Problem-of-Evil.html

imperfect beings as us humans or events such as tsunamis. Luther's answer is that evil in the world is the work of Satan, and his influence results in human sin and suffering. Moral evil is due to Satan's tempting humans so that they will eventually find themselves in his realm, i.e. fiery Hell. Satan wants to outdo God by enticing most of us to disobey Him and join. Satan, who didn't like the idea that God seemed to prefer humans to angels, in the first place. Satan is a jealous spirit who hated God for favoring us humans. After all, Christ, the Second Person of the Trinity gave up his very life to save all humankind. He certainly didn't do this for all jealous angels i.e. devils.

Blaming Satan for evil, however, simply pushes the Problem of Evil back to square one. Couldn't God have created humans in such a way that they would not sin? So that they would not be enticed into sin by the devil as was Eve. One option for Christians has, as we have seen, is to argue that God gave humans with freewill. Freewill is an essential aspect of humanity. It is also a very good thing for humans to be free. God had to make us capable of choosing the good but this then, by its very nature, means we can choose moral evil. The buck for moral evil (sometimes called sin) then stops with us humans.

But Luther rejected this option. For him, power is a zero-sum game. If humans had the power to decide to sin or not to sin, this implies a reduction in God's sovereignty, i.e. His infinite power. Also, according to Luther, humans do not have the freewill to choose to accept or reject salvation (this is in contrast to John Wesley's and Thomas Aquinas' view). For Luther, the responsibility for sin and salvation ultimately rest on God's shoulders. Both Luther and Calvin explained evil as the consequence of Adam and Eve's Original Sin and their subsequent fall from grace and eviction from the Garden of Eden along with the loss of all the superhuman qualities they possessed before the Fall. However, due to Luther and Calvin's belief in predestination[56] and God's omnipotence, the Fall is part of God's plan. Ultimately humans may not be able to understand and explain His plan. Often our inability to fathom the evil present in the world is blamed on the weakness of human understanding. We simply are not able to probe the mind of God. As it is said, "God works in mysterious ways".

In addition, we face the problem of why God allows the devil to perform bad deeds, tempt humans and take possession of human's freewill. One possible solution to the Problem of Evil that Luther could have used relates to God's logical inability to perform contradictory actions—the square circle conundrum. Human nature as defined requires humans to have freewill.

Luther in his doctrine of *solo fide* (faith alone) believed that evil deeds we committed could not be compensated for by meager, finite good deeds we as humans performed later. God as infinite cannot be appeased by finite, good works. As infinite, God can only be satisfied by an infinite act of which humans are not capable. Luther seems to be asking a lot of us limited humans. Also, God as infinite, does understand our limitations and can make adjustments for such weaknesses.

Ulrich Zwingli (1484 –1531) was a leader of the Reformation in Switzerland. Born during a time of emerging Swiss nationalism, he attended the University of Vienna and the University of Basel, a scholarly center of

---

[56] Calvin believed in a double election whereas Luther believed in a single election. This distinction is discussed elsewhere.

humanism. He was influenced by the writings of Augustine and Erasmus.[57]

In 1518, Zwingli became a pastor in Zurich where he began to preach on reforming the Catholic Church. In his first public controversy in 1522, he attacked the custom of fasting during Lent. In his publications, he pointed out corruption in the Catholic hierarchy. He promoted clerical marriage, and attacked the use of images in places of worship. He considered statues of saints as idolatrous. In 1524, Zwingli changed his belief about the Lord's Supper, experiencing a dream, which gave him confidence in his heterodox positions. In 1525, Zwingli introduced a new communion liturgy to replace the Catholic Mass. Zwingli also clashed with the Anabaptists, which resulted in their being persecuted in Switzerland.

Zwingli's ideas came to the attention of Martin Luther and other reformers. They met at the Marburg Colloquy in 1529 and although they agreed on many points of doctrine, they could not accept the doctrine of the Real Presence of Christ in the Eucharist. The Catholic Church believes that the bread and wine are transformed into the actual body and blood of Christ (transubstantiation). Luther claimed the Eucharist was a combination of bread and wine with the body and blood of Christ (consubstantiation) and Zwingli taught that the bread and wine were symbolic of the body and blood of Christ and his body and blood were not truly present in the Eucharistic host. Rather than, "This is my body" one should say, "This symbolizes my body."

Calvin also believed that those who partake of the bread and wine in good faith truly partake of the body

---

[57]   Desiderius Erasmus (1466–1536), was a Dutch Renaissance humanist, Catholic priest, and theologian. He was influential in the Protestant Reformation and Catholic Counter-Reformation. He wrote *The Praise of Folly*, his best-known work as a parody of humans generally and the Catholic Church specifically. He was critical of the abuses within the Church though he recognized the authority of the pope and rejected Luther's emphasis on faith alone as the source of salvation. Erasmus remained Catholic all his life.

and blood of Christ. Calvin explains this in terms of the believer's mystical union with Christ.

Significant antagonism developed between Zwingli's followers and other cantons[58] in Switzerland. Zwingli attempted an unsuccessful food blockade of the Catholic cantons in Switzerland. The cantons responded with an attack at a moment when Zurich was ill prepared. Zwingli was killed in battle at the age of forty-seven. His legacy lives on in the Reformed churches of today. Thus, though Luther, Zwingli and Calvin spearheaded the Reformation, and their approaches to the Problem of Evil were similar, they differed on a number of theological questions.

Zwingli and Calvin agreed with the Christian tradition that God created the Universe from nothing i.e., the doctrine of creation *ex nihilo*. This belief emphasizes God's total sovereignty. It also implies that anything wrong with the Universe cannot be attributed to the material Universe, since this, too, was created by God and it was, thus, created as good.

The reason for evil and suffering in the world is sin. Zwingli and Calvin agreed that sin is an act of human disobedience against God's commandments, and that this disobedience is entirely the responsibility of the person committing the sin. For Calvin, ever since the Fall (Eve and Adam's Original Sin), we have to accept that humans, and not God, are responsible for sin and thus also evil.

But human responsibility for sin, as we have seen, simply pushes the problem back as it does when blaming Satan for being the originator of human sin. Again, God could have, as all-powerful, all-knowing and all-good, created human beings with freewill but also with an intellect that always makes proper moral choices in spite of human passions.

Calvin was a thoroughly systematic theologian. In the end he had to maintain that we are not privy to God's

---

[58] Canton: a subdivision of a country established for political or administrative purposes like the States in America.

plans, and that it is inappropriate for us to question God's decisions–this would be blatant blasphemy. Our task is to trust that God knows what He is doing at all times.

But before Calvin got to this point, he spelled out all the things that God did for Adam and Eve. Prior to the Fall, they both had uncorrupted reason and totally freewill. Adam and Eve lived harmoniously in the presence of God. The one and only positive quality not bestowed on them by God, according to Calvin, was the gift of perseverance. In spite of their 'superhuman' intellect and physique, they could not resist the devil and persist in a state of total obedience to God.

Once again we are back to the same logical snag that we faced before. While these theological moves seem to delay assigning responsibility for sin to God, in the end it appears that Calvin cannot avoid this imposes, i.e. God in the final analysis is still responsible for human moral evil. As all-perfect, He failed to give humans, including the first humans in Paradise, the intellect, will, and grace to avoid sin and so it is God's fault that we are not free of sin, evil and suffering. If God had given us totally freewill, sufficient intellect and ample grace, we should be totally incorruptible free beings.

In fact, if we consider natural evil, the same reasoning applies. An all-perfect theistic God should be able to make a Universe without evil. This is the root of the Arminian controversy,[59] and was what eventually would separate Reformed Christians from Methodists. In the end, while continuing to assert that sin is a human responsibility, Calvin's emphasis on God's sovereignty means that his answer is a mystery, not to be questioned. Yet we do question it and have continued to do so for more than 2000 years!

---

[59] Arminius taught that Calvinistic predestination and unconditional election made God the author of evil. Arminius insisted that election was an election of believers and therefore was dependent on faith. Furthermore, Arminius argued that God's ultimate foreknowledge excluded a doctrine of determinism.

Here we see the influence of the medieval nominalists[60] and their arguments that we cannot use reason to gain knowledge of God, and we cannot draw analogies from human experience or from our nature to determine the nature of God. All we know about God is what we learn from Scripture, and today we know that the Bible is not inerrant.[61] Theologians and philosophers also try to explain God and what He is all about but all this is speculative and not based on any solid data. Calvin did not ask the question, "Why is creation the way it is?" He was simply aware of the fact of evil and suffering in the world, and the biblical account in Genesis of the Fall. The elect are given the gift of faith, which assures that their sins are forgiven, and provides the confidence that while we may not know why God does what He does, God surely has a good reason for all His actions.

Calvin identified one positive outcome of the Fall, that is, the elect enjoy the one benefit from God denied to Adam and Eve. The elect are given the gift of perseverance and they are going to Heaven for sure. For Calvin, once you are saved you cannot lose salvation. Zwingli and Luther believed this as well. Humans do not have it in their power to damn themselves, just as they do not have it in their power to save themselves. Again, this distinguishes Reformed theologies from Catholic and Methodist theologies. Calvin and Zwingli are willing to pay any

---

[60] Nominalists do not believe that every individual of a given species possesses an essential substance or essence that makes it a member of that species. Scholastic philosophers, on the other hand, believe the human soul possesses a universal essence that makes them a human being, a member of *Homo sapiens*. This essence is a universal substance that exists independent of a specific being. Nominalists believe there is no such universal substance or essence that is infused into an individual at birth, which determines ones essential nature. *Homo sapiens* is just a name (thus the label nominative) we use to identify a certain-group of like beings. We now know that DNA determines our nature not some spiritual essence.

[61] Ehrman, B., 2009, *Misquoting Jesus*, HarperCollins E-book

theological price to protect the doctrine of God's absolute and fatherly sovereignty.

Christian Science and Evil

Christian Scientists view evil as having no ultimate reality. Evil is due to mistaken beliefs held consciously or unconsciously by the faithful. Evils such as illness and death may be banished by correct religious understanding. This view has been questioned, along with the general criticisms of the concept of evil as illusory. Since the correct understanding by Christian Science members, put forth by its founder, Mary Baker Eddy, has not always prevented illness and death the question arises why this should happen. If proper belief heals all then the only answer can be that the afflicted person's beliefs are improper. Christian Scientists believe that the many instances of spiritual healing as recounted e.g. in Christian Science periodicals and their textbook, *Science and Health* with Key to the Scriptures by Mary Baker Eddy confirm their faith in spiritual healing. They are convinced that other approaches to the Problem of Evil are simply mistaken illusions. The evidence that is given for spiritual healing is based on anecdotal, not empirical data. However, most people cannot accept the Christian Science solution for diseases. There have been a number of cases in which the courts have mandated medical therapy when it seems apparent that a child may die if not given standard treatment for a disease. Prayer as the sole solution to all medical problems or, for that matter, the solution to all moral or all other natural evils has not been empirically verified. There have been studies in which patients in coronary care units (CCU) have been prayed for and compared to patients in alternate CCU's there has been no difference in outcomes. To view evils as illusory is also hard to accept in light of the very real and often harsh reality of day to day suffering experienced by all humans.

Jehovah's Witnesses and Evil.

Jehovah's Witnesses believe that Satan is the original cause of evil. Though once a perfect angel, Satan developed feelings of self-importance and craved to be worshiped by all creatures including humans, and eventually challenged God's right to rule the Universe. Satan caused Adam and Eve to disobey God, and humanity subsequently became participants in a challenge involving the competing claims of Jehovah and Satan to universal sovereignty. Other angels who sided with Satan became demons as well and have been tempting and tormenting humankind ever since in an effort to gain the soul's of all humans as demonic worshippers. For his infidelity and jealousy Satan was cast from Heaven into Hell.[62]

In addition, God's tolerance of evil is explained in part by the value of freewill. But Jehovah's Witnesses also hold that this period of suffering is based on the divine principle of non-interferences by God, which serves to demonstrate that Jehovah Witness's "right to rule" is both correct and in the best interests of all intelligent beings. Once again reaffirming God's right "of universal sovereignty". Further, it gives individual humans the opportunity to show their willingness to submit to God's ultimate authority.

At some future time, known only to God, He will consider His right to universal sovereignty to have been settled for all time. The reconciliation of the "faithful" will have been accomplished through Christ, and

---

[62] Revelation 12:9, "And the great dragon was cast out, that old serpent, called the Devil, and Satan, which deceives the whole world: he was cast out into the earth, and his angels were cast out with him." Also, John 8:44, "You are of [your] father the devil, and the lusts of your father you will do. He was a murderer from the beginning, and did not live in the truth, because there is no truth in him. When he lies, he speaks of his own: for he is a liar, and the father of it." There are other references in the NT to Satan fall but they are not as specific. Luke 10:18, "And he said unto them, I beheld Satan as lightning falls from heaven."

nonconforming humans and demons will be destroyed. Thereafter, evil (any failure to submit to God's sovereignty) will be summarily eliminated.

Jehovah's Witnesses do not believe in faith healing or healing by prayer as do the Christian Scientists, however, they hold that the Bible prohibits blood transfusions:

"This is a religious issue rather than a medical one. Both the OT and NT clearly command us to abstain from blood."[63, 64]

Also, God views blood as representing life.[65] So we avoid taking blood not only in obedience to God but also out of respect for Him as the Giver of life."[66] These quotes that are used by Jehovah's Witnesses to prohibit blood transfusions have created medical consequences when someone needs blood to avoid dying of severe blood loss. This results in more evil and since this dictum is based on Scripture and God is believed by Jehovah's Witnesses to have authored the Bible, this once again lays the blame for evil on God.

Islam and Evil

For the followers of Mohamed, suffering is either the painful result of sin, or it is a test of their faith in Allah. In the latter view, suffering tests belief; a true Muslim will remain faithful through the trials of life. Suffering also reveals the hidden self to God. Suffering is built into

---

[63] Deuteronomy 12:23 (NIV) "But be sure you do not eat the blood, because the blood is the life, and you must not eat the life with the meat.
Leviticus 17:10 (NIV) "'I will set my face against any Israelite or any foreigner residing among them who eats blood, and I will cut them off from the people."
http://www.jw.org/en/jehovahs-witnesses/faq/jehovahs-witnesses-why-no-blood-transfusions.
http://www.patheos.com/Library/Islam/Beliefs/Suffering-and-the-Problem-of-Evil.html#ixzz3ClroEzYX

[64] http://www.patheos.com/Library/Islam/Beliefs/Suffering-and-the-Problem-of-Evil.html#ixzz3ClroEzYX

the fabric of existence so that God may see who is truly righteous. In other words, God not only allows the various agonies and struggles of life, but He also has a purpose for evil. Suffering opens up the soul and reveals it to God. God uses suffering to look within humans and test their characters, and helps God to correct unbelievers.[67]

Islamic scholar Sherman Jackson states that the Mu'tazila school emphasizes God's omnibenevolence. Evil arises not from God but from the actions of His creatures that decide on their own actions independent of God's commands. The Ash'ari School, on the other hand, emphasizes God's omnipotence. God is not restricted to following some objective moral system centered on humans but has the power to do whatever He wants with His world. The Maturidi School argues that evil arises from God but that evil in the end has a wiser purpose for the future. Some theologians have viewed God as all-powerful and human beings as caught between the hope that God will be merciful and the fear that He will not treat them kindly.

Process Theology and the Problem of Evil

Process theology is a twentieth century theology that provides an alternate approach to the Problem of Evil. It limits God's omnipotence and/or omniscience as defined in traditional Christian theologies. Its God is not theistic.

Process theology is a system developed by Alfred North Whitehead (1861–1947). Process theology and process philosophy are collectively referred to as "process thought." Process theology is unrelated to the Process Church.

Whitehead saw God as an affective i.e. feeling being, that is, God feels emotions and induces emotions in humans. He is aware of, concerns by and, indeed, feels the emotions of His creatures. This is a temporal, that is, changing or evolving processes. At bottom, God suffers

---

67

along with He creatures. This is a God that contrasts sharply from the traditional theistic God who, in all respects, is non-temporal (eternal and not living in time as we humans do). The theistic God is unchanging (immutable) and unaffected (impassable) by the world He created. Process theology does not deny that God is in some respects eternal, immutable, and impassible, but it puts forth a modified view of the theistic God by insisting that God is in some respects temporal, mutable, and emotional. The process God walks the line between the theistic and anthropomorphic God. He is not totally transcendent like the gnostic God of antiquity who is totally unknowable. In a sense the process God is much like the traditional God of the Abrahamic religions. The Abrahamic God is both metaphysical and anthropomorphic. He meets the needs of all humans. He is all-everything while at the same time very caring, loving, aware of our every need and willing to answer our most sincere prayers. Whitehead's God, however, not only knows our feelings but also feels our feelings. He is the ultimate empathic being.

The God of Process Theology is not sovereign in the sense that His influence on humans is more persuasive than coercive. This is a friendlier, caring God. He is the polar opposite of the OT God, who is often mean spirited, jealous, vindictive and punishing: "Do it my way or else" is the absolute divine command that seems to be the OT God's usual *modus operendi.*

Process theologians all share certain ideas such as the existential concept of experiencing before being and the notion of divine 'relationality'. In other words, there is a strong existential element in process thought—existence comes before being. Our very being is created by our existence. How we act determines what we are. Reality is not made up of matter in motion, such as the atomists believed, but is rather composed of experiential events and these events are linked to one's relationship to God. Reality is a kind of dynamic, ever-changing existential series of happenings. These events have both a physical and mental aspects. All experiences are important and all contribute to the ongoing and interrelated processes of reality. God as feeling and emotional is, so to speak, walking with us throughout our lives. It is like holding the hand of our parent, spouse or friend as we travel across time. God is immanent and not transcendent. He is approachable and interested in our everyday life. Considered in a wider sense, Process Theology might be understood as referring to all forms of theology that embrace an active dynamic, temporal Godly existence. It looks to creative activity rather than mindless matter. It is an evolutionary growth process rather than changeless stagnation.

Process Theology would include the theology of Pierre Teilhard de Chardin (1881 –1955) and other theologies influenced by Hegel's dialectical method. De Chardin bases much of his theology on evolutionary theory. This is an ongoing, dynamic process in which God is wholly involved. Evolution is a temporal process. God is not timeless in the sense that everything is occurring outside of time. Rather God moves along with human happenings. We need 'time terms' to talk about timelessness, which, indeed, is a paradox. When speaking of everything happening for God at one and the same moment, we are caught in the middle of a divine contradiction. A timeless God, by definition, cannot experience 'moments'. There is no way we can get our mind or imagination around a concept such as a timeless, eternal God though many theologians use such verbiage.

Another related concept used in Process Theology is kenosis. This is a concept derived from the Bible. The term comes from Greek κένωσις, kénōsis) meaning emptiness and theologically involves the idea of 'self-emptying' of one's own will into the will of God and, thus, becoming entirely receptive to God's divine will. It originated in Paul's epistle to the Philippians 2:7, where it is written that Jesus is said to have "Emptied himself".

Kenosis can be applied in several different ways. In addition, to Christ emptying himself on the cross in order to save all humankind, several religions use it to indicate that humans must empty themselves into God as a means of gaining grace and submitting their souls entirely to the will of God and thus achieving salvation. Some view this as a mutual emptying: humans into God and God into humans. Pope Pius XII (1876–1958) condemned kenosis as suggesting that "The divinity was taken away from the Word in Christ". On the other hand, some see the emptying of the human soul into God as pantheistic. A God full of human souls would become a deity made up of billions of persons.

This smacks of Spinoza's idea, expressed in his *Ethics,* that humans are 'modes" of God. This seventeenth century Enlightenment theologian Baruch Spinoza (1632–1677) was excommunicated from his local synagogue for his views of God. In his *Ethics* he describes God as possessed of infinite 'attributes' two of which are 'thought and extension'. All humans are 'modes' within these two divine attributes and, thus, are part of God. This apparent pantheism brought down the wrath of Dutch Jewry, as well as many other religious groups, on Spinoza. The importance of Spinoza's work was not fully realized until years after his death. He helped lay the groundwork for the eighteenth century Enlightenment and rational biblical criticism, including modern notions of the self and, arguably, the Universe.

These views of God impact our understanding of the Problem of Evil. In one sense this compounds the Problem of Evil in that it raises the question of how we humans as intrinsically bound to God can experience evil. God as the ultimate good cannot contain evil as part of His essence. This would be an impossibility since God as defined is all-good and cannot be evil in any way. This would be self-contradictory, like having a square circle as noted above. In addition, if we humans are modes of God, that is, part of His very essence, we could not be evil. We could not sin, be responsible for moral evil or be affected in any way by the devil. We would not require Christ's salvific grace. He would not need to die on the cross. Adam and Eve could not have disobeyed God in Paradise. The very underpinnings of the Abrahamic religions would collapse. Theology as we know it today would be meaningless. Certainly we would all be heretics as viewed by the Catholic Church for holding such an idea of God and humans.

At any rate, kenosis and Spinoza's God and the several forms of Process Theology discussed above are some of the ways of viewing God as intimately bound to us humans making the Problem of Evil in some ways less of and in other ways more of a theological conundrum.

Figure 9. Teresa of Avila

Process Theology is one of the most recent approaches in our never-ending efforts to understand God. If we could fully comprehend Him, we would be able to solve the Problem of Evil. Mysticism, some claim, comes close to an understanding of the divine. Mysticism has been around a long time but in recent years neuroscience has provided a better understanding of this ineffable human experience. Most mystics and ordinary people, from time to time, experience spiritual feelings when praying, at church services, viewing a beautiful sunset or when in the presence of a host of other spiritual triggers including music, art works, the sight of a new born baby or when close to a loved one. Mystics, like Meister Eckhart (1260-1307), Catherine of Sienna (1347-1380) and Teresa of Avila (1515-1582) were all deeply moved by such human or divinely spiritual experiences. Even Mother Theresa (1910-1997) in the twentieth century reported such divine contacts i.e., states of communion with God. Experiencing God is, thus, a seemingly normal, even frequent, human activity. Even half of atheistic scientists report having spiritual feelings. With neuro-scientific support for such phenomena, it is hard to dismiss the reality of this 'sense of God' that so many mystics and average people report.

Neurotheology, also known as spiritual neuroscience, is the science that deals with the spiritual aspects of the human brain.[68] It attempts to explain religious experience and behavior in neuro-scientific terms. This science attempts to correlate neural phenomena with subjective experiences of spirituality by first developing hypotheses to explain these phenomena and then caring out neurological studies to confirm these hypotheses. Proponents of neurotheology say there is a neurological and evolutionary basis for subjective experiences traditionally categorized as spiritual or religious. The field has generated several popular science books,[69] but has also received criticism from psychologists.

In 1994, educator and businessman Laurence O. McKinney published the first book on the subject, titled "Neurotheology: Virtual Religion in the 21st Century", written for a popular audience but also promoted in the theological journal Zygon. [8] According to McKinney, neurotheology uses relatively recent developments in neurophysiology as the basis of neurotheology. According

---

68   Neurotheology, Wikipedia.

69   Alper, Matthew, *The "God" Part of the Brain: A Scientific Interpretation of Human Spirituality and God.*
James H. Austin. *Zen and the Brain: Toward an Understanding of Meditation and Consciousness.*
James H. Austin. *Zen-Brain Reflections: Reviewing Recent Developments in Meditation and States of Consciousness.*

to McKinney, pre-frontal brain development after the age three creates questions regarding earlier life experiences, which is a normal part of adult cognition. The inability of the adult brain to retrieve earlier images experienced by an infantile brain raises questions such as "where did I come from" and "where does it all go", which McKinney suggests led to the formation of various religious explanations for life before birth and after death. The experience of death as a peaceful regression into timelessness as the brain dies won praise from readers as varied as author Arthur C. Clarke, eminent theologian, Harvey Cox, and the Dalai Lama.

Andrew B. Newberg and R. Waldman[70] describe neurological processes that are driven by repetitive, rhythmic stimulation such as music, tapping, or other auditory, visual or sensory stimulation which are typical of human rituals such as religious liturgy. These repetitive sounds or touches can when combined with various thoughts or ideas can initiate brain activity associated with thoughts of God or other spiritual feelings. These authors insist that the physical, rhythmic stimulation must be combined with words, thought or ideas in order to produce what they call "transcendental unitize experiences", that is, spiritual feelings. Once this occurs "...ritual turns a meaningful idea into a visceral experience, emotion or feeling. A good example of such a stimulator of spiritual feelings is the Catholic rosary. This consists of five decades, that is, the recitation of an Our Father, ten Hail Marys and one Glory Be To God five times. This includes praying a preliminary Apostle's Creed, three Hail Marys and an Our Father. Each decade has an intention and a full rosary involves saying twenty decades with thoughts about Christ, such as his death and resurrection. Twenty decades might take an hour to pray. The repetition is rhythmic and the ideas about Christ energize certain parts of the brain and

---

[70] Newberg, A. and Waldman, R, 2009, *How God Changes Your Brain*, Kindle e-book.

thus stimulate a sense of spirituality. The rosary is almost hypnotic in its effect and induces a sense of God as well as spiritual feelings.

Newberg and Waldman note that when we think, talk about or try to imagine God multiple brain circuit are activated or under certain stances some are deactivated. Thinking about God may relax or stimulated you. Awareness if God alters brain circuitry and may thicken the outer surface (cortex) of the brain. The brain is very plastic, that is, it is always changing and the idea of God will increase brain connections between millions of brain cells (neurons). These connections occur within a short time and may last for long period of time. These changes will occur in religious persons but also agnostics and atheists. These changes are associated with spiritual feelings that occur in everyone no matter how religious or non-religious they are.

Moreover, Newberg and Waldman suggest that humans are compelled to act out myths by biological operations of the brain through what they call the "inbuilt tendency of the brain to turn thoughts into actions". Thus, myths, which would include religious doctrines and prayers, can function as rhythmic stimulation in activating brain function and subsequent behaviors.

Various theories regarding the evolutionary origin of religion and the psychology of religion have been proposed. It has been suggested that religion and certain genes have evolved over time because they provide natural selective advantages. These include emotional, cognitive, social and or physiological advantages that religion provides. We may feel more secure, comforted, and protected by belonging to a religious group. Religious doctrines have long provided "answers" for unexplained phenomena such as how did the world begin and subsequently evolve. As a result, we have developed a healthier physiology related to religious elements in our lives.

Some scientific studies have helped to support these notions. One controversial proposal, the God gene hypothesis, states that a specific gene, the VMAT2 gene, predispose to spirituality. During the 1980's Michael Persinger stimulated the temporal lobes of human subjects with a weak magnetic field using an apparatus that popularly is known as the "God helmet" and reported that many of his subjects claimed to experience a "sensed presence" during stimulation.[71] This work has been criticized and has, to date, not been replicated by other researchers. It has been noted that Persinger's work was not "double-blind." Participants' subjects were often graduate students who knew what sort of results to expect, and there was the possibility that the experimenters' expectations would be transmitted to subjects by unconscious cues. The participants were frequently given an idea of the purpose of the study by being asked to fill in questionnaires designed to test their suggestibility to paranormal experiences before the trials were conducted. Other double-blind studies have failed to replicate Persinger's results, and concluded that the presence or absence of the magnetic field had no relationship to any religious or spiritual experience reported by the participants, but results were entirely dependent on the subjects' suggestibility and personality traits. Following the publication of this study, Persinger has disputed these critiques.

Newberg and Waldman's studies at the University of Pennsylvania on the other hand have been extensive and thorough and support a brain-God connection. These studies include:

1. Each part of the brain constructs a different view of God.

---

[71]   Persinger, M.A., *The Sensed Presence Within Experimental Settings: Implications for the Male and Female Concept of Self.* The Journal of Psychology: Interdisciplinary and Applied, vol. 137.

2. Each person's brain develops a unique perception of God.
3. Spiritual practices even in non-religious persons enhance brain function and thus improve physical and emotional health.
4. Intense, long term contemplation of God and other spiritual values appears to permanently changed the structures of the brain that control our moods, conscious sense of self, and the world.
5. Meditation promotes peacefulness, social awareness, and compassion for others.
6. Cognition, communication, creativity, and perception of reality can also be augmented by spiritual practices. Survival skills are also enhanced.

All these experiences and research studies do not prove there is a God, but the feeling of a fatherly figure is certainly a real human phenomenon. However, the brain in many instances has been shown to 'care little' about the reality of its conscious experiences. The brain is mainly interested in the survival value of these experiences. So brain activity doesn't mean that it is experiencing any true spiritual or material reality. Many brain responses have evolved because they have natural selective advantages that help us as individuals and as a species to survive and evolve to higher more adaptive levels.

In the past several years there has an emerging Neo-atheism in the writing of such authors as Richard Dawkins', *The God Delusion,* Sam Harris', *The End of Faith* and Christopher Hitchens's, *God is Not Great.* These authors not only deny the existence of God, but also maintain that religious beliefs are personally and societally dangerous. Newberg, and Waldman along with many other authors provide solid evidence that such is not the case. We live in an evolving world. Religion provides a natural selective advantage for us humans. Religion of one sort or another

has, as best we can tell, been around since prehistory.[72]
There is some evidence that H. sapiens as early as 300,000
years ago and more formal forms of religions existed
between 50,000 and 30,000 years ago practiced religion
of some early types. Since the development of farming
around 12,000 years ago religious formats have become
more pervasive and powerful with architecturally advance
temples as seen in the Middle East and Peru. There is some
evidence from Neanderthal burial sites that they may have
had religious ideas before did humans.

Without some benefit, religion or we humans would
have disappeared long ago. Religion, as we have seen and
continue to see is not all good but it provides enough pluses
to outweigh its negatives.

Nonetheless, to dismiss God out-of-hand is not easy to
do. However, a modified dystheistic notion of God, if valid,
would go a long way in solving the Problem of Evil. Such
a non-theistic God is, of course, hard to accept for many
religious believers. However, knowing what we do about
the connection between subjective experiences, objective
brain activity and the natural selective advantages of many
mental experiences, it would make sense that the benefit
gained from such feelings, are helpful for most humans and
will not soon go away. We are seeing diminished church
attendance over the past one hundred years and a fairly
marked change in Europe and North America over the
past twenty or thirty years, however, though attendance is
down there is no evidence as of yet that spiritual feelings or
a sense of God have declined.

In terms of the Problem of Evil, the evidence is fairly
solid that religion can help with the Problem of Evil by
strengthening our ability to deal with challenges in our
environment and help us survive longer as individuals and
as a species.

---

72 Menzies, Allan, 2012, *History of Religion A Sketch of Primitive Religious Beliefs and Practices, and of the Origin and Character of the Great Systems* Kindle e-book.

Part III

Chapter 7

Greater Good Solutions for the Problem of Evil

The 'Greater Good solution' argues that some greater good will come out of an evil act or event. The proponents of this solution claim that God cannot bring about some greater good without permitting a specific moral or natural evil. An example of the 'Greater Good' argument might be one that is often mentioned in regards to the Mayo Clinic that is located in Rochester, Minn. The Mayo Clinic is the one of the largest and best-known medical clinics in America and possibly the world. It provides high-quality medical care for thousands of patients worldwide ever day and is the largest employer in Rochester providing jobs for nearly 40,000 people. In 1864, a tornado struck Rochester and the Franciscan nuns who were working here at the time, asked Dr. William Worrall Mayo, to come to Rochester to care for the injured victims of the tornado. In due course his sons Drs. William James Mayo and Charles Horace Mayo joined him in 1883 and 1888. The Mayo Clinic celebrated its 150th anniversary in 2014. Many consider the foundation of the Mayo Clinic as a greater good that arose out of a natural evil.

The Freewill Response for the Problem of Evil

Related to the greater good response is the freewill argument that appeals to human moral freedom. The freewill defense asserts that the existence of beings with freewill is of great moral value, because with freewill comes the ability to make morally significant choices. This entails the possibility of making both good and bad moral decisions, but to have freewill allows humans to perform good acts for individuals and society as a whole. This far outweighs the evil that may ensue. God, therefore, is justified in creating a world that allows freewill. A world with free beings and no evil would be even better, however, this would require that people function as automatons and thus they would not be truly human. It is logically impossible for God to prevent evil without curtailing human nature. It is the old square circle conundrum.

In addition, according to many religions, Heaven is a most wondrous place, that awaits those who use their freewill to do good deeds and follow God's commands. Meriting Heaven through morally good acts is a greater good, outweighing the potential evil that results from evil acts free humans perform.

Critics of the freewill argument suggest that such evils as murder, rape, pedophilia, and the like, far out weigh the benefits of human freewill. One option would be for God, who is infinitely resourceful, to create humans with freewill but also make their capacity to evaluate potential outcomes of their actions so astute that they would never err in their decision-making. Is this possible even for a theistic God with all His knowledge and power or would this be equivalent to making all humans divine? Some, like Spinoza, believe that we humans are 'modes' of God as noted above. However, if we are part of the essence of God, why don't we function like 'little gods'? After all, the Bible says we are made in His 'image and likeness'. (Genesis 1:26).

God could limit evil by making moral actions especially pleasurable, so that good deeds would be immediately pleasurable options for us. He could also punish immoral actions immediately with pain or some sort of discomfort. Or He could allow us to make bad moral decisions, but intervene to prevent the harmful consequences of such acts. This approach would mean that freewill has less or no real value. In a sense, we wouldn't really be free. The debate depends on how we define freewill and determinism, humanity and automatons. These concepts are not always easy to separate.

Genetics and environment play important roles in how ethical an individual may ultimately turn out to be. There is mounting evidence that a child's environment during his or her formative years will influence their moral decision-making ability. As an example, serial killers tend to come from abusive homes though obviously not all abused children end up serial killers. It is likely that genetics influences their adult moral behaviors as well. There are some factors in most criminal's early life that impact their relationships as adults. How much these factors determine moral behaviors and mitigate responsibility for evil deeds is uncertain. So the question remains, just how free is human freewill?

The Individual versus Society

Humans, since prehistory, have been struggling to survive. This struggle pits two human elements against each other: individual needs and societal needs. Much of what we base moral decisions on relate to our perceived individual needs and wants. If we are starving and find some food, will we eat all the food ourselves or offer some to others. If we are scavenging for food all by ourselves and a starving total stranger wanders by, we are less likely to share the food. We might even steal what food he has hunted down or gathered up. On the other hand, if we have a spouse or children, it is more likely that we will share the food with them. This phenomenon is labeled "kin selection". Kin selection is the evolutionary strategy that favors the reproductive success of an organism's relatives even at some cost to the organism's own survival. Kin altruism is behavior that drives kin selection.[73] This is an evolutionary response that maintains and improves our survival as well as that of genetically related individuals.

---

[73] Wikipedia.

Darwin mentions this in *The Origin of Species*. Kin selection and altruism favor survival of those closely related to the person performing helpful acts. Some frame this in terms of protecting and maintaining the genetic profile of ones family. In Richard Dawkins' terminology it's the "selfish gene" at work. [74]

The other side of this equation is societal survival. Our personal needs and that of our kin come first. However, we all (unless we are anchorites that exist alone in some desert cave) live in a society and that society helps us live well and happily. Society provides jobs, resources, community, comfort and a host of other benefits. As a result, we need to support the society in which we live in order for us as individuals to live better and survive longer.

Societies have needs just as individuals do. Often times these individual and societal needs come into conflict and that is why society develops cultural mores and laws. There are some things we can and cannot do. Generally we can't drive on the left side of the road unless we live in the UK or Japan. We stop at red and go on green lights. We own a house and other people can't come in unless invited. As the Declaration of Independence proclaims, we have a right to life, liberty and the pursuit of happiness. Actually Thomas Jefferson took this from John Locke who sanctioned life, liberty and property. So we all have to give a little so we can live a little happier, healthier and more peacefully.

When our individual needs and wants bump up against other's needs and wants compromises need to be made and that is what society is all about. In the end we, or most of us, can live productive and peaceful lives. It is through this give and take that *Homo sapiens* has survived and improved as a species over the last 200,000 years or so. This is Darwin's natural selection at work.

---

[74] Dawkins, Richard, 1976, *The Selfish Gene*, Kindle ebook.

Freewill and Natural Evils

Another argument against the freewill defense is that it fails to address natural evils, such as earthquakes, hurricanes, epidemics, and the like. Advocates of the freewill response may offer a different explanation for these natural evils. As an example, Alvin Plantinga has famously suggested that natural evils are caused by the free choices of supernatural beings such as demons or Satan. Others have argued that natural evils are the result of our biblical 'parents', who corrupted the perfect world created by God when they, Adam and Eve, sinned. Others say that natural laws are prerequisites for the existence of intelligent free beings and these natural laws are ne, in turn, necessary to run the world properly. Others claim that natural evils provide us with knowledge of evil, which in turn makes our free choices more significant and valuable. It has also been claimed that natural evils are a means of divine punishment for immoral acts that humans have committed, and so natural evil is are justified as God's retribution for our voluntary misdeeds.

It seems, nonetheless, that a theistic God ought to be able to create this world, along with its most intelligent beings, so that we humans would function in a perfectly rational way. This would include Adam and Eve who would not have disobeyed God over one piece of fruit, and not have reduced an ideal world to this imperfect planet, Earth, some 6004 years ago, at least according to Genesis 1 & 2 and Bishop James Usher.[75]

---

[75] Bishop James Usher (1581 –1656) in 1650, after studying the genealogy of Christ as presented in the Bible, declared the Earth had been created in 4004 BCE and thus was under 6000 years old at the time.

Irenaeus' Theodicy:[76]

The Soul-Making Defense

Irenaeus (d. 202 CE) was an early Church Father and bishop of what is present day Lyon, France. His solution to the Problem of Evil is referred to as the "soul-making" defense. Essential to the human soul-making theodicy is the claim that evil and suffering are necessary for spiritual growth. For anyone to grow spiritually and morally we must suffer in order to better understand what suffering is all about and how it affects all of us. Evils teach us how to help our family, friends and even strangers. We become more virtuous as a result of such suffering. In a way this is another form of the greater good theodicy. The greater good in this instance, however, is spiritual growth.

Irenaeus' approach to the Problem of Evil was expanded upon some eighteen hundred years later by the influential philosophers of religion, John Hickson (1922-2012), whom we have seen before, believed an inadequacy of this theodicy is that personal evils do not always promote positive moral growth and, in fact, evil can have a negative effect on the human spirit. Recall the serial killers abused as children. A second issue concerns the distribution of evils suffered. Were it true that God permits evil in order to facilitate spiritual growth, then we would expect evil to disproportionately befall those in poor spiritual health. This does not seem to be the case, since decadent people may enjoy affluent and happy lives, which protects them from evil, whereas many pious and morally good persons may suffer excess worldly evils when they seemingly are already spiritually strong people. There is an accepted biased view that the rich are less ethical than the poor while, in fact, studies show that economically stressed

---

[76] Theodicy is a term coined by Leibniz (see below) and literally means God's justice. A theodicy is an argument justifying God's choice to allow evil in the world.

persons are more often involved in crimes. At least, they are more often convicted of crimes. It does not appear that this level of criminal behavior is always due to bias on the part of courts or that the rich are able to obtain better legal advice, though this certainly happens. The fact is that the poor more often commit crimes because they are simply more in need of funds to stay afloat on a day to cay basis. If soul-making is promoted by suffering why are so many poor in our prisons?

A third issue associated with Irenaeus' 'soul-making' theodicy is that the qualities developed through experiencing evil are useful because they help humankind evolve to a higher level. In favor of a modified soul-making argument it may be said that the desired moral qualities are intrinsically valuable. There is empirical verification of this view. As will be discussed later, evil is essential to the evolutionary process. If there were no suffering over the 4.6 billion years Earth has been around, we would not have evolved to the level we are at today. We are better humans and live in a more advanced society because of the difficulties we have faced over the centuries. Human growth and improvement in more than spiritual ways has occurred because we have overcome many challenges. In this sense, Irenaeus was right but it is not just soul-making that has been affected; it is the soul, the body, the mind and society as a whole that have grown and improved over the tens of thousands of years humans have been on Earth.

Afterlife and the Problem of Evil

The belief in an afterlife has also been cited as justifying evil. Christian theologian Randy Alcon in *Heaven, The Purity Principle*, (2011), argues that the joys of Heaven will compensate for our sufferings on Earth, and writes:

"Without this eternal perspective, we assume that people who die young, who have handicaps, who suffer poor health, who don't get married or have children or who don't do this or that will miss out on the best life has to offer. But this assumption [that there is no afterlife] has a fatal flaw. It presumes that our present Earth, bodies, culture, relationships and lives are all there is...[but] Heaven will bring far more than compensation for our present sufferings."[77]

The Bible, ancient and modern religious authorities, human desires and the vast majority of humankind all maintain that there is a Heaven to look forward to if we are morally good and Hell is the destination for those who are morally bad. Most all of us want to live forever. We want a peaceful, trouble free life that goes on eternally. We hope to be loved by all our friends, family and most especially by God forever. No matter how much we want such a life and no matter how many people believe in an afterlife, the fact is that there is no certainty that there is such a place. There is no empirical evidence to support such a concept.

There have been many people who claim to have died and then come back to life on Earth. Recently, Alex Malarkey who had written a bestselling book along with his father, Kevin Malarkey, *The Boy Who Came Back From Heaven,* in 2010, just recently (Jan. 16, 2015) admitted he made up this tale after he was seriously injured in an accident. He was in a coma for two months following which he had difficulty speaking and walking and thought the story would get him some needed attention and sympathy. We simply have no way of verifying any of these "death and back to life" stories.[78]

If there is no afterlife then, of course, Randy Alcon's Problem of Evil argument is without merit.

---

[77] Alcon, Randy, 2009, *If God Is Good: Faith in the Midst of Suffering and Evil,* Kindle ebook, p. 243.

[78] http://www.washingtonpost.com/blogs/style-blog/wp/2015/01/15/boy-who-came-back-from-heaven-going-back-to-publisher/.

The Soul-Body Dualism Problem

Alcorn's, *The Purity Principle*,[79] is an epilogue to his, *If God Is Good*. In his *Purity Principle* Alcorn presents a somewhat novel view of Heaven that is based on an updated interpretation of the Bible. He paints a most blissful picture of life in Heaven. It is not a boring place floating in the clouds with everyone lounging around playing a harp. Rather, it is an earthly place, in which everyone enjoys the pleasure of God i.e. His beatific vision, while involved in a multitude of enjoyable activities. Alcon makes this a life after death a place that fully compensates for any sufferings endured during life on Earth.

This compensatory Heaven is based on Alcon's interpretation of the Bible, which he admits may seem heretical to some Christians. Unfortunately, there is no empirical certitude that such a heavenly place exists or that it is as Alcon describes it. Philosopher Stephen Maiden has called this the "Heaven Swamps Everything" theodicy, arguing that such a description of afterlife is invalid because it combines compensation and justification for all evils suffered and committed. He observes that this reasoning may stem from imagining an ecstatic or forgiving state of mind on the part of the blissful souls in Heaven. In Heaven no one bears grudges, even the most horrific earthly suffering is as nothing compared to infinite heavenly bliss. All past wrongs are forgiven. But "are forgiven" doesn't mean, "Are justified". The blissful person's disinclination to dwell on his or her earthly suffering doesn't imply that a perfect being, i.e. God, is justified in permitting such earthly suffering. In addition, Alcon's view of Heaven is anthropomorphic. If we humans live on in Heaven as spirits, as is the usual religious view of our afterlife, then we aren't in a given place and we can't enjoy activities anything like the activities we enjoyed on Earth.

---

[79] Alcorn, R. L., 2009, *The Purity Principle,: God's Safeguards for Life's Dangerous Trails* (LifeChange Books), Kindle ebook

We can't sit around and look at God enjoying His divine presence. As spirits we are not able to "sit around", "look" at anything (we aren't in space-time and spirits don't have eyes). We can't be involved in earthly activities. Activities imply complex natures. Spirits are 'simple', that is, they don't have parts. Theologians tell us that anything that has parts, such as eyes, arms, hearts, brains and atoms/molecules are mutable and thus corruptible. Such beings come to an end at some point in time. In other words, they die. But once we, as humans, die and our soul (spirit) goes to Heaven, we no longer are corruptible and will persist for all eternity. As spirits we can't even think because this involves brain activity and we no longer have a brain.

As young Christians we are taught that the soul acts through the brain and the other parts of our body. This implies that there is a 'soul-body' connection—a dualistic union. This means there are two spheres that make up our world. One is immaterial (spiritual) and one material. The soul is spiritual and immaterial. The body is material and in space-time. The soul and body belong to two entirely different spheres. The soul is 'simple'; it has no working part and thus is incorruptible and eternal. The body has trillions of working parts (cells, tissues and organs) and is thus corruptible. Anything with parts can come apart. Spirits are not corporeal or material and thus cannot exist in space-time. By definition only material things reside in space-time. Since these two 'spheres' are limited to their separate spheres or realms, they cannot interact. How is it that they can connect with one another? How is it that the soul can influence the body and in turn, how can the body relay information, images and feelings back to the soul? As currently defined the soul and body can't 'talk' to one another.

This is the body-soul dualism with which Rene Descartes (1596-1650) struggled five hundred years ago. He and many philosophers/theologians have anguished over this issue without resolution ever since.

Stephen J. Gould (1941–2002) of Harvard attempted to resolve this enigma by simply saying there is no resolution to this dualism. Religion and science reside in two entirely different 'magistaria' as he calls their two spheres, and these spheres or magistaria are 'non-overlapping'. We can never discuss religion (the spiritual world) and science (the material world) at one and the same time and in the same way. They are "non-overlapping magistaria" (NOMA). They reside in separate worlds never to be united.

Descartes tried to overcome this dualistic impasse by suggesting that the human soul resides in the pineal body—a small organelle situated in the center of the brain. Unfortunately, the pineal is material and is situated in space and time. The soul on the other hand is 'spiritual' and cannot be located anywhere in space and time. In addition, the soul has no way of communicating with anything material. We have been told by (in my case) priests and nuns that God, angels and even devils can interact with us. In essence we were led to believe that spirits can do anything from create the material world, keep the world going, stand by our side (as guardian angels), hear and respond to our prayers, and hover over us with caring kindness. The problem with these images is that spirits, as defined, are incapable of doing any of these things. To be able to connect with us, they have to be able to talk, touch, and comfort us. As material beings we have no means of experiencing such behaviors and spirits have no way of relaying such behaviors to us without being in some way material beings. However, if material, they cannot be eternal, all-knowing, all-powerful etc. as is God said to be and to a lesser extend are other spirits supposed to be. We've been told that spirits basically can do anything in some magical way. This is a comforting concept but logically impossible. God can't make square circles and He can't, as a spirit, create or connect with material beings– this is just logically impossible. Likewise, how many angels can dance on the head of a pin? None, they have no feet with which to dance!

We humans love myths. They explain things otherwise inexplicable. They help guide our lives, provide moral principles, and make the world a little more meaningful but they are after all fictional stories that comfort and guide us but are most often simply myths and nothing more. They don't describe the real world.

Most of us no longer believe in polytheistic gods. Science has clearly established that the Universe arose out of a 'Big Bang' 13.8 billion year ago and that it was 4.6 billion years ago that Earth evolved and another billion years or so before life began to emerged on Earth. Not everyone believes these scientific facts but the reality is that there was no Great Flood that wiped out all but Noah's family. The world wasn't created in six days and the first day of creation didn't begin at nine o'clock Sunday morning, October 23, 4004 BCE as Bishop Usher claims. The problem with this day and date, is that there was no time before creation and if James Usher was correct, then the calendar should have begun on day one and it should be reset to reflect the number of days and years since then. So since Usher proclaimed this in 1650, then our calendar today should read 6019 (4004 + 2015) and Christ would have been born in the year 4004 although the exact year of Christ's birth is uncertain. It probably was 4 BCE. And, of course, there have been adjustments before and since Christ's birth. Julius Caesar made changes some forty years earlier and Pope Gregory XIII skipped ten days in 1582 to get the calendar back on track.

The fact is that the Universe began with the Big Bang about 13.8 billion years ago and this may be as close as we can come to the time of creation. The point is that as science advances we need fewer myths to help us understand the world in which we live. It's difficult to give up ancient ideas even when they have become outdated. We like the comfort of simple, easily grasped stories that have been with us for millennia. It is so much easier to believe in a magically made Universe that popped into existence from nothing with a few divine words or the gentle waving of God's hand. The fact is that a spirit, even if divine, can't speak any words or wave His hand because He has no lips nor hands by definition.

To understand the Big Bang is not easy. First of all, how did the Bid Bang get started in the first place? Somebody or something had to set it in motion, right? So we need a first mover or first cause, as Aristotle suggested, or gods or a God as religions over the centuries have posited. And if this first cause were an anthropomorphic God such as a deistic God, or a theistic God He wouldn't be capable of creating a material Universe. In my, *Problem Gods: In Search of a Meaningful Deity*, I offer a deity more in line with todays science, including relativity and quantum theory that could initiate a Big Bang. But everything proposed about God is in the end speculative. Some even suggest that the Big Bang could have occurred without a cause!

The prevailing scientific model of how the Universe developed over time from the instant in which the Universe is thought to have begun, rapidly expanded from a singularity[80], estimated to have begun 13.798 ± 0.037 billion years ago. It is convenient to divide the evolution of the Universe so far into several phases:

→Beginning 0 to 10^{-43} seconds after the Big Bang started, the four physical forces as we now know them (weak, strong, electromagnetic and gravitational) were but one force, and the nascent Universe was unimaginably hot. There was only intense energy and no matter, i.e. no atoms. In time as the Universe cooled the energy was converted into matter including quarks and antiquarks, electrons, protons and neutrons. After about 379,000 years the electrons and protons combined into atoms

---

[80] Singularity. This is a complex physical phenomenon that I won't go into here. Wikipedia offers a reasonable discussion of the "initial singularity".

(mostly hydrogen). E=mc² is the formula Einstein developed showing the amount of matter that can be created out of a given amount of energy.

There was a period of rapid expansion of the Universe called the Inflationary Period. Residual radiation produced during this time spread through space largely unimpeded. This relic radiation is known as the cosmic microwave background radiation and it is one of the ways we know of the Big Bang. We can still detect this background radiation today. Eventually the Universe ended up composed of 75% hydrogen and 25% helium.

In time gravity caused hydrogen and helium to collect into large masses of matter that we now know as suns or stars. The gravitational force of a sun is huge and this causes the hydrogen to 'ignite' as atomic energy. There are literally millions of hydrogen bombs in each sun producing the light and heat that comes from our Sun and all stars. The first stars and all stars thereafter were and are composed of these many hydrogen 'bombs' exploding continuously. Over time these stars run out of fuel, i.e. hydrogen and implode. In a matter of minutes, if massive enough, they collapse forming a supernova and then explode. During this brief implosion of the supernova, hydrogen and helium are crunched together with such force that they form larger atoms including lithium, carbon, oxygen, sodium, potassium, calcium, iron and even silver and gold. Many other new atoms are formed this way leaving stardust scattered in space. Then the sun-making process begins all over again.

Our Sun is a second-generation descendant of a supernova. But now this new Sun of ours contains all the ingredients for life including us humans. This happened about 4.6 billion years ago as noted earlier. It took another billion years or so before life began to emerge on Earth and since then evolution has given Earth all the millions of species that have lived or are living here today. We are literally made of stardust!

There is much more to this process that began with the Big Bang but we need not go into to this presently. The basic point is that this is all very complex and not completely understood even today. It is reasonable that a large percentage of humans prefer the Genesis version of creation. It is not such a brain busting process to comprehend and it is the physicists who love to play with such mathematical and physical complexities.

With all this evolution has come the many problems that all living beings face on a daily basis and which form the basis for this book.

Karma, Previous Lives and the Problem of Evil

→The Eastern religious concept of karma holds that good acts result in pleasure and bad acts in suffering. The doctrine of karma is part of the theology of Buddhism, Hinduism and other eastern religions. The theology of karma holds that there is suffering in the world, but there is no undeserved suffering, and thus no evil that is unjustified. The obvious objection to this approach is that some people suffer misfortunes that are undeserved. This objection is answered by coupling karma with reincarnation, so that such suffering is the result of immoral behaviors in a previous life. This view eliminates any divine responsibility for the evil that is justified punishment for individual human immoral freewill behaviors.

Buddhism holds that all humans must gain nirvana by performing good deeds (good karma). Nirvana is the ultimate state obtained after death and it is achieved after ample good karma is built up during ones life or series of lives after repeated incarnations. If there is not enough good karma and too much bad karma then following death a person is doomed to be reincarnated as a lower level being. Instead of being a human in its next life, a person may be a dog, a bird or even such low life as a worm. But if he or she is able at this lower level to perform enough good deeds they may be reincarnated at a higher level and possibly after several reincarnations may make it back to being a human and finally with proper karma achieve nirvana for all eternity.

Nirvana is not like the Heaven of Christianity but rather is seen as a transcendental, "deathless" state, in which there is no time and no "re-death." By following the Noble Eightfold Path, which culminates in the practice of *hyena* the mind is brought to rest and all three desires of passion, hatred and delusions are extinguished. They, in fact, lose their sense of self.

In essence nirvana is a quiet peace of mind unfettered by turmoil and worldly cares. In Buddhism the suffering and evils of life are explained as part of a process of cleansing oneself of those aspects of one's being that prevent us from entering into nirvana—the final ultimate peaceful state of mind. This quietude is thought to be worth all the hassle of reincarnations. In the end, this is one solution to the Problem of Evil. The Buddhist God, however, is not like the theistic God of Christianity. He is much less well defined and thus not so difficult to exonerate from creating such an evil world.

Human Limitations Regarding our Knowledge of God and the Problem of Evil

Another so-called 'skeptical theistic' argument holds that due to human's limited knowledge we cannot expect to understand God or His ultimate plan. When a parent takes an infant to the doctor for a routine vaccination, it's because the parent cares for and loves that child. The infant, however, will be unable to appreciate the need for a needle stick and cries in response to the pain. It is argued that just as an infant cannot possibly understand the motives of the parent due to its cognitive limitations, so too we are, even as adults, unable to comprehend God's reasoning. Given this view, the difficulty or impossibility of finding a plausible explanation for evil in a world created by a theistic God is to be expected.

Related to this argument is the concept of God as a transcendent being. As transcendent, God lives in a realm beyond our own. His nature is beyond not only the physical world in which we live but also our spiritual and intellectual world. God as such is totally beyond our comprehension, imagination, and sensory world and thus this limits our comprehension to the world around us.

A related argument is that good and evil are strictly beyond human comprehension. Since our concepts of good and evil as instilled in us by God are only intended to facilitate ethical behavior in our relations with other humans, we can have no expectation that these ethical concepts are accurate beyond what is needed to fulfill this societal ethical function and therefore these perceptions cannot presume to be sufficient to determine whether what we call evil really is truly evil in the greater scheme of things. Evil for one person may be viewed as good by another. Though many believe in absolute ethical standards, this is a view that is hard to support empirically. If ethics is culturally and genetically based then they tend to change over time. If ethics is based on Darwinian natural selective advantages and these selective advantages are continually evolving as our environment evolves, then ethical standards must also change and evolve. This makes our understanding of the world along with good and evil just that much more enigmatic. It is said, the only constant is change.

With our inability to identify God's reasons for permitting evil, there remains a question as to why we have not been given clear and unambiguous assurances by God for allowing evil; answers that we could understand. Here discussion of the Problem of Evil moves to the atheistic argument for the Problem of Evil. Does God really exist? Is what we call evil just an integral part of a purely materialistic world?

Denial of the Existence of God and the Problem of Evil

The atheistic view of the Problem of Evil can be simply stated as follows:

1. If the theistic God were all-good, all-knowing and all-powerful, then He would be capable of preventing all earthly evils.
2. There are earthly evils.
3. Therefore, there can be no theistic God.

This syllogism has been discussed before. It is simple and clear-cut but only applies to a theistic God. Any deity defined as less than infinite in all respects, can be accepted, as a being that allows evil without logical inconsistencies. We can have a non-theistic God and evil existing together. The atheist's argument doesn't prove that God doesn't exist; it only proves the non-existence of a theistic God. Any other type of God could allow natural and moral evil.

Such a God is, of course, unacceptable to followers of the three Abrahamic religions who are all theists. If theists are true to their various theologies, they must espouse a God that is capable of everything that is not logically self-contradictory, like creating a "round square". There has been some decline in dogmatic rigidity for many Jews, Christians, and Muslims in recent decades and as a result theism is not as strongly held and as pervasive as it once was and there is less of a problem with worldly evil for many believers as a result. Still nearly 90 percent of Americans believe in God and the majority hold to the classical theistic God of the past two to three millennia. As many as 45 percent of Americans still believe in the biblical account of creation. These classic theological tenets meet many emotional and spiritual needs and in spite of recent scientific advances resist changing their views of creation and God.

Evil as a Test of Our Faith

In the Book of Job, we read about a man that was good and faithful to God but as is the case in many OT parables, Job is tested by God who allows the devil to devastate Job monetarily, physically and emotionally. He loses all his cattle, crops, family and health. All these evils are allowed by God as a test of his faith in God. Job passes the test with flying colors and God then returns all his goods and gives him a new family. (Job 1.1-2.7 & 42.7-42.16).

Also in Job 14:1 the OT reads:

"Man that is born of a woman is of few days, and these full of trouble."

It is an obvious fact that all of us suffer to some degree or another on a daily basis. Either the weather isn't quite to our liking or we worry about money or our job or health. And the list goes on and on. We have many happy minutes, hours or days as well but some experience a life full of emotional and/or physical pain so that for many only suicide seems to offer any relief.

At this moment of writing, a good friend is in the hospital undergoing treatment for acute myelogenous leukemia. This is a very serious "blood cancer" with a limited prognosis. He is faced with the question, "Why is this happening to me." He's 58 and has been generally healthy, but now he may be dying with this devastating disorder; a disease that took his wife just a few years ago.[81] Is God allowing this to test his faith? He is understandably very depressed over all this and is searching for the reasons, "why me, why now, why my wife?" He is a good person, very caring and compassionate—a modern day Job; so why, why, why?

---

[81] Since writing this, his leukemia has been treated with several courses of chemotherapy and he is now in remission and may be cured!

If God is all-good, all-knowing and all-powerful, He knows that this man is faithful and God fearing. No divine test should be necessary. God, with His infinite nature, knows all past, present and future happenings. He knows what my friend will do always and everywhere. So why would God choose to enlist such a despicable demon as Satan to do these dirty deeds to Job, my friend and the billions of human beings throughout the ages and all over the Earth?

We might pose the same questions as well for the suffering that all sentient animals endure daily.

Chapter 8
A Historical View of the Problem of Evil

In ancient Mesopotamia the Problem of Evil was based on polytheistic religious thought. There were multiple anthropomorphic gods. Their behaviors, like the behaviors of us humans, were often chaotic, self-centered, and emotional. These multiple gods were constantly battling for control. Their interests lay not with mere earthlings but with power over other gods, womanizing and punishing all those who fail to honor and obey them. There was no Problem of Evil because the ancient gods were not theistic. They were not all-everything gods. They could err. They were like us humans, given to failings of reason, the passions and behaviors that the theistic God is not, b y definition, allowed to display.

In Ancient Egypt, it is thought the Problem of Evil took at least two forms, as found in the extant manuscript, *Dialogue of a Man*. In this treatise a man accuses his soul of wanting to desert him, and of dragging him towards death before his time. He says that life is too heavy for him to bear; that his heart would come to rest in the West (i.e. the afterlife), his name would survive and his body would be protected. He urges his soul to be patient and wait for a son to be born to make the offerings he needs in the afterlife. His soul describes the sadness death brings and responds to the man's complaints about his lack of value; his being cut off from humanity; and the attractiveness of death. His soul exhorts him to embrace life and his soul promises to stay with him.[82] This man appears to be extremely depressed and pulled down by the worries of the world. He seems not to be suicidal according to the translator of the papyrus.

Egyptian gods are seen as far removed from ordinary humans. They are portrayed as distant and anthropomorphic and are not responsible for creation and thus not responsible for human acts. These gods were not theistic. As non-creators and finite, they could not be blamed for evil.

The Gnostic Response to the Problem of Evil

Gnosticism refers to several early (Christian?) sects that competed with the Proto-Catholic Church. They saw the world as evil because it was created by an imperfect demiurge, Sophia[83]. The Gnostic God was transcendent, that is, totally above and beyond the reach of humans. God, as transcendent, can have no interaction, contact or intercourse of any sort with material beings. As we have seen, a spirit is by definition, devoid of any material elements. Because of this limitation God had to create a creator who was capable of interactions with material beings and for the Gnostics this was Sophia. However, since Sophia is not a god in the fullest sense, she is imperfect and as a result made an imperfect world—a world full of suffering and evil. The Problem of Evil in our world is, therefore, not directly due to an all-knowing, all-good and all-powerful God. Evil is due to this imperfect demiurge

---

[82] Egyptian religion, Wikipedia.

[83] Demiurge: In Gnosticism and other theological systems, a heavenly being, subordinate to the Supreme Being that is considered to be the controller of the material world and antagonistic to all that is purely spiritual.

that God made. Does this solve the Problem of Evil? I think not, it just adds one step to the process of the Problem of Evil.

As noted above, our body precludes any intellectual or physical awareness of God. God must, as transcendent, be beyond our understanding. I suppose our soul as spiritual could conceivably perceive God since one spirit ought to be able to connect with another spirit such as God and angels, however, this takes us into the mind-body dichotomy that has plagued us for centuries. Since psychologists maintain that all human knowledge comes through the five senses, there has to be some interaction between the soul and body, so far even our best psycho-physiological thinkers have not solved this mind-body dualism problem.

Theologians tell us that the soul mediates its functions though the body. Our sensations, emotions, imagination and consciousness are all combined functions of both our body and soul. This is said to occur through mind-body interactions. Without the body a person cannot collect information through the five senses. This data is then delivered to the soul where it is processed, and then returned to the body especially the brain but also other parts of the body so that we can use this information in activating the nerves, muscles, enzymes, hormones etc. to respond to the information obtained from the five senses. This is accomplished by stimulating behaviors that are beneficial to all of us. The body collects data via the senses, feeds it to the soul which in turn analyzes it; decides how the body should respond to this data in such a way that is most helpful in maintaining life, keeping us secure, allowing us to propagate, and interact with others in socially beneficial ways so that we and those around us live better more productive lives. This to and fro interaction between body, mind and back to the body allows for freewill decisions and behaviors that help all of us.

The problem with this system is: How does the physical, sensory input get transferred to the soul? The spiritual and physical realms are entirely separate. Descartes tells us the soul is situated in the pineal gland, a structure in the middle of the brain. But how can a spirit like our soul be anywhere? It is not a 'space-time' entity. Likewise the soul cannot function in space or time. Our brain and body are time limited biological entities. We do everything sequentially. We are mutable, that is changeable, and live in an ever-changing world. We can't be out of step with the cosmos. The microcosm has to be in tune with the macrocosm.

Our soul has to be timeless or it could not be eternal as it must be in order for any of us humans to live eternally in Heaven (or for those unfortunate souls in Hell). Physical beings cannot, by definition, live forever. Physicality implies change or mutability and this means an end to our physical existence at some time in the future. The soul cannot be located in the pineal gland. It can't be situated anywhere in space or time.

This mind-body relationship problem involves a logical issue just as our interaction with God faces a spirit-matter boundary that is insurmountable. The physical is tied to space and time; the spiritual is not of space and time. So how can these two entities connect with each other?

We cannot ask God to make a square circle. The very nature of square and circle makes such a geometric figure impossible even for God. The two concepts are mutually exclusive. The same logic applies to the mind-body problem. If a spirit could interact with a physical body, then it could not be eternal, be capable of viewing the beatific vision (seeing God in Heaven) or live forever. As a corollary, if a body could connect with a spirit such as our soul, then it could not exist in space and time and it could not possess the five senses and live in our physical Universe. We couldn't be born, walk, talk, eat, sleep and love our spouse, children, friends and colleagues. Love is an emotion and emotions are of the body not the soul. We couldn't shake hands or hug one another. To have a soul and body interact in any way would be like having a square circle. As a consequence of these limitations, the whole idea of a soul (spirit) working with a body (matter) is logically impossible. It would be nice of these two realms could interact. This would solve a lot of problems but this simply is not possible. Spirits have been invented without any empirical evidence for their existence because it answers a lot of questions we have about the world and we humans who live in it. It solves the problem of where we came from and whence we are to go after we die. But these solutions run up against the reality of material and spiritual as they are defined. Matter we understand fairly well. Spirit, on the other hand, is a pure concoction of the human mind that cannot be studied or precisely known. The spiritual is devised simply to meet emotional needs and answer unresolved questions about us and the world in which we live.

The omnipotence of God raises questions as to the extent of God's infinite powers. Some solutions for the Problem of Evil suggest that God's omnipotence allows Him to do anything and everything that is not logically impossible. This would exclude such actions as allowing evil. God's very nature as theistic prohibits this. It is easy to say that God can do anything, but theologians tell us this is only true if the actions required are not self-contradictory.

Now I recognize the above arguments against a soul-body pairing is hard to grasp and even harder to accept. Most of us have been told from childhood that we are made up of a body and a soul and that God is a pure spirit as are the angels, devils and ghosts. It is a difficult task to undo all this past history and adopt a new paradigm that does not admit of a soul. We know we have a body. That is quite evident when we stub our toe. These ideas of soul, spirit and God meet deep-seated emotional needs. They provide answers to ancient questions that we have not otherwise been able to solve. These spiritual answers are, however, magical, mystical solutions that are based on the Bible, ancient authority and the teachings of parents, pastors and other people we believe are trustworthy. Such solutions, nonetheless, do not meet the demands of reason and logic. There is absolutely no empirical, scientific evidence for the existence of spirits or souls. The concept of spirits, until definite evidence is gathered to support the notion of spirits and souls, cannot be considered anything more than myths just as the ancient gods of Greece and Rome are now viewed as myths.

We've been told since early childhood that we can't have everything we want. The fact is that we want an eternal life. Few of us want to die. We want a fatherly God that we can pray to and from whom we receive the many gifts that make life easier. We want someone who can make all our daily anxieties, sufferings and evils go away. Life is so difficult and we would like all these pains and problems to just disappear and leave us living a leisurely, comfortable life. Unfortunately, our world doesn't work that way. We humans have created myths, theologies and spiritual beings to make all of life seem better. To toss out our religious and magical beliefs that have provided emotional comfort for us for so many years is neigh impossible but if we are to be true to God, the world in which we live, and ourselves, this is a rational necessity.

Manichaeism

Mani or Manichaeus (c. 216–276 BCE) taught a dualistic theology that involved two equal deities, the one good and the other bad. These two divine beings are in an ongoing spiritual struggle. The good god rules over a world of light, and the bad god over a material world of darkness. The god of light fought to bring light into our world and the god of darkness wrestled to maintain cosmic darkness. Our human world under this scheme was created in darkness. Since the beginning, darkness has been transformed f gradually rom a world of matter and darkness to a world of spirit and light. We seemingly are slowly evolving into a spiritual world—a spiritual, non-material world that is without evil. It would be a stretch to make this into a Darwinian evolutionary system though Teillard de Chardin in his *Phenomenon of Man* suggests that such a process is ongoing in the cosmos and will eventually reach the *Omega Point* at which time we will be one in Christ.

Manichaeism was widespread throughout the Aramaic, speaking regions in antiquity. Christ spoke Aramaic. It reached its peak between the third and seventh centuries CE, and at its height was one of the most widespread religions in the world. Manichaean churches and scriptures existed as Far East as China and as far West as the Roman Empire. It was briefly the main rival of Christianity in the struggle to replace classical polytheistic paganism. Manichaeism survived longer in the East than in the West, and it appears to have finally faded out in southern China after the fourteenth century.

Manichaeism is considered a dualistic philosophy in which a moral course of action involves a clear black and white choice between good and evil. Augustine of Hippo (354-430) was a Manichaean before converting to Christianity. Following this change of heart, he was a fierce opponent of this sect.

Mani's system is based on Mesopotamian theology. It has the advantage of solving the Problem of Evil by allowing for a bad god that is responsible for all evil and a good god that remains pristine and thus not responsible for any evil. The catch, of course, is that the good god is not a theistic god and doesn't coincide with the Abrahamic God of the OT or NT. We have to revise our concept of God to use this solution for the Problem of Evil. This would be difficult for the reasons noted above. The God of Judaism, Christianity and Islam has been around a long time. We are bonded to Him and He satisfies many human needs.

Tertullian and the Problem of Evil

Tertullian (c.160 – c. 225 CE) was a Christian theologian from Carthage, North African. As a Christian apologist and a polemicist, he wrote against early Christian heresies. Tertullian has been called "the Father of Latin Christianity" and "the founder of Western theology." He influenced the Church's nascent doctrines in many ways. He originated and advanced many doctrines of the early Church. He is perhaps best known for being the oldest extant Latin writer to use the term "Trinity" and gave the earliest formal description of Trinitarian theology. He coined the phrase, "three Persons, one Substance" which was to provide the doctrinal basis for what has become the most important of all Christian tenets. As with so many Christian beliefs, the Trinity was not specifically defined in the NT and only gradually developed over the first several centuries of Christianity.

Tertullian opposed the teachings of Mani and wrote against Manichaeism because it ran counter to his view of the Trinity. There was but one God with three equal or consubstantial persons: Father, Son and Holy Spirit. The Trinity created problems for those who believed that all three Persons were all-good, all-powerful and all-knowing. The three persons of the Trinity were not three Gods, rather they were three "persons in one God" and this God was a theistic God as discussed above.

Tertullian's solution to the Problem of Evil runs as follows:[84] Evil exists, not because God ordained all evil acts as a necessary part of creation, but because God, by His own authority, gave humans two gifts. The first is the gift of freewill; the second gift is the ability to use the freewill as we see fit. Because God gave us freewill, He withholds

---

[84] http://evangelicalarminians.org/tertullian-on-the-problem-of-evil-and-free-will/. An interview with John Frame when asked about God's relationship to evil.

His power to prevent evil that God knows will occur when humans freely and recklessly employ these gifts.

Tertullian's defense of God in allowing evil in the world is based solely on the "freewill" defense and is found in his, *The Five Books Against Marcion*, Book 2.

Tertullian makes the following key points regarding the Problem of Evil:

- God's purpose was to be known by humans and this is the *'first goodness'* as he labels it. Knowledge and the enjoyment of God are good. This purpose led God to create the Universe and make humans with the ability to pursue 'the knowledge of Himself', which Tertullian explores in detail.

- Tertullian believed humans were created in the image and likeness of God and this means that 'man was constituted by God [to be] the free, master of his own will and power', which allows humans to know God and to oversee creation (ii.5 and ii.6). This might be interpreted to mean humans are involved in their evolution and the evolution of the world as a whole.

- God gave 'man freedom of will and mastery of himself' and 'He from His very authority in creation permitted these gifts to be enjoyed'.

- This gift of freewill allows humans to choose freely because 'man is free, with a will either for obedience or resistance'.

- It is this freewill that is the basis for responsibility for 'the reward neither of good nor of evil could be paid to the man who should be found to have been either good or evil through necessity and not choice'. The last part of this statement that is hard to follow seems to make humans as free and responsible for their good or bad choices and the rewards or punishments that follow. What do you think?

- This freewill given to humans enables them to be a "rational being, capable of intelligence and knowledge, yet still being restrained within the bounds of rational liberty' and 'subject to Him who had subjected all things unto Him". In other words freewill allows humans to be rational beings, which is superior to being non-rational automatons.

- Since humans have 'unshackled power over their will', it must be concluded that they and not God are responsible for the evil that occurs. Nothing evil could possibly have come forth from God.
- Evil exists because God has 162afforded room for a conflict' between humans and the devil which started at the time of the Fall of Adam and Eve. In this conflict humans are able to conqueror the same devil and crush this enemy with the same freedom of his will as had made him succumb to him (the devil)'. Humans must choose which side they will take in this conflict, just as they had to choose in the beginning, thus proving that the fault of the Fall and evil was *all our own, not God's, and so worthily* recover his (human) salvation by a victory'. (ii.8 and ii.10).
- The victory is achieved by Christ and received by humans through faith.

He enjoins those who are justified by faith in Christ and not by the law to have peace with God.

Tertullian's view anticipates Calvin and Luther. Faith plays a major role in Tertullian's solution to the Problem of Evil. If freewill and faith are not the answer to the Problem of Evil and God does indeed determine all events, then reconciling a good God with the occurrence of evil is, as one Calvinist admits, 'more difficult'. The question, though, is whether God merely permits evil, or whether, in addition, He actually brings evil about in some way. I think the latter is true. Scripture often says that God brings about sinful decisions by human beings. This is a harsh teaching in Scripture, and on one level it makes the Problem of Evil more difficult. The early Church, however, had no such problem affirming that God does not cause evil. He only permits it because He allows us to exercise freewill, which is necessary for us to be truly human and not just automatons, i.e. we have freewill. The issue still remains that if God is all-good, etc. then He ought to be able to make us so reasonable that we would always choose good rather than bad. Give us enough grace or smarts and we would be free, fully human and morally good. Right?

Tertullian wrote his Trinitarian treatise after becoming a Montanist. Montanism was a religious system characterized by ecstatic prophecies. Montanus (c. 135 –177 CE) made predictions about the future often while in a frenzied state of mind much like charismatic Pentecostals do today. The early Church was not opposed to prophecies but Tertullian's style and ultimately his Montanistic theology ran up against the Church's more conservative views in the second century. Montanism recognized female bishops and presbyters. Women and girls were forbidden to wear ornaments, and virgins were required to wear veils. There was an emphasis on ethical standards and asceticism. Montanists prohibited remarriage following divorce or the death of a spouse. They also emphasized keeping strict fasts and added new fasts to those mandated by the Catholic Church.

Although many Church Fathers were ultimately canonized by the Catholic Church, Tertullian never was and in fact he was excommunicated as a result of his Montanistic views.

Augustine of Hippo and the Problem of Evil

Augustine of Hippo (354–430 CE) in his theodicy[85] focuses on the Genesis story that claims God created the world and when reviewing all His work, saw it as "good"(Genesis1, 37). Evil for Augustine is essentially the consequence of the Fall of Adam and Eve as described in Genesis when they disobeyed God and thus stained all

---

[85] Hick's, John, 2010, *Evil and the God of Love*, Palgrave Macmillan.

humans thereafter with Original Sin. By eating fruit from the 'Tree of Knowledge' all of humanity was doomed to all the failings of humans as we see them today: diminished understanding, physical and mental diseases, natural and moral evils. Humans became less rational, more immoral and if not baptized with mortal sins on their souls were doomed to Hell for all eternity. The Bible doesn't specify what the fruit was that Eve took a bite of after being tempted by the devil. Satan, as devils are prone to do, lied to Eve, suggesting that God had forbidden eating of the Tree of Knowledge because she would gain knowledge of the sort God Himself possesses (Genesis 3,4).

Augustine was the first theologian to propose the concept of an Original Sin. It is a very special kind of sin according to Augustine. First of all, Adam and Eve alone committed this first sin.[86] Secondly, we are all tainted by Original Sin. None of the billions of people that came after Adam and Eve committed any sins while *in utero* yet everyone, according to Augustine, who dies without having this sin cleansed from their soul by baptism, will never enter Heaven. Thirdly, in the past, Catholic theologians taught that these unbaptized babies would go to Limbo. This was a pleasant enough place; nothing like Purgatory or Hell, but since these babies could not get into Heaven they would be denied the Beatific Vision of God, which is, according to Christian theology, the essential joy of Heaven. Fourthly, in recent years there has been more debate about infants who are not baptized before they die, especially if they die *in utero*. Some theologians say that if the mother "wishes that her baby be baptized" *in utero*, this would satisfy the sacramental requirement for baptism and if aborted before birth would go straight to Heaven. Cardinal Karol Józef Wojtyła when head of the Congregation of the Doctrine of Faith stated in 1984 that he rejected the claim that children who die unbaptized cannot attain salvation.

---

[86] Of course, Satan and the other devils had sinned against God before Adam and Eve's Original Sin.

Subsequently, as Pope John Paul II, he was quoted as saying that Limbo was not a firm doctrine of the Church and that we needed to rely on the infinite wisdom and goodness of God to provide for such unbaptized babies and adults. The 1992 Catechism of the Catholic Church states that, "God has bound salvation to the sacrament of Baptism". In 2007, Pope Benedict XVI terminated the concept of Limbo.

The best one can say now is that Original Sin in infants is still a debated question. This issue has evolved over the centuries and remains part of the Problem of Evil.

Can we imagine that a theistic God would allow a totally innocent child, who has never sinned, be stained by the sin of Adam and Eve and end up in Limbo for this? Or --would He send an unbaptized adult to Hell if not baptized. And, of course, we are dealing with a mythological set of parents that never existed in the first place. We humans evolved through a complex series of random mutations, natural selection and a lineage of prehistoric species to get to where we are today. Theologians often create problems that don't help solve the Problem of Evil. Such machinations only make things worse for us Earth bound humans who are limited by a less than divine intellect! I often wonder what happened to all the babies when the Catholic Church closed the doors to Limbo!

Augustine claims that natural evil, as found in disasters such as earthquake, is caused by fallen angels i.e. devils, whereas moral evil (evil caused by the freewill of human beings) is a result of humans having become estranged from God, and as a result, choose to deviate from God's designated path.

Augustine also argues that God could not have created evil, since the world was created as good, and all notions of evil are simply a deprivation or privation of goodness. Evil cannot be a separate and unique positive action or thing. For example, blindness is not a separate entity, but is merely a lack or privation of sight. Thus the Augustinian theodicy claims that evil, including all suffering, is the absence of good because God did not create evil; it is we humans who chose to deviate from the path of perfect goodness.

This, however, raises a number of questions involving genetics. If evil is merely a consequence of our choosing to deviate from God's desired path, then genetic dispositions to evil must surely be in God's plan and thus cannot be blamed on human choice. Some people have genetic profiles that are associated with criminal behavior. In addition, as mentioned at the beginning of this book, I have Stargardt's Disease, an autosomal recessive (inherited) disorder that is purely genetic in origin. It has resulted in the gradual loss of my vision. It is a type of macular degeneration that has progressed over the years. I am fortunate in the sense that, though my central vision is gone, I will always have some peripheral vision. This disorder has had a significant impact on my life and one could call it an evil. However, it is not my fault that I have Stargardt's Disease. I did nothing to deserve this disorder. It just happened that each of my parents had the allele (gene) for this problem and there is a 25 percent chance that any of their offspring would end up with the disease. My brother was not affected. The occurrence of Stargardt's Disease in this situation is simply the luck of the draw. Nor are my parents to blamed for giving me this disease. It just happened. There was no freewill decision on their part. There is no moral evil involved; it is simply a natural evil. God must be blamed because He set up the genetic laws that led to my Stargardt's.

In addition, this disorder is not just the absence of good eyesight. There are two alleles that cause the disease. There are definite changes in my ocular fundi (back of the eyes) that are present. This disease or evil is caused by something definitely bad! There are bad genes and bad yellow scars on my retinae. I have pictures of the back of my eyes and they look awful. Augustine's argument from the 'absence of good' just doesn't hold up in light of modern science.

Pelagianism and Semi-Pelagianism

Pelagianism is the belief that Original Sin did not taint human nature and freewill is still capable of choosing good or evil without special divine help i.e. God's grace. This theological theory is named after Pelagius (c. 390-418 CE) although he denied many of the doctrines associated with his name today. Pelagianism ran afoul of Catholic ethical doctrine as it was generally defined following the Nicaea Council of 325 CE. Divine sovereignty was a major principle of theology then as it is even today. God is in control of everything. We humans are totally dependent on God for all things and this includes even the good deeds we do. Only through God's grace can we do good and ultimately gain Heaven. This is affirmed by Augustine who supported the orthodox view of human behavior although there is, in fact, an element of predestination in his approach to Gods sovereignty. Pelagianism proposes a moral system that allows for human behaviors that depend largely on human freewill. Good deeds are determined largely based on person's reason and freewill according to Pelagius.

On the other hand, according to Luther, we can do nothing in the way of good works to "buy" or "earn" Heaven. Ultimately, Luther claimed that only through God's free gift of grace are we able to act in meritorious ways. We need only believe, that is having faith, in order to make our way to Heaven. We are all elected i.e. determined by God for either Heaven or Hell and this is decided by God's inscrutable will. We have nothing to say about what path we will take according to Luther. All is determined before we are even born. This doesn't seem very fair but who are we to question God's ways as Luther reminds us.

"All things whatever arise from, and depend on, divine appointment; whereby it was foreordained who should receive the word of life, and who should disbelieve it; who should be delivered from their sins, and who should be hardened in them; and who should be justified and who should be condemned." The doctrine of predestination or election depends largely on this sovereignty principle.

Election comes in "two sizes' and this double doctrine of election, has caused divisions within Christianity, perhaps more than any other doctrine, and in particular, has historically driven a wedge between Calvinists and Lutherans. Why is this? What is the difference between Lutheran and Calvinist thought concerning election?

→John Calvin and his followers taught the doctrine of 'double' election, whereas Martin Luther and his followers support the doctrine of 'single' election. Double predestination states that in 'eternity past', prior to the creation of the Universe, God elected, that is, chose a portion of humankind for God Himself. These people God will actively save over time, but He also chose to pass over all remaining humans, allowing them to follow their sinful ways, and suffer the consequences of their sins, i.e. eternal Hell fire.

Double predestination affirms both God's election of some in eternity for salvation and His reprobation, i.e. rejection of a certain percentage of all humans in past eternity. God decrees that some souls will be saved, and others will be lost. Calvinist theologian Louis Barhop defines reprobation as:

"That eternal decree of God whereby He has determined to [pass over] some people by denying them His special grace, and to punish them for their sins, [as a] manifestation of His justice. These people are lost from the very beginning of creation. They are elected by God at the very beginning of the Universe to be damned to Hell. Then again, when they are born this election to Hell is set in motion. This is double election. They are doomed from the first moment the Universe is formed by God and then at the moment of their birth the decision by God to condemn them to Hell is reconfirmed."

Such is Calvin's stance on election. Lutherans, on the other hand, teach single predestination. While God, in eternity past, did indeed elect some people for Himself whom He would actively save in the course of time, He did not decree that the rest of humankind would absolutely be lost. Thus, while affirming an initial election, Lutherans reject eternal divine damnation by God. Although He denies electing some humans for salvation, at the same time He does not necessarily maintain their sinfulness, and ultimate suffering in Hell. Robert G. Hoerber writes:

"According to Ephesians 1, our salvation is the result of our election by God from eternity, which is a gospel message. To deduce by logical reasoning that therefore some people must be predestined to damnation is law - a clear instance of mingling law and gospel. On the other hand, the 'unreasonable' doctrine of election to salvation (but not to damnation) Is a particularly comforting part of the gospel message."

It is clear that the motive of Lutheran theology at this point is to preserve the goodness of God and to refrain from making God the author of evil and sin. Lutherans see the reprobate as being eternally punished on their own merit, not because of God's eternal decree that they should be punished. Thus, the sinner is the author of his or her own sin, not God. Though elected in eternity past for Hell, they at birth and during their lives may gain salvation.

It is clear that the Calvinists wish to make humans the author of their own sins, not God, but the ways in which this question is answered take two very different paths. The Calvinist approach would seem to make the Problem of Evil more of a problem and less of a solution. That is, in double predestination certain people are doomed by God twice—first from all eternity and secondly from their birth. In single predestination they are doomed from eternity but after birth are allowed enough grace to make it to Heaven if they are so inclined, i.e. if they have faith in Jesus Christ.

The Reformation, as previously mentioned, consisted in the recovery of ancient doctrines, especially those of Augustine of Hippo. Augustine wrote extensively on the issue of predestination, and has thus been the subject of both admiration and scorn. The vigorous debate that resurfaced on the subject during the Reformation makes this a subject relevant to today's disciples of the Reformation. With Calvin's view of double election it is, I think, very difficult to resolve the Problem of Evil satisfactorily. Using Luther's single election a solution is possible.

Erasmus, Luther and the Problem of Evil[87]

The difference between Desiderius Erasmus (1466–1536) and Luther regarding the Problem of Evil boils down to the question of freewill. Erasmus had generally avoided involving himself in theological disputes, however, he was urged by many of his contemporaries, particularly by his good friend Thomas More, and Pope Clement VII, to apply his skill and learning to Luther's polemic regarding the Problem of Evil. Luther had become increasingly more aggressive in his attacks on the Roman Catholic Church. The debate between Erasmus and Luther came down to differences regarding the doctrines of divine justice as well as divine omniscience and omnipotence. While Luther and many of his fellow reformers emphasized the control and power that God held over creation, Erasmus stressed the justice and liberality of God regarding humankind.

Luther and other reformers proposed that humans were stripped of freewill by sin and as a result divine predestination ruled all activity within the mortal realm. Luther held believed God was completely omniscient and

---

[87]   Erasmus and the Problem of Evil, Wikipedia.

omnipotent; that anything which happened had to be the result of God's explicit will, and that God's foreknowledge of events brought events into being.

Pelagianism and Semi-Pelagianism

The teachings of Pelagius are generally associated with the rejection of Original Sin and the practice of infant baptism. Pelagianism is the belief that Original Sin does not taint human nature and that human will is still capable of choosing good or evil without special divine aid, i.e. grace. Pelagius taught that the human will, as created by God, is sufficient to live a sinless life, although Pelagius believed that God's grace assists all good works. Pelagianism has come to be identified with the view, (whether Pelagius would agree or not), that human beings can earn salvation by their own efforts. This theological theory is named after Pelagius (354 – c. 420), although he denied, at some point in his life, many of the doctrines associated with his name today. In essence, Pelagius took away God's total sovereignty and this is not an acceptable orthodox Catholic view. God's sovereignty is a sacrosanct doctrine. Giving too much freedom to humans limits God's power.

The writings of Pelagius are no longer extant but they were condemned at the Council of Carthage (418 CE) and the Council's records provide some idea of Pelagius' tenets. Pelagianism stands in contrast to the official hamartiological[88] system of the Catholic Church that is based on the theology of Augustine of Hippo.

Semi-Pelagianism is a modified form of Pelagianism that was condemned by the Catholic Church at the Second Council of Orange in 529 CE. Semi-Pelagianism is an early Christian theological and soteriological[89] school of thought through which humanity and God are restored to a right

---

[88] Hamartiological: of the branch of Christian theology that studies sin.

[89] Soteriology is the study of salvation theology i.e. how we are saved and get to Heaven.

relationship. Semi-Pelagianism varies from Pelagianism in that instead of being totally capable of effecting our own salvation, Semi-Pelagianism in its original form is a compromise between Pelagianism and the orthodox teachings of the Church Fathers. They taught that humans cannot be saved without the freely given, grace of God whereas in Semi- Pelagianism, a distinction is made between the beginning of faith and the subsequent increase of faith. Semi-Pelagianism teaches that the latter half of salvation, is the growth of faith through the work of God, while the beginning of faith is an act of freewill, with grace supervening only after a person makes some voluntary, non-grace based movement toward God. After this freewill movement on the part of a person is initiated, God is said to shower grace upon the person who then is able to move on the final path to God and salvation. Because this system did not maintain God as the sovereign actor in salvation, Semi-Pelagianism was labeled heretical.

The Roman Catholic Church condemns Semi-Pelagianism because it claims that the beginning of faith involves an act of freewill on the part of humans. In contrast, the Church maintains that the initiative must come from God, but requires 'free synergy' (collaboration) on the part of humans: "God has freely chosen to associate humans with the work of His grace. In the Catholic view God gives us grace and good works play a minimal role in salvation. No one can merit the initial grace of God. After grace is showered on us, we can then moved by the Holy Spirit, we can then merit for ourselves and for others [in purgatory] the graces needed for our sanctification and the increase of grace needed for the attainment of eternal life."[90]

Basically Semi-Pelagianism is heretical because God doesn't have control over the initial process of giving grace to a human. In orthodox teachings God must give the initial nudge toward the acquisition of grace following which

---

[90]   Quote from Wikipedia.

humans can carry on the process of gathering grace. This is a truly fine line but in the mind of some theologians this view maintains God's sovereignty. Semi-Pelagianism, on the other hand, takes away at least part of God's responsibility for evil.

In a real sense, the Church's view of salvation only complicates the Problem of Evil for if God is always sovereign. He then retains all responsibility for moral evil that humans perpetrate. Once again it is God who is responsible for evil in the world both human moral evil and natural evil. God has failed to give humans enough grace in order that they can follow through with morally good acts. In this system, though the person uses freewill after God's initial gift of grace, a more powerful injection of grace by God would allow the person to avoid moral evil and act in a morally beneficial way. The notion of divine sovereignty makes the Freewill Solution to the Problem of Evil untenable because human will is not truly free. God determines our will by providing or not providing the proper spiritual drive i.e. grace toward moral behaviors. In addition, God chooses to allow Satan to tempt and draw humans into sin.

There is another issue related to God's sovereignty. Since the Catholic Church, and specifically the pope is the ultimate interpreter and propagator of God's message, and since God is always sovereign then the Church can claim to be eternally sovereign i.e. infallible as well. The pope has claimed to be infallible in matters of faith and morals sine 1870 when the First Vatican Council proclaimed:

"The holy Roman Church possesses the supreme and full primacy and principality over the whole Catholic Church. She truly and humbly acknowledges that she received this from the Lord himself in blessed Peter, the prince and chief of the apostles, whose successor, the Roman pontiff, is together with the fullness of power. And since before all others she has the duty of defending the truth of the faith, so if any questions arise concerning the faith, it is by her judgment that they must be settled."

The pope has functioned as *de facto* infallible for centuries before this statement. Although papal infallibility is said to apply only to matters of faith and morals, in fact, the Church has extended its interpretive powers to other intellectual areas. Examples include the condemnation of Galileo because he approved of the Copernican view of the Solar System, which is, we now know, a strictly scientific matter. If infallible, the Church should have known that that the issue was not one of faith or morals. For this breech of heavenly "faith and morals" he was sanctioned by the Inquisition, barely avoiding a death sentence by renouncing this heliocentric view of the heavens in 1633.

Giordano Bruno (1548 -1600 CE) was put to death for his view of the cosmos although he also held that the Trinity, the divinity of Christ, the virginity of Mary, and Transubstantiation were not valid theological doctrines. Bruno also correctly proposed that the Sun was just another star moving in space, and claimed as well that the Universe contained an infinite number of inhabited worlds, i.e. planets orbiting other stars. Today he would have been excommunicated but not burnt at the stake. We might ask why killing someone for heresy was an infallibly correct decision in 1600 CE when it wouldn't be considered such today. Why is the Church not burning people at the stake today when it did so infallibly up to 1813 CE?

Bruno was not so lucky as Martin Luther because Bruno was a Dominican friar who lived in Naples and had no protector as Luther had in Frederick the Wise of Saxony who kidnapped Luther and hid him in Wartburg castle for two years after he was condemned at the Diet of Worms in 1521.

We could also ask why the Church was infallibly correct when it denied Copernicus' heliocentric world in 1543 CE (*De revolutionists orbium coelestium*). He was denounced because this contradicted Genesis' version of creation and the motion of the Sun as portrayed in Joshua 10:13: "And the Sun stood still". One could say this wasn't a matter of faith, however, contradicting the Bible would be considered a matter of faith by most any believer including the pope, one would think. The Church also claims to be the final interpreter of the Bible. If infallible why was its interpretation of the Bible in 1543 correct though it chose to exonerate Galileo in 1992, thus changing its infallible mind regarding the Bible?

The Inquisition was responsible for burning thousands of 'heretics' at the stake for their views on a host of doctrinal issues that weren't always related to matters of faith or morals. What the Church considered evil in the Middle Ages are now merely "errors" deserving only expulsion from the "true" Church. There are many "mistakes" the Church has made relating to matters of faith and morals over the centuries forcing the Church to reverse its views. This should never happen if it were truly infallible. The most famous of these mistakes was the Galileo affair. One might say his belief that Copernicus was right regarding the heliocentric view of the Sun a scientific issue and not faith based but the Church based its decision on the Bible, (Joshua 10:13) making it a matter of faith.

Thomas Aquinas and Evil

Thomas Aquinas (1222-1284 CE) systematized the Augustinian conception of evil, supplementing it with his own perspective. Evil, according to Thomas, is a privation, or absence of some good, which belongs properly to the nature or essence of a creature such as wo/men. There is therefore no positive source of evil, corresponding to the greatest good, which is God. Evil is not real but rational, i.e. it exists not as an objective fact, but as a subjective concept. Things are evil not in themselves, but by reason of their relation to --other things or persons. All realities are in themselves good; they produce bad or evil only incidentally, and consequently the ultimate cause of evil is fundamentally good, as are the objects in which evil is found.

Aquinas bases his theodicy on two major points. First, all beings made by God are essentially good and only accidentally bad. The term 'accidentally' in scholastic parlance means that the essential nature of all Gods creatures is good. So God only makes good beings. Creatures are 'accidentally' bad means that the badness is not part of its nature. We are all humans but some of us are white skinned or black or brown. The color of ones skin is an accident, that is, skin color is not part of our human nature. So too, evil is not part of our nature but an unessential part of us. Thus, we are by our very nature good. Secondly, Aquinas claims, humans by nature possess a freewill. A human without freewill is not human. By definition all humans can only make freewill moral decisions. It would be self-contradictory for a person not to have freewill just as it is self-contradictory for a circle to be square. Having freewill means that we humans can choose to perform morally evil acts. Therefore, God must make humans beings as good and He must give them freewill. God, therefore, is not culpable for moral evil. Having a philosophy degree from the University of St. Thomas, St. Paul, Minn. almost all my readings in philosophy were Scholastic treatises written by Aristotle and Aquinas. If you have a driving desire to ponder some Scholastic verbiage see Appendix A.

Thee Catholic View of the Nature of Evil

The Catholic Church's view of evil is largely based on Aquinas, who is the official theologian of the Catholic Church. Evil is, according to Aquinas, threefold, viz., metaphysical[91], moral, and physical, the consequence of moral evil is guilt and guilt promotes the perfection of the

---

91 Author: Bill King, Quodlibet Journal: Vol. 4 No. 2-3, Summer 2002.

'whole person'. Of course this doesn't apply to sociopaths who do not ordinarily have a sense of guilt or shame after evil deeds. The Universe, Aquinas maintains, would be less perfect if it contained no evil and evil's sequelae. Thus fire could not exist without the corruption of what it consumes; the lion must slay the fawn in order to live, and if there were no wrong deeds, there would be no place for patience and justice. God is said, as in Isaiah 45, to be the author of evil in the sense that corruption of material objects in nature is ordained by God as a means for carrying out the design of the Universe; and on the other hand, the evil which exists as a consequence of the breach of divine laws is in the same sense due to the divine will. The Universe would be less perfect if its laws could be broken with impunity. Thus evil, in one aspect, i.e. as the counter-balancing of sin, has the nature of good. But the evil of sin, though permitted by God, is in no sense due to Him. Denying divine omnipotence is not necessary in this solution of the Problem of Evil. God could have created another equally perfect Universe in which there would be no place for evil but he chose to create an evolutionary world that allows the Universe and all its creatures to progressively evolve into more perfect beings both physically, emotionally and morally. This view is in line with the thesis of this book, although Aquinas lived centuries before Darwin. Aquinas also mirrors the soul-making solution discussed above.

Because Aquinas' approach to the Problem of Evil is based on Aristotle's metaphysics, which is, indeed, "very philosophical" I have chosen to include the details of Aquinas' proof in Appendix A at the end of the book as noted above. In its most simple form we can consider Aquinas' approach as the absence of good solution.

Aquinas remains, even today, the Catholic Church's primary source of theology, I felt his approach to the Problem of Evil needed to be part of this book so I have include a short section here as an introduction to his argument regarding evil.

The thesis of this book does not follow a teleological approach to the Problem of Evil.

Since the solution proposed here is based on Darwin's evolutionary system and since evolution is a random, probabilistic science, then this implies that a deistic God has initiated all things including the evolutionary forces that have made for an ever-evolving world full of ever-changing creatures. We humans are here today because we have responded to environmental change utilizing individual, cultural and societal adaptations that have included a system of morality that, though continuously changing, helps us humans as individuals and as a species to survive and improve over time. What we call evil forms part of the evolutionary pressures that force us to adapt, improve and survive as a species. Aquinas sees this as an ethical rather than an evolutionary process but nonetheless there are elements of evolution in his solution.

Luther, Calvin, Zwingli and Evil

Like all monotheists, Lutherans are faced with the dilemma created by evil and suffering that all of us face daily.[92] Does God want to relieve suffering, but is unable to do so? In such a case, God is good but not all-powerful. Is God able to relieve suffering but unwilling or too unconcerned? Then God is all-powerful but not all-good. We have seen this dilemma before and Luther also faced these questions and now they are issues for his followers today.

Luther accepted most of the Christian ideas including the notion that God created the Universe from nothing. This belief emphasizes God's omnipotence. This also means that anything wrong with the Universe cannot be attributed to anyone except God. The material Universe, as

---

[92] Patheos, http://www.patheos.com/Library/Lutheran/Beliefs/
Suffering-and-the-Problem-of-Evil.html

created by God must be good, but many natural events that God has created such as tornadoes and the like cause evil. So if God made all material things and events, why do so many of His creations produce evil? He is omnibenevolent and should not have made such imperfect beings as us humans or events such as tsunamis.

For Luther evil and suffering in the world are the work of Satan, and his influence results in human sin and suffering. So moral evil is due to Satan's tempting humans so that they will end in his realm of fiery Hell. Satan wants to outdo God by enticing most of us to disobey Him and join. Satan, who didn't like the idea that God seemed to prefer humans to angels in the first place. Satan is a jealous spirit who hated God for favoring us humans. After all, Christ, the Second Person of the Trinity gave up his very life to save all humankind. He certainly didn't do this for all jealous angels i.e. devils.

Blaming Satan for evil, however, simply pushes the Problem of Evil back to square one. Couldn't God have created humans in such a way that they would not sin? One option for Christians has, as we have seen, been to argue that God created humans with freewill. Freewill is an essential aspect of human nature. It is also a very good thing for humans to be free. God had to make us capable of choosing the good but this then by its very nature meant we could choose moral evil. But this consequence of freewill was worth the good that freewill brought to humankind. The buck for moral evil (sometimes called sin) then stops with us humans. Of course, one might ask why God didn't make angels so that they wouldn't sin. After all they are superior spirits and spirits aren't supposed to have emotions. Emotions after all are limited to material beings and thus angels can't really be jealous. Right?

For Luther, power is a zero-sum game. If humans had the power to decide to sin or not to sin, this implied a reduction in God's sovereignty i.e. His omnipotence. Also, according to Luther, humans do not have the freewill to

choose to accept or reject salvation (this is in contrast
to John Wesley and Thomas Aquinas). For Luther, the
responsibility for sin and salvation ultimately rests on
God's shoulders. Both Luther and Calvin explained evil as
the consequence of Adam and Eve's Original Sin and their
subsequent fall from grace and eviction from the Garden
of Eden along with the loss of all the superhuman qualities
they possessed before the Fall. However, due to Luther and
Calvin's belief in predestination and God's omnipotence,
the Fall is part of God's plan. Ultimately humans may not be
able to understand and explain His plan. Often our inability
to fathom the evil present in the world is blamed on the
weakness of human understanding. We simply are not
able to probe the mind of God. As it is said, "God works in
mysterious ways".

In addition, we face the problem of why God allows
the devil to perform bad deeds, tempt humans and take
possession of human's freewill. One possible solution to the
Problem of Evil that Luther could have used relates to God's
logical inability to perform contradictory actions—the
square circle conundrum once again.

Ulrich Zwingli (1484 –1531) was a leader of the
Reformation in Switzerland. Born during a time of
emerging Swiss patriotism, he attended the University of
Vienna and the University of Basel, a scholarly center of
humanism. He was influenced by the writings of Augustine
and Erasmus.[93]

In 1518, Zwingli became a pastor in Zurich where he
began to preach on reforming the Catholic Church. In his
first public controversy in 1522, he attacked the custom

[93] Desiderius Erasmus (1466–1536), was a Dutch Renaissance humanist,
Catholic priest, and theologian. He was influential in the Protestant
Reformation and Catholic Counter-Reformation. He wrote *The Praise
of Folly*, his best-known work as a parody on humans generally and the
Catholic Church specifically. He was critical of the abuses within the
Church though he recognized the authority of the pope and rejected
Luther's emphasis on faith alone as the source of salvation. Erasmus
remained Catholic all his life.

of fasting during Lent. In his publications, he pointed to corruption in the Catholic hierarchy. He promoted clerical marriage, and attacked the use of images in places of worship. In 1524, Zwingli changed his belief about the Lord's Supper, and experienced a dream, which gave him confidence in his heterodox positions. In 1525, Zwingli introduced a new communion liturgy to replace the Catholic Mass. Zwingli also clashed with the Anabaptists, which resulted in their being persecuted in Switzerland.

Zwingli's ideas came to the attention of Martin Luther and other reformers. They met at the Marburg Colloquy and although they agreed on many points of doctrine, they could not accept the doctrine of the Real Presence of Christ in the Eucharist. The Catholic Church believes that the bread and wine are transformed into the actual body and blood of Christ (transubstantiation). Luther claimed that the Eucharist was a combination of bread and wine with the body and blood of Christ (consubstantiation) and Zwingli taught that the bread and wine were symbolic of the body and blood of Christ and his body and blood were not truly present in the Eucharistic host. Rather than "This is my body" one should say, "This signifies my body."

Calvin, on the other hand, believed that those who partake of the bread and wine in good faith truly partake of the body and blood of Christ. Calvin explains this in terms of the believer's mystical union with Christ.

Significant antagonism developed between Zwingli's followers and other cantons[94] in Switzerland. Zwingli attempted an unsuccessful food blockade on the Catholic cantons in several cantons. These cantons responded with an attack at a moment when Zurich was ill prepared. Zwingli was killed in battle at the age of forty-seven. His legacy lives on in the Reformed churches of today. Thus, though Luther, Zwingli and Calvin spearheaded the Reformation, and their approaches to the Problem of Evil

---

[94]   Canton: a subdivision of a country established for political or administrative purposes like the States in America.

were similar they differed on a number of theological questions.

Zwingli and John Calvin agreed with most of the Christian tradition such as that God created the Universe from nothing i.e., the doctrine of creation *ex nihilo.* This belief emphasizes God's total sovereignty. It also implies that anything wrong with the Universe cannot be attributed to the material Universe, since this was created by God and it was created as good.

The reason for evil and suffering in the world is sin. Zwingli and Calvin agreed that sin is an act of human disobedience against God's commandments, and that this disobedience is entirely the responsibility of the person committing the sin. For Calvin, ever since the Fall (Eve and Adam's Original Sin), we have to accept that humans, and not God, are responsible for sin and thus also evil.

But human responsibility for sin, as we have seen, simply pushes the problem back as it does when blaming Satan for being the originator of human sin. Again, God could have, as all-powerful, all-knowing and all-good, created human beings with freewill but also with an intellect that always made proper moral choices in spite of human passion and Satan's devious ways.

Calvin was a thoroughly systematic theologian. In the end he had to maintain that we are not privy to God's plans, and that it is inappropriate for us to question God's decisions. This would be blatant blasphemy. Our task is to trust that God knows what He is doing at all times.

But before Calvin got to this point, he spelled out all the things that God did for Adam and Eve. Before the Fall they both had uncorrupted reason and totally freewill. Adam and Eve lived harmoniously in the presence of God. The one and only positive quality not bestowed on them by God, according to Calvin, was the gift of perseverance. In spite of their 'superhuman' intellect and physique, they could not resist the devil and persevere in a state of total obedience to God.

Once again we are back to the same logical snag as we faced before. While these theological moves seem to delay assigning responsibility for sin to God, in the end it appears that Calvin cannot avoid the conundrum that God in the final analysis, is still responsible for human moral evil. As all-perfect, He failed to give humans, including the first humans in Paradise, the intellect, will, and grace to avoid sin. Once again, it is God's fault that we are not free of sin, evil and suffering. If God had given us totally freewill, sufficient intellect and ample grace, we would be totally incorruptible freewill beings.

In fact, if we consider natural evil, the same reasoning applies. An all-perfect theistic God should be able to make a Universe without even natural evil. This is the root of the Arminian controversy,[95] and this was what eventually would separate Reformed Christians from Methodists. In the end, while continuing to assert that sin is a human responsibility, Calvin's emphasis on God's sovereignty means that his answer is a mystery, not to be questioned. Yet we do question it and have continued to do so for more than 2000 years!

---

[95] Arminius taught that Calvinist predestination and unconditional election made God the author of evil. Arminius insisted that election was an election of believers and therefore was dependent on faith. Furthermore, Arminius argued that God's ultimate foreknowledge excluded a doctrine of determinism

Here we see the influence of the medieval nominalists[96] and their arguments that we cannot reason our way to knowledge of God, and we cannot draw analogies from human experience and from our nature to determine the nature of God. All we know about God is what we learn in the Scriptures, and today we know that Scripture is not inerrant.[97] Calvin did not ask the question, "Why is creation the way it is?" He was simply aware of the fact of evil and suffering in the world, and the biblical account in Genesis of the Fall. The elect are given the gift of faith, which assures that their sins are forgiven, and provides the confidence that while we may not know why God does what He does, God surely does know and has a good reason for all His actions.

Calvin identified one positive outcome of the Fall, that is, the elect enjoy the one benefit from God denied to Adam and Eve. The elect are given the gift of perseverance and they are going to Heaven for sure. For Calvin, once you are saved you cannot lose salvation. Zwingli and Luther believed this as well. Humans do not have it in their power to damn themselves, just as they do not have it in their power to save themselves. Again, this distinguishes Reformed theologies from Catholic and Methodist theologies. Calvin and Zwingli are willing to pay any theological price to protect the doctrine of God's absolute and fatherly sovereignty.

---

[96] Nominalists do not believe that every individual of a given group or species possesses an essential substance or nature that makes it a member of that group or species. For example, scholastic philosophers believe the human soul is a universal essence that resides in each human and makes every human a human. This essence is a universal substance that exists independently somewhere outside of the beings it makes a specific being. Nominalists believe there is no such universal substance or essence that is infused into an individual at birth, which determines ones essential nature. *Homo sapiens* is just a name (thus the label nominalist) we use to identify a certain-group of like beings. We now know that DNA determines our nature not some spiritual essence.

[97] Ehrman, B., 2009, *Misquoting Jesus*, HarperCollins E-book

Christian Science and Evil

Christian Scientists view evil as having no ultimate reality. Evil is due to mistaken beliefs held consciously or unconsciously by the faithful. Evils such as illness and death may be banished by correct religious understanding. Since the correct understanding by Christian Science members, put forth by its founder, Mary Baker Eddy, has not always prevented illness and death, this view has been questioned, along with the general criticisms of the concept of evil as illusory. Christian Scientists believe that the many instances of spiritual healing as recounted for example in Christian Science periodicals and their textbook, *Science and Health with Key to the Scriptures* by Mary Baker Eddy, confirm their faith in spiritual healing. They are convinced that other approaches to the Problem of Evil are simply mistaken illusions. The evidence that is given for spiritual healing is based on anecdotal cases of cures. However, most people cannot accept the Christian Science solution without empirical evidence to support the Christian Scientist's view. There have been a number of cases in which the courts have mandated medical therapy when it seems apparent that a child may die if not given standard treatment for a disease. Prayer as the sole solution to all medical problems or, for that matter, the solution to all moral or all other natural evils has not been empirically verified. In fact, empirical studies of prayers for Coronary Care patients have not supported the Christian scientist's view of prayerful healing. To view evils as illusory is also hard to accept in light of the very real, and often harsh reality of day to day suffering experienced by all humans.

Jehovah's Witnesses and Evil.

Jehovah's Witnesses believe that Satan is the original cause of evil. Though once an angel, Satan developed feelings of self-importance and craved to be worshiped

185

by all, and eventually challenged God's right to rule the Universe. Satan caused Adam and Eve to disobey God, and humanity subsequently became participants in a challenge involving the competing claims of Jehovah and Satan to universal sovereignty. Other angels who sided with Satan became demons as well and have been tempting and tormenting humankind ever since in an effort to gain the soul's of all humans as demonic worshippers. For his infidelity and jealousy Satan was cast rom Heaven.[98]

In addition, God's tolerance of evil is explained in part by the value of freewill. But Jehovah's Witnesses also hold that this period of suffering is based on the divine principle of non-interferences by God, which serves to demonstrate that Jehovah Witness's "right to rule" is both correct and in the best interests of all intelligent beings. Once again reaffirming God's right "of universal sovereignty". Further, it gives individual humans the opportunity to show their willingness to submit to God's ultimate authority.

At some future time, known only to God, He will consider His right to universal sovereignty to have been

---

[98] Revelation 12:9: "And the great dragon was cast out, that old serpent, called the Devil, and Satan, which deceives the whole world: he was cast out into the earth, and his angels were cast out with him."
Also, John 8:44: "You are of [your] father the devil, and the lusts of your father you will do. He was a murderer from the beginning, and did not live in the truth, because there is no truth in him. When he lies, he speaks of his own: for he is a liar, and the father of it." There are other references in the NT to Satan fall but they are not as specific.
Luke 10:18: "And he said unto them, I beheld Satan as lightning fall from heaven.
Genesis 9:4 (NIV): "But you must not eat meat that has its lifeblood still in it."
Deuteronomy 12:23 (NIV): "But be sure you do not eat the blood, because the blood is the life, and you must not eat the life with the meat."
Leviticus 17:10 (NIV): "'I will set my face against any Israelite or any foreigner residing among them who eats blood, and I will cut them off from the people."
http://www.jw.org/en/jehovahs-witnesses/faq/jehovahs-witnesses-why-no-blood-transfusions.

settled for all time. The reconciliation of the "faithful" will have been accomplished through Christ, and nonconforming humans and demons will be destroyed. Thereafter, evil (any failure to submit to God's sovereign will) will be summarily eliminated.

Jehovah's Witnesses do not believe in faith healing or healing by prayer as do the Christian Scientists, however, they hold that the Bible prohibits blood transfusions:

"This is a religious issue rather than a medical one. Both the Old and New Testament clearly command us to abstain from blood.[99] [100]

Also, God views blood as representing life.[101]

So we avoid taking blood not only in obedience to God but also out of respect for Him as the Giver of life."[102]

These quotes that are used by Jehovah's Witnesses to prohibit blood transfusions have created unfortunate consequences when someone needs blood to avoid dying of severe blood loss. This creates more evil and since this dictum is based on Scripture and since God is believed by Jehovah's Witnesses to have authored the Bible, this once again lays the blame for evil on God.

[99]   36 Deuteronomy 12:23 (NIV) "But be sure you do not eat the blood, because the blood is the life, and you must not eat the life with the meat.
Leviticus 17:10 (NIV) "'I will set my face against any Israelite or any foreigner residing among them who eats blood, and I will cut them off from the people."
http://www.jw.org/en/jehovahs-witnesses/faq/jehovahs-witnesses-why-no-blood-transfusions.
http://www.patheos.com/Library/Islam/Beliefs/Suffering-and-the-Problem-of-Evil.html#ixzz3ClroEzYX

[100] http://www.patheos.com/Library/Islam/Beliefs/Suffering-and-the-Problem-of-Evil.html#ixzz3ClroEzYX

[101]

[102]

Islam and the Problem of Evil

For the followers of Mohamed, suffering is either the painful result of sin, or it is a test of their faith in Allah. In the latter view, suffering tests belief; a true Muslim will remain faithful through the trials of life. Suffering also reveals the hidden self to God. Suffering is built into the fabric of existence so that God may see who is truly righteous. In other words, God not only allows the various agonies and struggles of life, but He also has a purpose for evil. Suffering opens up the soul and reveals it to God. God uses suffering to look within humans and test their characters, and helps God to correct nonbelievers.[103]

Islamic scholar Sherman Jackson states that the Mu'tazila school emphasizes God's omnibenevolence. Evil arises not from God but from the actions of His creatures, who decide on their own actions independent of God. The Ash'ari school, on the other hand, emphasizes God's omnipotence. God is not restricted to following some objective moral system centered on humans but has the power to do whatever He wants with His world. The Maturidi School argues that evil arises from God but that evil in the end has a wiser purpose as a whole for the future. Some theologians have viewed God as all-powerful and human beings as caught between the hope that God will be merciful and the fear that He will not treat them kindly.

Hinduism and Evil

Hinduism is a complex religion with many different schools of thought. As such the in Hinduism answers the Problem of Evil in several different ways. Hinduism is considered by many to see the divine as polytheistic. It has been claimed that there are 330 million deities or Devas, however, a more often quoted figure is that there are

---

[103] Vicas: Ancient Hindu scriptures, written in early Sanskrit.

thirty-three Devas mentioned in the Vedas.[104] At any rate, it may be fair to say that Hinduism is a polytheistic religion with one supreme deity, the Ishtar of Parambrahamn.

The key to understanding the existence of suffering and evil in Hinduism is the central concept of karma. Karma is at once the simplest of concepts and the most complex. The word itself simply means "action," and originally referred to the sacrificial action that was at the center of the Vedic world. Karma gradually took on the meaning of both action and the effect of action.

Karma is understood within Hinduism—and Buddhism and Jainism as well—as the fundamental and universal law of cause and effect. When a person does something, it has an effect. Good actions have good effects; bad actions have bad effects. Thoughts have effects as well. An individual person carries around these accumulated effects of their karma. Over the course of a single lifetime, an individual performs countless actions, and has countless thoughts. All of these bits of karma—good and bad—are something like spiritual baggage, or deposits or debits in a spiritual bank account. When a person dies, all of his or her karma is, in a sense, added up. A "positive balance" leads to a more positive rebirth; a "negative balance" leads to a more negative rebirth. All three eastern religions, Hinduism, Buddhism and Jainism believe in rebirth, also known as transmigration of souls, reincarnation or metempsychosis.

If a person has primarily good karma during his or her lifetime, then they will either move up to nirvana, which is a state of union with all souls that have had good karma. This is a state in which the person is eternally liberated from the recurrent cycles of rebirth and death. If the karma is on balance mostly bad during ones lifetime, they will be placed in the body of a lesser being such as a worm, ant, or dog etc. Then, if during one of these lower lived cycles they manage a better karma then they move to a higher level

104

hoping to eventually make it to nirvana where there is no suffering, anxiety or other evils.

In the Buddhist context nirvana refers to the imperturbable stillness of mind after the fires of desire, aversion, and delusion have been finally extinguished. In Hindu philosophy, nirvana is the union with the divine ground of existence, Brahman (Supreme Being) and the experience of blissful 'agelessness'. Jainism holds similar views of karma with varying terminology. Ones individuality is limited in nirvana.

Two concepts are essential here: the first is that of the *atman*, the permanent self; the second is that of *samsara*, the cycles of rebirth and death. Hinduism holds that just as the world is created, maintained, destroyed, and recreated endlessly, so too people are born, live, die, and are reborn endlessly. Although samsara is often called "reincarnation" in the West, it is important to note that it is not the "person" who is reborn, but the permanent self, the *atman* (which includes elements of personality).

The quality of each rebirth depends on the accumulated karma from prior rebirths; this karma "sticks" to the *atman*, and determines what form it will take in each rebirth. Thus, if a human being does particularly good deeds while alive, he or she might be reborn as a "better" human being such as a Brahmin. But if one does particularly "bad" deeds he or she might be reborn into a lower life form—a member of a lower caste, say, or even as an animal or insect. One might also be reborn outside of the earthly realm, as a demon or even, according to some schools, as a god or goddess.

According to this worldview, there is no such thing as evil. There are "bad" people, who are bad because they have done or continue to do bad things. Bad events happen as a result of bad karma.

For Buddhists, the Problem of Evil, or the related problem of *dukkha* (suffering)[105] is one argument against a benevolent, omnipotent creator i.e. a theistic God. The notion of such a God is a false concept according to the Hindus.

Denial of Omnibenevolence and the Problem of Evil

Dystheism is the belief that God is not wholly good. Pantheists and panentheists,[106] who are dystheistic may also avoid the Problem of Evil by defining God as other than theistic, i.e. God as not totally metaphysical and at the same time is totally anthropomorphic. Pantheism views God and the Universe as one. They are, if one can use the term in reference to God, coextensive. Panentheism, on the other hand, considers God as 'extending' beyond our Universe. God in this view is bigger than our known Universe. God includes our Universe but much more. Again, as pointed out above, a spirit by definition is not limited by space and time and, thus, God as a spirit, cannot be viewed as extending anywhere in space. Just as God is eternal and thus not of or in time, He is 'spaceless', and cannot exist in or be of space. Nonetheless, theists see God as residing throughout the Universe and infinitely beyond it and existing eternally in time. Any 'spiritual' being, by definition simply cannot do

---

105 Dukkha: commonly translated as "suffering", "anxiety", "stress", or "unsatisfactoriness".

106 Panentheism (from Greek πάν (pân) "all"; έν (en) "in"; and θεός (theós) "God"; "all-in-God") is a belief system which posits the d ivine being be He a monotheistic God, polytheistic gods, or an eternal cosmic animating force, that penetrates every part of nature and timelessly extends beyond all of nature. Panentheism is differentiated from pantheism by claiming the divine is synonymous or co-extensive with the Universe but does not extend beyond the known Universe. Unlike pantheism, panentheism is the belief or doctrine that God is greater than the Universe and though God includes the Universe, He also extends infinitely beyond it. From the Google dictionary.

these things. If you redefine God as partially spiritual and partially material then you would have to redefine 'spirit' and 'matter'. If 'spirit' is a little bit material, such a spirit cannot be immortal because anything that is even partially material is mutable and cannot be immortal. Matter is changeable and thus cannot be immortal. In addition, if 'spirit' has some material elements then we are faced with the age-old problem of Descartes' dualism. How do you connect a spirit that is 'spaceless' to a material element that exist only in space? They 'live', so to speak, in two entirely different realms.

The dystheistic God, as opposed to the theistic God, is not 'all-everything' including not all-good, not all knowing and not all-powerful. Dystheism, thus, eliminates the Problem of Evil but leaves us with a God that isn't capable of doing all the things that traditional religions and most humans want: a God to create the world, care for us, answer all our prayers and personally attend to our every need.

Figure 10. Teresa of Avila

Mysticism and Evil

Process Theology is one of the most recent approaches in our never-ending efforts to understand God. If we could fully know God, we would be able to solve the Problem of Evil. The notion of mysticism has been around a long time but in recent years neuroscience has provided a better understanding of this ineffable human experience. Most mystics and ordinary people, from time to time, experience spiritual feelings when praying, at church services, viewing a beautiful sunset or when in the presence of a host of other spiritual triggers. Mystics, like Meister Eckhart (1260-1307), Catherine of Sienna (1347-1380) and Teresa of Avila (1515-1582) were all deeply moved by such divinely spiritual experiences. Mother Theresa (1910-1997), frequently experienced states of communion with God. Experiencing God is, thus, a seemingly normal, even frequent, human activity. Half of atheistic scientists report having spiritual feelings. With neuro-scientific support for such phenomena, it is hard to dismiss the reality of this 'sense of God'. This, as many have noted, does not prove there is a God, but the feeling of a fatherly being is certainly a real natural phenomenon. To dismiss God out-of-hand is not easy to do. However, a modified dystheistic notion of God, if feasible, would go a long way in solving the Problem of Evil. Such a non-theistic God is, of course, hard to accept for many religious believers. Nonetheless, knowing what we do about the connection between subjective experiences, objective brain activity and the natural selective advantages of many mental experiences, it would make sense that the benefit gained from such feelings, are helpful in the short term for most humans and in the long term for our species, *Homo sapiens.* More will be said about mind and matter later.

Part VI

Chapter 9
Philosophy and the Problem of Evil

Philosophy and theology are intrinsically connected and often cover the same material though in somewhat different ways. As we saw in the last several chapters, scholars such as Thomas Aquinas use both philosophy and theology to clarify a topic such as the Problem of Evil.

Aquinas' approach is Aristotelian and minimizes the Bible as a resource for solving the problem. In Part III, we will look at philosophers who have approached the Problem of Evil over the centuries. Ancient Greek philosophers had had little if any exposure to the OT and certainly no awareness of the NT.

Figure 11. Epicurus

Epicurus

Epicurus (341–270 BCE) was an ancient Greek philosopher and founder of the school of philosophy named after him, i.e. Epicureanism. Only a few fragments and letters of Epicurus's 300 written works are extant. Much of what is known about Epicurean philosophy is derived from later followers and commentators.

For Epicurus, the purpose of philosophy was to attain the happy, tranquil life as characterized by ataraxia— peace and freedom from fear—and aponia—the absence of pain—and by living a self-satisfactory life surrounded by friends. Hinduism contains some of these same elements. He taught that pleasure and pain are the measures of what is good and evil. Death is the end of both body and soul. Thus a person should not be afraid; the gods neither reward nor punish humans. The Universe is infinite and eternal; and events in the world are ultimately based on the motions and interactions of atoms moving in empty space. Epicurus was an atomist following Leucippus and Democritus, the ancient Greek founders of the atomistic school of philosophy.

Epicurianism is often portrayed as a hedonistic way of life where any form of pleasure, debauchery and unlimited passion is acceptable. This view, however, is a misinterpretation of Epicurus' philosophy. He was an atomist, as noted, and this school of thought is often viewed as atheistic. Nonetheless, as is the case with modern atheists, this does not necessarily include an unethical way of life. In general, atheists are more moral and less criminal than are religious fundamentalists. Epicurus simply teaches a happy, meaningful life with as little anxiety, suffering and evil as possible. It involves kindly caring for oneself and ones neighbor. If anything, his philosophy was a forerunner of Christ's message. In contrast to the Abrahamic religions, Epicurus cautioned against worrying about the gods and their interactions with humankind. Epicurus believed the gods, in today's terminology, 'could care less' about us earthlings.

Epicurus is generally credited with first expounding the Problem of Evil, and it is sometimes called "the Epicurean paradox" or "the riddle of Epicurus", which is stated today as:

"Is God willing to prevent evil, but not able? Then He is not omnipotent. Is he able, but not willing? Then He is malevolent. Is He both able and willing? Then from where does evil come? Is He neither able nor willing? Then why call him God?"

We have seen this paradox many times before but Epicurus was apparently the first to so state the Problem of Evil in this form. Epicurus himself did not leave any written form of this argument. It can be found in the Christian theologian Lactantius's, *Treatise on the Anger of God*, where Lactantius critiques the argument. Epicurus's argument as presented by Lactantius actually argues that a god that is all-powerful and all-good does not exist and that the gods are distant and uninvolved with humans' daily concerns. The gods are neither our friends nor enemies. As a polytheist, Epicurus viewed the Greek gods as fully anthropomorphic. They are just as fickle, jealous, vain, vindictive, immoral and given to passion as the worst of us humans. Epicurus was certain that the gods were totally self-centered and consequently were only concerned about themselves and their world. They were too taken up with their own desires and needs to be bothered about humans that lived below Mt. Olympus. So why worry about the gods? Take care of yourself and those family and friends who are important in your life.

Philo of Alexandria and Evil

Philo of Alexandria (c. 25 BCE – c. 50 CE) was a Greek philosopher living in Egypt. In antiquity, religious movements in philosophy, of which the Babylonians and the Assyrians are well known, there was a sharp distinction between the principles of good and evil. Philo thought that the spiritual part of man, his mind or soul, is the seat of good, and his body, the material part, is the seat of evil. Consequently, when the soul is incorporated in the body it suffers a fall from divine perfection and becomes predisposed to evil. Thus the goal of man is freedom from matter and a return to God who is perfect goodness.

Other Ancient Greek Philosophers and Evil[107]

Heraclitus (535-475 BC). This Greek philosopher believed that good and evil are two notes in a symphony. He found that many things change into their opposites: for example, hard ice melts into water, which is soft. This led him to believe that the combination of opposites resulted in a harmonious whole. In music, harmony results from the combination of low and high notes, while in the Universe harmony flows from the combination of opposites: good and evil.

Democritus (460-370 BC) believed that the goal of life is happiness. What is conducive to happiness is good; whatever yields unhappiness is evil. According to him, happiness is an inner condition or state of tranquility. He thought that one should not depend upon material things alone as these are transient and a lack of them causes unhappiness. Goodness, to him, was not only a matter of action but depends upon human's inner desire. A good man is not one who does good things, but who always wants to do good acts.

Sophism: An important sophist, Protagoras, considered humans as the standard of good and evil. As he put it, "Man is the measure of all things" and so humans were the standard of good and evil. Everybody has the right to determine for him/herself what is good and what is evil. Some other philosophers of this school, such as Thrasymachus (459 – c. 400 BCE) and Callicles (c. 484 – c. 410 BCE) went a step further claiming there are no moral laws, no all-inclusive principles of right and wrong. Good or evil are a matter of mere tradition and habit and humans are not bound by moral codes, they are free to live as they desire and to get what they want by any means possible and to frame their own code of life. However, since the outcome was moral anarchy, pure individualism

---

[107] http://www.renaissance.com.pk/jafelif987.html

and selfishness, Callicles went as far as saying, "To Hell with morality, this has been propounded by the weak to debilitate the power of the strong."

→Socrates (470-390 BCE). This great Greek philosopher thought that the most important question that confronts us is the determination of good and evil. According to him, knowledge of good and evil and its criteria are imbued in humans and they can differentiate between the two if they wish. With sustained thought and guidance of nature we are in a position to know what is good and what is evil. The saying, "O man! Know thyself", also indicates that the basic principles of good and evil are innate in humans and can be discovered by deliberation. Socrates believed firmly that there are basic principles independent of individual desires and beliefs for measuring good and evil and right and wrong. According to him, the greatest good is knowledge and the treasure of knowledge is hidden in a person and it can be discovered after thoughtful deliberation. Socrates' emphasis on self-realization was due to his belief that it is our innate knowledge that a person cannot disregard. Knowledge alien to a person does not have a significant impact on that person. Self-realization brings real happiness. Other sources of happiness are not real according to Socrates. If someone acts contrary to his or her knowledge, it is only transitory, just as a clean and holy person happens to soil herself but she does not live with it and cleanses herself at the earliest opportunity. Socrates said, "No man is voluntarily bad. He turns bad when he does not know what is good and what is evil. If he knew what were good, he would be sure to choose it." Knowledge is essential to goodness in Socrates' view. We just have to look within ourselves to find it.

Plato (428-348 BCE) thought that a person is endowed with the knowledge of good and evil before coming to this world. Knowledge exists in his or her soul but during the period between their creation and descent into this world, they forget most of these things, but this knowledge can be recollected either by wise sermons or through meditation on nature. Experience also helps in recollecting forgotten knowledge. All good and evil is innate in a person. For Plato, the life of reason and good behavior is a happy life. Good itself is happiness and the soul's paradise. It is its own reward.

Aristotle (384-322 BCE). He thought that reason is the greatest bounty of God, and called it the `Divine Spark'. If a woman uses her reason and other capabilities properly, she can attain self-realization after which she hardly needs any measure for good and evil. The position of self-realization is sufficient for her guidance. Aristotle also considers reason and nature sufficient for human guidance. He said that goodness is in harmony with nature and its principles have been set by reason, which a wise man can easily find.

For the Greeks 'Man is the measure of all things' as noted earlier. Morals come from innate knowledge contained within each person. One needs only resurrect this knowledge that is part and parcel of each person's nature. The ancient Greek gods had nothing to do with morality. After all these gods were not particularly moral themselves. In addition, according to the Greeks, the gods had little interest in us mortals and we are pretty much on our own. Thus, the Problem of Evil for the Greeks was not a problem. Their gods were not only not theistic; they also didn't bother with humans unless humans directly antagonized them.

Figure 12. Gottfried Wilhelm Leibniz

Theodicy and the Problem of Evil

Gottfried Leibniz

Gottfried Wilhelm Leibniz (1646-1716) was a German mathematician and philosopher. He occupies a prominent place in both the history of mathematics and philosophy. Leibniz developed the Calculus independent of Isaac Newton, and Leibniz's mathematical notation (y = fx) has been widely used ever since it was first published. He was the first to describe a pinwheel calculator in 1685 and invented the Leibniz wheel, used in the arithmometer, the first mass-produced mechanical calculator. He also refined the binary number system, which is the foundation of virtually all digital computers. He indeed had a brilliant mind!

In philosophy, Leibniz is best known for his optimism. He concluded that our Universe is, in a restricted sense, the best possible world that God could have created. Leibniz, along with René Descartes (1596-1650), and Baruch Spinoza (1632 –1677), was one of the three great seventeenth century advocates of rationalism.[108] Leibniz anticipated modern logic and analytic philosophy, but his philosophy also looks back to the scholastic tradition, in which conclusions are produced by applying reason to first principles or prior definitions rather than to empirical evidence. He was a traditional logician rather than a modern empirical scientist, though many of his ideas look forward to modern thought.

Leibniz made major contributions to physics and technology, and anticipated notions that surfaced much later including probability theory, biology, medicine, geology, psychology, linguistics, and computer science. He wrote works on philosophy, politics, law, ethics, theology, history, and philology[109]. Leibniz's contributions to this vast array of subjects were scattered in various learned journals, in tens of thousands of letters, and in unpublished manuscripts. He wrote in several languages, but primarily Latin, French, and German.

Leibniz introduced the term theodicy in his 1710 work, *Theodicy Essays on the Benevolence of God, the Free Will of Man, and the Origin of Evil*, which was directed mainly against his contemporary, Pierre Bayle (1647 –1706), who had denied the goodness and omnipotence of God based on the daily suffering experienced by all humans. Bayle was

---

[108] Rationalism: a belief or theory that opinions and actions should be based on reason and knowledge rather than on religious notions or emotional responses.

[109] Philology: the branch of knowledge that deals with the structure, historical development, and relationships of a language or languages.

a Protestant, and as a fideist[110] he advocated a separation between the spheres of faith and reason, on the grounds that God is incomprehensible to humans. Leibniz, on the other hand, was an advocate for toleration of divergent belief systems and maintained we could comprehend some aspects of God. Leibniz's works subsequently influenced the development of the Enlightenment.

Leibniz argued that the world we live in "is the best of all possible worlds" that God could have created. As a junior in college, I remember writing on this topic for a philosophy class. I can't remember if it was for or against the idea of á "best of all possible worlds" but it did seem something of a stretch for the world to be the best God could do.

Imitating Leibniz, other philosophers also called their treatises on the Problem of Evil, theodicies as well. Theodicy literally means 'God's 'justice' or 'judgment' and deals with the vindication of divine goodness and providence in view of the existence of evil. Voltaire's popular novel, *Candide* (1759), satirizes Leibnizian optimism through the fictional tale of a naive youth, Candide, and his scholastic philosopher-teacher Dr. Pangloss, who presents the world as good and evil as illusionary.

The Problem of Evil took up much of Leibniz's thought. This is evident in the first and last books that Leibniz authored, the *Philosopher's Confession* (1672) and *Theodicy* (1759) that were both devoted to this issue. He also published shorter treatises on the Problem of Evil over the years. This issue is possibly the primary philosophical concern of Leibniz's career.

If God is, as claimed by the theists, infinite in all respects including omnipotence, omnibenevolence and omniscience, then He must, by definition, be all-loving, and

---

[110] A fideist believes that there are two realms of thought, faith and reason. Both are valid but faith is superior to reason in getting at truth according to Leibniz. Stephen J. Gould, who will be discussed later, held that faith and reason were entirely separate realms never to be united.

wishes no evil to impact His creatures. He must also be all-knowing, and capable of designing a world without evil and as all-powerful capable of making our world devoid of all evil.

However, since there obviously is evil in the world, Leibniz had to devise a God and a world that explains persistent evil without negating His infinite goodness, knowledge and power. Leibniz attempted to resolve this apparent divine inconsistency by claiming that God had made our world the best of all possible words. No better a world could be imagined or created given the limitations and evident contradictions imposed on God by the intrinsic nature of human beings and our material world.

Leibniz needed to reconcile human freedom (and God's own freewill) with the determinism inherent in His theoretical construct of the Universe. Leibniz's solution casts God as the "optimizer" of all the possible worlds of which God's infinite mind can imagine. Since He is all-good and omnipotent and since He chose this world out of all possible worlds, this world must be good—in fact the best of all possible worlds. This view helped Leibniz understand the evident evil in the world. The world is made of good and evil. The best possible world would have the most good and the least bad. As this world is a mixture of good and evil and as God, with His infinite goodness, power and understanding is able to choose to create the best of all possible options, He must have done so in order to optimize universal good and minimize universal evil. Humans as free are doomed to choose evil acts at times. If we were not free beings then God would have created us as deterministic automatons. We, as part of the best of all possible worlds, must be the best of all possible creatures. Free beings are metaphysically and practically better than automatons.

For example, courage is better than pusillanimity (cowardice). It might be observed, then, that without evil to challenge us, there can be no courage. Since evil, suffering and/or injustice, brings out the best in us humans, evil can be viewed as necessary in making us good and in promoting ever increasing virtue. So in creating this world it was necessary for God to mix in some evil in order to make our world the best of all possible worlds and to make us the best of all possible beings. Leibniz's explains evil not by denying it or even rationalizing it, but simply by declaring it to be part of the optimum mix that makes for the best of all possible worlds that God could create. Leibniz thus does not claim that the world is solely good, but that because freewill requires elements of human good and evil, God, though omnipotent, could not improve it in one way without making it worse in some other way. We would all be wimps without some evil. Leibniz relies on an early form of the "freewill defense" for his solution for the Problem of Evil. He also enlists the 'soul-making' defense for the problem. His solution, which is especially pertinent to the main theme of this book, makes one of the first attempts at explaining evil by enlisting evolutionary theory, though, of course, he lived before Charles Darwin (1809-1882) and Jean-Baptiste Lamarck (1744 –1829) who proposed evolutionary ideas. Though Leibniz is primarily known for his best of all possible worlds" approach to the Problem of Evil, it may be that he deserves some credit for opening the door to the idea of evolution in solving the Problem of Evil.

David Hume and the Problem of Evil

David Hume's (1711–1776) formulation of the Problem of Evil in *Dialogues Concerning Natural Religion* is as follows:

"Is He [God] willing to prevent evil, but not able? Then is He impotent? Is he able, but not willing? Then is He malevolent? Is He both able and willing? Then why is their evil? [God's] power we allow [is] infinite: Whatever He wills is executed: But neither man nor any other animal is happy.

Therefore, He does not will their happiness. His wisdom is infinite. He is never mistaken in choosing the means to any end. But the course of nature tends not to human or animal felicity. Therefore, it is not established for that purpose. Through the whole compass of human knowledge, there are no inferences more certain and infallible than these. In what respect, then, do His benevolence and mercy resemble the benevolence and mercy of men?"

David Hume was one of the eighteenth century's leading thinkers. His statement of the problem is clear and simple. If God is all good, all-powerful, etc. then He could do a better job of making us humans and all other animals happy. Hume's God is theistic. He is a traditional perfect God. There should be no difficulty for God in making the world a better place. Something is wrong, however. If God is all-everything, then we ought to be living in lighthearted, happy world. In Hume's view it seems apparent that God isn't all that He's supposed to be. Either God isn't theistic or we humans are so evil that we don't deserve much good and are due lots of evil for the evil we do.

Robert Malthus

Robert Malthus (1766 –1834) was a population and economic theorist who argued that evil exists to spur human creativity and production. Without the necessary evil of strife, mankind would have remained in a savage state because all human needs would be provided for.

Malthus was an English cleric and scholar, who was influential in the fields of political economy and demography. Malthus became widely known for his theories about changes in population numbers. His, *An Essay on the Principle of Population*, observes that sooner or later the world's population will be limited by famine and disease, leading to what is known as a Malthusian Catastrophe. He wrote in opposition to the then popular view in eighteenth century Europe that saw society as improving and in principle as ultimately on the right economic track. However, he believed that the dangers of population growth precluded progress towards a utopian society:

"The power of population is indefinitely greater than the power in the earth to produce subsistence for man".

As a cleric, Malthus saw this situation as divinely imposed to teach virtuous behavior: a form of soul-making. Malthus wrote:

"That the increase of population is necessarily limited by the means of subsistence. That population does invariably increase when the means of subsistence increase, and, that the superior power of population is repressed, and the actual population kept equal to the means of subsistence, by misery and vice."

Malthus placed the longer-term stability of the economy above short-term expediency. He supported the Corn Laws, which introduced a system of taxes on British imports of wheat. This helped support England wheat farmers. His views became influential, and controversial, across economic, political, social and scientific thought.

He remains a much-debated writer. His thought concerning suffering and evil focused on uncontrolled population expansion and the resultant famines and other limited resources that result.

We have seen, especially in the twentieth and twenty-first centuries, an ever-expanding knowledge of genetically modified foodstuffs (gmos). This label, 'genetically modified', has taken on a pejorative flavor in recent years as something unhealthy. Medical studies do not support this negative view of "gmos". In addition, without improved crop production, Malthus' predictions might already have come true at a pace swifter than we are seeing with the millions of people, many of them children, dying each year of starvation and tainted water supplies. In addition, if gmos are unhealthy, why are we living longer and healthier over the 100years or more that they have been around?

Malthus' ideas have echoed over the years and are
heard even louder today. Pioneers of evolutionary biology,
Charles Darwin and Alfred Russell Wallace were influenced
by his views.

Figure 13. Immanuel Kant

Immanuel Kant

Immanuel Kant (1724-1804) argued for "skeptical
theism". He claimed there is a reason that all theodicies
must fail. Evil is a personal challenge to every human
being and can be overcome only by faith. Kant set out the
principles of moral conduct based on his philosophical
account of rational thought, what he calls "Pure Reason"
and then based on this concept defines virtue as the
freewill decision to act according to the principles of pure
reason. Although Kant speaks of faith, he is at bottom a
metaphysical rationalist. All his arguments are based on
reason, not the Bible nor science. The highest good, he
says, is arrived at by reason. Virtue and its consequence,
happiness, is the natural result of his rational ethics. If we
act virtuously, happiness automatically follows and this
functions as a motivator to future virtuous acts. True good
or the "highest good" as Kant labels it, is not motivated by

personal gain; rather it flows directly from virtue based on pure reason.

In *The Critique of Practical Reason*, Kant argues that the highest good for humanity is complete moral virtue together with complete happiness; virtue the condition of our deserving happiness. If we think rightly we will act rightly. Unfortunately, Kant says that virtue does not insure wellbeing and may even conflict with it. We know this from experience. Even if we are virtuous we may not be happy. Further, there is no real possibility of moral perfection in this life and indeed few of us fully deserve the happiness we may be lucky enough to achieve.

Reason, he also claims, cannot prove or disprove the existence of Divine Providence, nor the immortality of the soul. Nevertheless, Kant argues for an unlimited amount of time to perfect ourselves, that is, immortality and that God insures that we will have an adequate amount of time for achieving individual wellbeing.

The most basic aim of moral philosophy is, in Kant's view, to "seek out" the foundational principles of metaphysics of morals. He proceeds by analyzing and elucidating commonsense ideas of morality. The point of this is to come up with a precise statement of the principle upon which all of our ordinary moral judgments are based. The judgments in question are supposed to be those any normal, sane, adult human being would accept. This moral principle is based on each person's own rational freewill. We are autonomous, very rational beings with freewill according to Kant and, most importantly we each can reason our way to Kant's ultimate moral principle; what he labels the Categorical Imperative.

The Categorical Imperative is the central philosophical concept in Kant's deontological[111] moral philosophy. It was introduced in Kant's 1785, *Grounding for the Metaphysics of Morals*. This may be defined as a way of evaluating

---

[111] Deontology is the study of "duty and obligation". Kant uses this as a basic approach to his ethics—what reason tells us our duties are.

motivations for moral action. According to Kant, human beings occupy a special place in creation, and, in addition, morality can be summed up in an imperative, or ultimate commandment of reason from which all duties and obligations are derived. He defines an imperative as any proposition declaring a certain action (or inaction) that is necessary and not contingent. In other words, virtuous behaviors are derived from human reason and these behaviors are based on absolute standards accepted by all rational beings. A categorical imperative denotes an absolute, unconditional requirement that must be obeyed in all circumstances and is justified as an end in it. It is best known in its first formulation or definition:

"Act only according to that maxim whereby you can, at the same time, will that it [the standard] should become a universal law."

Examples include:

- Lying, or deception of any kind, would be forbidden under any circumstance.
- Theft: Taking some other person's property without their permission.
- Suicide: killing oneself if the person is still rational.
- Laziness: failing to cultivate one's talents.
- Charity: Helping others in need.

Kant expresses dissatisfaction with the popular moral philosophy of his day, believing that it could never surpass the level of hypothetical imperatives, which is a rule of action that applies only to individual needs of the moment such as studying for an immanent exam. A categorical imperative applies at all times and in all situations. One could question these examples but Kant felt they were universal in their ethical applications.

Ever since Aristotle, happiness has been used as the moral end.[112] This is so called utilitarian ethics. Kant claims that this ethical system sees murder as wrong

---

[112] Aristotle, *Nicomachian Ethics.*

because it does not maximize good for those involved, but this is irrelevant to people who are concerned only with maximizing the positive outcome for themselves. Consequently, Kant argues, hypothetical moral systems such as a happiness based system cannot be regarded as a basis for moral judgments against others, because the imperatives on which they are based rely too heavily on subjective considerations. He presents a deontological moral system, based on the demands of the categorical imperative, as an alternative.

Throughout his career, Immanuel Kant addressed many of the major issues that contemporary philosophy group together under the heading of "philosophy of religion." These include arguments for the existence of God, the attributes of God, the immortality of the soul, the Problem of Evil, and the relationship of moral principles to religious beliefs and practices. In the writings from his so-called "pre-critical" period, i.e., before the publication of the *Critique of Pure Reason* in 1781, Kant was interested principally in the concept of God and less so in ethical principles. In developing a new role for philosophical principles in understanding the order and structure of the Universe, he went from his, *Critique of Pure Reason* to the *Critique of Practical Reason*; from the analysis of God to an analysis of moral behavior. Chief among these are the moral and the religious issues relating to the relationship between human beings and God. This shift in Kant's thinking then expanded to include not only the concept of God, arguments for the existence of God, but also the relationship between morality and religion, and the role of religion in the dynamics of human culture and history.

Relative to the Problem of Evil I will discuss Kant's view of freewill and his concept of God as viewed by Kant. As we have seen, Kant emphasizes individual freedom of will and human intellectual capacity. He believes that God creates humans as totally autonomous in our decision-making capabilities, i.e. we have freewill. Divine sovereignty was not an issue for Kant. So we are totally free to choose good or evil. Thus, one element in Kant's handling of the Problem of Evil is the freewill defense that we have seen before and will see again when discussing Plantinga's solution to the Problem of Evil.

The second major element in Kant's concept of God is that we humans do not have the intellectual capacity to understand, define or imagine God. God is transcendent and cannot be imagined, intuited or in any way comprehended by human cognition. God is neither sensible, capable of being perceived by the senses, nor being grasped by the understanding. Kant employs an analogical approach to our view of God. Several early Christian philosopher/theologians such as Augustine and Aquinas state categorically that we cannot 'know' God and then they go forward to define God as infinite, benevolent, omniscient etc. The OT paints a picture of a very tough, jealous, often angry, vengeful Father that helps the early Jews invade Jericho and kill all within the walls of the city, committing genocide in killing as many Canaanites as they can. (Joshua 6:1-27) In the NT Christ speaks of condemning sinful souls to the fires of Hell for all eternity. If we cannot 'know' God, how come, so many theologians are able to describe Him in such detail? Maybe the Bible is inerrant after all. At any rate, if God is truly a spirit and doesn't exist in time/space, just how does He connect to us and how can we 'know' Him, space and time bound as we are?

Kant's approach to the Problem of Evil makes all the terms we use to define God, analogical. When we speak of God as good, we are only using the term in the sense that humans understand it. The same is true of other adjectives applied to God, such as, loving, caring, responsive to our prayers, fatherly, etc. In approaching God analogically, can Kant truly solve the theistic Problem of Evil?

David Hume and Evil

David Hume (1711-1776) was a contemporary of Kant and one of the first Deists. Hume denies that God is theistic. If He is not all-everything, as a theistic God must be, then there is no Problem of Evil. A deist believes that God created the world and its laws and then left the world to roll along on its own. Whatever happens is not directly attributable to God. He only made the world including its workings (rules and regulations) and what happens thereafter is based on chance. As we will see later, the world is a chancy place and though Einstein denied that God plays dice with the Universe, the fact is, that He does. We live in a probabilistic world not a deterministic one so what happens on Earth and in the heavens is variable and unpredictable for the most part. Just as DNA mutates in a random fashion so too the Universe as a whole performs in the same way. Quantum and relativity physics have demonstrated earthly randomness with a high degree of certitude.

So whenever we deny that God is theistic, the Problem of Evil automatically goes away, because if God is not all-everything, then God is fallible in at least some way, and our problem disappears. If He is not omniscient, omnipotent and/or omnibenevolent then He can be responsible for evil. If God is not theistic, however, there are other issues that surface for traditional religious believers but these are topics for another time.

In spite of being a deist, David Hume's formulation of the Problem of Evil as presented in *Dialogues Concerning Natural Religion*, takes on a theistic flavor:

"Is He [God] willing to prevent evil, but not able? Then is He impotent? Is he able, but not willing? Then is He malevolent? Is He both able and willing? Whence then is evil?

God's power we allow [is] infinite: Whatever He wills is executed: But neither man nor any other animals are happy.

Therefore He does not will their happiness. His wisdom is infinite: He is never mistaken in choosing the means to any end. But the course of nature tends not to human or animal felicity. Therefore it is not established for that purpose. Through the whole compass of human knowledge, there are no inferences more certain and infallible than these. In what respect, then, do His benevolence and mercy resemble the benevolence and mercy of men?"

Hume is thus harder on God than a strict deist ought to be but theology doesn't always follow nicely defined rules of logic.

Thomas Henry Huxley and Evil[113]

Thomas Huxley (1825–1895) was an English biologist or more specifically a comparative anatomist, who is best known as "Darwin's Bulldog" for his staunch advocacy of Charles Darwin's theory of evolution. Huxley's famous debate in 1860 with Samuel Wilberforce came one year after Darwin published, *On the Origin of Species*. This debate was a key moment in the wider acceptance of evolution and in Huxley's own career. Huxley had been planning to leave Oxford on the day prior to the debate, but after an encounter with Robert Chambers, the author of *Vestiges*[114], he changed his mind and decided to join the debate. Wilberforce was coached by Richard Owen, against whom Huxley had previously debated whether humans were closely related to apes. Huxley was slow to accept some of Darwin's ideas, such as gradualism[115], and natural selection, but despite these concerns he was wholehearted

---

[113] Wikipedia.

[114] The full title is *Vestiges of the Natural History of Creation*, published in 1844 and was a work of speculative natural history and philosophy by Robert Chambers. Published anonymously in England, and was one of several works that antedated Darwin's *Origins*.

[115] Gradualism: a theory of gradual change rather than sudden change during evolution of species.

in his public support of Darwin. Huxley was instrumental in developing scientific education in Britain. He fought against the more extreme versions of biblical creationism.

In 1869 Huxley coined the term 'agnostic' describing his own views on theology, a term whose use has continued to the present day. Thus, though most consider Huxley a deist, he maintained some doubts about the very existence of God. This indeterminism is evident in his deistic/theistic view of the Problem of Evil noted above.

Huxley had little formal schooling and was virtually self-taught, but his intellect and broad knowledge is evident in his extensive writings. He became perhaps the best comparative anatomist of the latter nineteenth century. He worked on invertebrates, clarifying relationships between species previously little understood. Later, he worked on the relationship between apes and humans. After comparing *Archaeopteryx*[116] with *Compsognathus*[117], he concluded that birds evolved from small carnivorous dinosaurs, a theory widely accepted today. The tendency has been for this fine anatomical work to be overshadowed by his energetic and controversial activity in favor of Darwin and evolution, and by his extensive public work on scientific education, both of which had significant effects on society in Britain and elsewhere. He was trained as a physician especially in ophthalmology. He learned Latin, and enough Greek to read Aristotle in the original Greek.

At age twenty, Huxley was too young to apply to the Royal College of Surgeons for a license to practice medicine, yet he was 'deep in debt'. So, at a friend's suggestion, he applied for an appointment in the Royal Navy. He had references on character and certificates showing the time spent on his apprenticeship and on requirements

---

[116] Archaeopteryx is a genus of bird-like dinosaurs that is transitional between non-avian feathered dinosaurs and modern birds.

[117] Campsognathus is a genus of small, bipedal, carnivorous theropod dinosaurs. Members of its single species *Compsognathus longipes* could grow to the size of a turkey. They lived about 150 million years ago

such as dissection and pharmacy. Sir William Burnett, the Physician General of the Navy, interviewed him and arranged for the College of Surgeons to test his competence and he got the job as a ship's surgeon.

Huxley and Darwin in many ways ran parallel paths through life. They both were naturalists, studied medicine and were competent writers and speakers. In the debate that marks the apotheosis of his career Huxley soundly defeated Samuel Wilberforce in their debate on evolution. It is important to remember that at the time Darwin proposed his theory of evolution the idea of humans evolving from apes was beyond the understanding of most people who had lived by the biblical version of creation for three thousands years so that making a shift from humans "made in the image and likeness of God" (1 Genesis 26-27) to beings whose 'grandparents' were harry beasts that walked on all fours was unthinkable. As noted earlier, about 45% of Americans still believe in the Bible's version of human creation. Just today I saw a letter to the editor in our local paper that in a rambling way reasserts the creationists view. See Appendix B.

Thus, Huxley played an important role in moving Darwin's dream on its path to acceptance at least in the scientific community.

Plantinga's Solution to the Problem of Evil

Alvin Plantinga (b. 1932) used a version of the freewill defense in an attempt to refute the logical problem of evil. He begins by accepting that the existence of an omnipotent, omniscient, omnibenevolent God in an evil world is a logical contradiction. Then Plantinga goes on to say, "It is possible that God, even being omnipotent, could not create a world with free creatures that never choose evil. Furthermore he says, "it is possible that God, even being omnibenevolent, would desire to create a world which contains evil if moral goodness requires free moral creatures." In other words, creatures with freewill can and will choose to act in evil ways. Freewill by its very nature implies such creatures will at times elect to act immorally. Creatures with freewill by their very nature may make evil decisions and behave in evil ways. It is the old square circle problem. By definition 'freewill creatures' includes the concept of evil acts as well as good acts. As a consequence, if God chooses to create human beings, they must have freewill and must at times behave immorally.

While Plantinga's freewill defense has received fairly widespread acceptance among philosophers, many still contend that it fails to adequately resolve the Problem of Evil. Additionally, the defense only addresses moral evil, not natural evil.

Arthur Schopenhauer (1788-1860) famously said (as paraphrased by Einstein later):

"Man can do what he wills but he cannot will what he wills." In other words, although an agent may often be free to act according to a certain *motive* or *motives*, the nature of that motive is determined by many factors other than will itself. The arguments against Plantinga's freewill defense is complex, difficult to understand, as I am freely willing to admit, and delves into metaphysical issues that, it would seem, don't apply to ethical issues which as Kant says relate to practical reason rather than pure (metaphysical) reason. Current empirical studies indicate that decision making in humans and other animals are influenced by both genetic and environmental factors so that freewill is rarely totally free. We do not live in a deterministic world but rather in a probabilistic world. There are no absolutely certain outcomes. There are only percentage chances that some event will happen in one defined way. We are not automatons nor are we totally free. As discussed in my, *Problem Gods: In Search of a Meaningful Deity*, relativity and quantum theory have established that our world is not deterministic and our freewill not deterministic either.

Thus, if God created us, He did not create us so that He knows exactly what anyone of us will do under a given circumstance. Plantinga's freewill defense is valid but only if our will is truly free, which it is not. If the world is probabilistic then God, it would seem, is not responsible for moral evil. Again contrary to what Einstein once claimed, God does play dice with the Universe.

Having looked at evil throughout time and across the world, the nature of evil, the religious and philosophical solutions to the Problem of Evil we now turn to the solution that I think all of this points to i.e. evolution.

Part IV

Chapter 10

The Science of Evolution

Fig.ure 14. Charles Darwin (1809-1882) the Father of Evolution Theory. A naturalist, who developed the basic tenet of evolution, that is, natural selection.

The following chapters attempt to outline the scientific and thus empirical evidence for evolution. This may be 'too much information' for some readers, nonetheless, this information is key in understanding the Neo-Natural God as defined in my prior book, *Problem Gods: In Search of a Meaningful Deity* and it must be dealt with in some detail in order to convince the reader of evolution's validity as a solution to the Problem of Evil. Using Darwinian theory and the evidence for natural selection that is based solidly on geology, physics, archeology, molecular biology and other scientific disciplines, there can be no question about the reality and utility of evolution in solving the Problem of Evil. Evolution is no longer a 'theory' but rather a firmly established fact. At any rate, this is a gentle warning that the next few pages may be tough going for some. Good luck!

The theory of evolution begins with Charles Darwin's, *The Origin of Species*, first published in 1859 and last revised in 1872.[118] Darwin freely admits his indebtedness to earlier workers such as Jean Baptiste de Lamarck, who first proposed the idea of evolution in the early part of the nineteenth century. Lamarck, however, believed that environmentally induced characteristics, such as tanned skin, resulting from exposure to the Sun, could be passed on to ones offspring. Darwin's grandfather, Erasmus (1731-1802), had actually proposed the theory of evolution in the late eighteenth century but his ideas were not generally circulated. Charles Darwin also openly gave due credit to Alfred Russel Wallace (1823-1913) who developed the theory of evolution nearly contemporaneously with Darwin though Darwin appears to have been first and did publish ahead of Wallace. It was Darwin, who first developed the concepts of "modifications" or "change in character" as something that developed within a species or variety which, if beneficial, was then passed on from generation to generation as a result of natural selection.[119] Darwin knew nothing of genetics including Gregor Mendel's Laws of inheritance. We now know that DNA mutates randomly but if the mutation promotes increased offspring that do better in their environment than other offspring of a competitive species then the individual and species as a whole will persist and prosper.

---

[118] Darwin, C. 197 9, *Origin of Species* (New York: Hillard Wang).

[119] Ibid, Chapter 4.

Darwin was initially a theistic[120] evolutionist. He did not deny God's hand in the workings of nature[121] but did not believe in 'special creation' as described in Genesis 1 and 2. Rather, he believed that all species including *Homo sapiens*, evolved from lower animal forms. Darwin did not have the benefit of Mendel's laws of genetics nor the concept of genetic mutations but he did understand that changes or modifications, useful to an individual and thus the individual's species, will persist rather than die out. In other words, all species are in competition within their environment, including local predators and those preyed upon. In order to continue as a species all species must adapt to the world around them. The environment is always changing and in order to survive the individuals of a given species have to change as well. Mutations, which are random genetic events, if beneficial, help individuals and thus their species adapt to the environment in which they live. Adaptation may include such changes as successfully battling with predators, finding food better than other individuals of a given species, running faster, hunting in herds rather than alone, being more attractive to the opposite gender or managing in colder or hotter climates among many other adaptations to their local environment.

All of Darwin's ideas were based on his or other naturalists' observations of the flora and fauna of England and other parts of the world, including the Galapagos Islands, where Darwin studied for five weeks in the 1830's. The varieties of species, he found there and elsewhere, along with their local environments, convinced him that natural selection worked to improve species or, more precisely, helped them adapt to their environment in a

---

[120] Some say Darwin was an agnostic or atheist, but this is not true. He wrote, "That a man can be an ardent theist and an evolutionist...In my most extreme fluctuations I have never been an atheist in the sense of denying the existence of a God. https://www.google.com/#hl=en&q=was+darwin+an+agnostic

[121] Ibid, pp. 14, 57.

beneficial way, Huxley coined the term "survival of the fittest", but it might be better to think of these species as "survival of the most adaptable". It is the most adaptable individuals that survive which leads to their species surviving. On this point, Darwin differs from the strict creationists who do not believe that there has been any 'improvement' in species since the original creation described in Genesis. The creationists also deny the extinction of species. Extinct fossils are considered to be unreal—misinterpretations of geological findings.

Although Darwin's theory of evolution is based on observations, much of his theory has to be considered speculative, at least initially. Very frequently, he makes statements such as, "it seems reasonable" or "these observations would suggest" followed by some conclusion based on his observations. Thus, all of his ideas are founded on empirical data. His conclusions, however, could be faulted as not necessarily following from these data. The causal relationships he develops are not always correct. Nonetheless, the great majority of his concepts have held up in light of modern genetics and molecular research. He did have access to Charles Lyell's *Principles of Geology*, the benchmark work on paleogeology, before he left for the Galapagos Islands on the H.M.S. Beagle in 1831.[122] Thus, Lyell's concepts played a major role in his theory of evolution, even though geological time-scales were not well understood then. Lyell was convinced that the 4004 BCE date proposed by Archbishop James Usher in 1650 for the origin of the Earth, was not consistent with the geological record.[123]

In addition to the concept of natural selection, the theory of evolution rests on the fossil record, geological dating methods and modern genetics. These are the four 'warrants,' as philosophers would say, that support the

---

[122]   Lyell, C. 1997, *Principles of Geology* (London: Penguin).

[123]   Ibid, p. 13.

notion of evolution and its many ramifications as we shall see.[124]

[125]Natural Selection

Natural selection was fully developed by Darwin in his *Origin of Species*. Darwin's numerous observations of nature made it clear that natural selection was the driving force behind "modification" of the species. He puts it this way:

"When we see leaf-eating insects [that are] green and bark-feeders, mottled-grey, the alpine ptarmigan [126], white in winter, the red grouse the color of heather, we must believe that these tints are of service to these birds and insects in preserving them from danger."[127]

Darwin gives many such examples in great detail and his most famous 'proof' of natural selection deals with the finches of the Galapagos Islands. These finches are geographically isolated on several Galapagos islands and their eating habits have led to modifications of their beaks, depending on the type of food they consume–large beaks for eating seeds, small sharp beaks for insects and so on.[128]

In order to strengthen the case for natural selection as envisioned by Darwin, one needs access to modern methods for establishing the role of evolution in nature. That a hierarchy of species exists is not enough to support the theory of evolution, as proposed by Darwin and his nineteenth century colleague, Thomas Huxley, his strongest

---

[124] Hutton, N. 1968, *The Evidence of Evolution* (New York, NY: American Heritage Publishing).

[125]

[126]

[127] Ptarmigan: a species of grouse.

[128] Op. cit. Darwin, C. 1979, p.78.

supporter.[129] It was not until the fossil record became more complete and geological dating appeared on the scene that the theory of evolution matured into a true science.

Fossil Evidence

Natural selection is evident in the macroscopic, microscopic and molecular worlds. The fossils that have been discovered over the last 150 years or more have helped to fill in the gaps of our human genealogy, although there are still manifold mysteries to be solved and many actors on the stage of evolution are yet to make their appearance. The evolutionary record of *Homo sapiens* and its progenitors is complex and marked by many twists and turns, some of which lead to dead ends.[130] Life appears to have begun on Earth some 3.6 billion years before the present epoch when unicellular (one celled) organisms first appeared. Metazoans (multicellular organisms) emerged 2.5 billion years ago.[131] The first organisms were anaerobic,[132] since there was essentially no oxygen (O_2) in the atmosphere at the time. The Ediacarans[133] developed later, after the Cyanobacteria[134], which could make oxygen

---

[129] Although Darwin spends more time dealing with the Galapagos mockingbirds the Peter R. Grant & B. Rosemary Grant in *40 Years of Evolution: Darwin's Finches on Daphne Major Island*, have more recently clarified Darwin's work on the finches.

[130] Tattersall, Ian, 2015, The Strange Case of the Rickety Cassack: and Other Cautionary Tales, Kindle e-book.

[131] Knoll, A.H., & Carroll, S.B. 1999, *Early Animal Evolution: Emerging Views from Comparative Biology and Geology*, Science, 284:2129-2137.

[132] Anaerobic: not requiring oxygen.

[133] Ediacaran: of or relating to a soft-bodied marine organism of the Precambrian Era (before 540 million years ago) thought to be the earliest multicellular form of life.

[134] *Cyanobacterium*: a photosynthetic bacterium of the class *Coccogoneae* or *Hormogoneae*, generally blue-green in color and in some species capable of nitrogen fixation. Cyanobacteria were once thought to be algae. Also called *blue-green algae*.

out of carbon dioxide, produced enough oxygen to allow this oxygen consuming form of life to evolve, that is, adapt to the changing environment with its ample oxygen and thus survive.[135] Beginning with the Cambrian Period, 540 million yeas ago, there was a mushrooming of many new phyla.[136] In addition, over the course of many eons, there have been numerous mass extinctions, some occurring as the result of climate changes,[137] catastrophic events, such as asteroid or comet strikes,[138] volcanic eruptions or the impact of humans on the environment.[139] After each mass extinction, new forms of life evolved to fill the ecological niches that then became available. An example of evolution related to climatic change is that of the Woolly Mammoth, whose evolution has recently been worked out.[140] They came on the scene as an adaptation to Ice Age conditions and later disappeared as a result of over-hunting by Neanderthals and humans.

The genera of our human lineage have been partially elucidated over the past 150 years.[141] And, of course, new *Homo* species are being found in Africa and Asia on a regular basis.[142][143], There are hominids dating to four

[135] Brasier, M., & Antclife, J., 2004, *Decoding the Ediacaran Enigma*, Science, 305:1115-1117.

[136] Op. cit. Knoll, A.H., & Carroll, S.B., 1999.

[137] Bains, S., et al. 2000, *Termination of Global Warmth at the Palaeocene/ Eocene Boundary through Productivity Feedback*, Nature, 407:171-174.

[138] Ward, P.D., & Brownlee, D., 2000, *Rare Earth: Why Complex Life is Uncommon in the Universe*, New York: Copernicus Books.

[139] Barnsky, A.D., et al., 2004, *Assessing the Causes of Late Pleistocene Extinctions on the Continents*, Science, 306:70-75.

[140] Lister, A.M., & Sher, A.V., 2001, *The Origin and Evolution of the Woolly Mammoth*, Science, 294:1094-1097.

[141] Cela-Conde, C.J., & Ayala, F.J., 2003, PNAS, 100:7684-7689.

[142] Brown, P., et al. 2004, *A New Small-Bodied Hominin from the Late Pleistocene of Flores, Indonesia*, Nature, 431:1055-1061.

[143] Gibbons, A. 2002, *In Search of the First Hominids*, Science, 295:1214-1219.

million years ago. However, the earliest *Homo sapiens* fossil dates to 200,000-160,000 years ago.

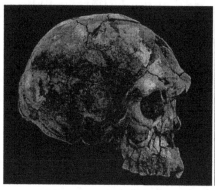

Fig.ure 15. One of the oldest know *Homo sapiens* skulls dating to 160,000 years ago. The skull shows typical modern human features with a high forehead, small supraorbital ridges and no prognathism (prominent Jaw).

From the fossil record there is ample evidence of human evolution. There are a number of early hominins[144] The earliest humans are usually classified as *Archaic H. sapiens* because there are some minor anatomical variations present when compared to present day humans. There are a number of *Homo* species that date to several millions of years ago including *Homo habilis, Homo erectus* and *Homo heidelbergensis* that antedate *Homo sapiens*. However, the exact lineage and evolutionary connection to *Homo sapiens* of these species are not entirely clear. Beginning around 50,000 years ago, truly modern humans emerged and this is confirmed, in part, by the evidence of cultural advances, such as cave paintings found in Europe and Africa.[145] Evidence of a developing human culture is seen as early as 2.5 million years ago.[146] Thus, there is not only evidence of anatomical evolution, but also cultural

---

[144]   Hominin: the group consisting of modern humans, extinct human species and all our immediate ancestors (including members of the genera *Homo, Australopithecus, Paranthropus* and *Ardipithecus*).

[145]   Balter, M. 1999, *Restorers Reveal 28,000-Year-Old Artworks*, Science, 283:1835.

[146]   Ambrose, S. 2001, *Paleolithic Technology and Human Evolution*, Science, 291:1748-1753.

evolution as well.[147] Such cultural changes are found in many activities, including sewing,[148] burial rites,[149] fire making,[150] flint mining,[151] jewelry making,[152] hunting equipment, such as spears,[153] the fashioning of knives and finally the development of farming.[154] In addition, there are anatomical changes that suggest evolutionary developments in cognitive function, beginning around 50,000 years ago.[155],[156]

There are literally thousands of studies indicating evolutionary processes in animals, plants and humans,

---

[147]   Klein, R.G., & Edgar, B. 2002, *The Dawn of Human Culture* (New York: Hahn, Wiley & Sons). Culture in this and other papers, refers to all information transmitted to subsequent generations by other than genetic means. Technology, language, writing, art and all types of learning would be included in the definition of 'culture'.

[148]   Balter, M. 2004, *Dressed for Success: Neanderthal Culture Wins Respect*, Science, 306:40-41.

[149]   Op. cit. Klein, p. 147.

[150]   Goren-Inbar, N., et al. 2004, *Evidence of Hominin Control of Fire at Gusher Beano Ya'aqov, Israel*, Science, 304:725-727.

[151]   Verdi, G., et al. 2004, *Flint Mining in Prehistory Recorded by in situ-Produced Cosmogony ^{10}Be*, PNAS, 101:7880-7884.

[152]   Kuhn, S., et al., 2001, *Ornaments of the Earliest Upper Paleolithic: New Insights from the Levant*, PNAS, 98:7641-7646.

[153]   Ibid, p. 159.

[154]   Denham, T.P., et al., 2003, *Origins of Agriculture at Kuku Swamp in the Highlands of New Guinea*, Science, 301:189-193.

[155]   Chou, H. H., et al., 2002, *Inactivation of CMP-N-acetylneuraminic acid Hydroxylase Occurred Prior to Brain Expansion During Human Evolution*, PNAS, 99:11736-11741.

[156]   Conroy, G.C., et al., 1998, *Endocranial Capacity in an Early Hominid Cranium From Sterkfontein, South Africa*, Science, 280:1730-1731.

not to mention evolutionary developments in the Universe including the evolution of planets,[157] stars[158] and galaxies.[159]

Geological Dating

Until the discovery of geological dating techniques in the early twentieth century, many of the claims made by evolutionists remained unproven. After one hundred years experience with radiometric dating methods, along with stratigraphy (the study of geological sedimentary layers), dendrochronology (counting tree rings), glacial ice core studies (counting ice layer) and other non-radiometric methods, the science of geological dating now rests on firm experimental foundations.[160] There are about 40 radiometric methods currently available. The first to be used was the Uranium/Lead system. Certain elements are physically unstable and will 'decay', that is, are converted into different elements or isotopes over precisely

[157]   Buckle, R. van, et al., 2004, *The Building Blocks of Planets Within the "Terrestrial Region" of Protoplanetary Discs,* Nature, 432:479-482.

[158]   Abel, T., et al., 2002, *The Formation of the First Star in the Universe,* Science, 295:93-98.

[159]   Buser, R., 2000, *The Formation and the Early Evolution of the Milky Way Galaxy,* Science, 287:69-74.

[160]   Wiens, R.C., 2002, *Radiometric Dating: A Christian Perspective,* http://www. Talkorigins.org/faqs/dating.html.

predictable time periods.[161] There is a defined 'half-life' of each of these unstable elements. One half-life is the time it takes for one-half of a given amount of an element to be converted into another isotope or element. Fig.3. shows several radiometric systems and their half-lives.

Their Half-Lives

Radioactive Isotope (Parent)	Product (Daughter)	Half-Life (Years)
Samarium-147	Neodymium-143	106 billion
Rubidium-87	Strontium-87	48.8 billion
Rhenium-187	Osmium-187	42 billion
Lutetium-176	Hafnium-176	38 billion
Thorium-232	Lead-208	14 billion
Uranium-238	Lead-206	4.5 billion
Potassium-40	Argon-40	1.26 billion
Uranium-235	Lead-207	0.7 billion
Beryllium-10	Boron-10	1.52 million
Chlorine-36	Argon-36	300,000
Carbon-14	Nitrogen-14	5715
Uranium-234	Thorium-230	248,000
Thorium-230	Radium-226	75,400

Table. 3. Radiometric isotopes commonly used in geological dating of sedimentary strata and fossils of various types. The isotope is produced by radioactive decay and its half-life is shown. Note that each isotope has a different half-life–some very long, others much shorter. Many of these half-lives overlap in time and, thus, can be used to check the accuracy of other radiometric techniques.

The half-life of a given isotope can be used to determine the age of a fossil or rock that contains the fossil, even if the isotope is present in very small amounts. If the amount of the 'parent' isotope is known and the 'daughter' isotope is determined, then the age of the fossil or rock (or both)

---

161 In the nucleus of an element, there are protons and neutrons (with the exception of hydrogen which has only one proton and no neutrons). If a uranium atom loses one or more of its neutrons it will have the same 'atomic number' i.e. same number of protons in the nucleus, and thus will still be an uranium atom, though with a lighter nucleus, that is, its atomic weight will be less. Uranium with a total of 238 protons and neutrons in its nucleus is U^{238}. If this molecule loses three of its neutrons, it is converted into the isotope U^{235}. On the other hand, if, by radioactive decay, (because U^{238} is unstable) it loses a total of 32 protons and neutrons, it is converted into a new element, that is, lead (Pb^{206}). Loss of neutrons makes an element lighter becoming an isotope of the same element. With the loss of one or more protons it becomes another element entirely.

can be determined.[162] The half-lives of over 40 isotopes have been determined directly, either by using a radiation detector to count the number of atoms decaying in a given period of time or by measuring the ratio of parent to daughter isotopes, where the original amount of parent material is known. These measurements are very precise and can give accurate dates up to 10 half-lives, so that carbon dating is valid to 45,000 years and several of the isotopes listed in Table 3 can give accurate ages for the Earth, meteorites or Moon rocks. Potassium 40/Argon 40 is often used to date hominid[163] fossils. Usually the value obtained by one dating method is compared to one or more additional me thods in order to verify a given result. This makes geological dating a highly reliable research tool.

Radiometric methods can also be checked by non-radiometric methods, such as counting tree rings. Using long-lived trees, carbon dating has been verified to 6800

---

[162] A 'parent' isotope is the original form of the element present in a fossil or rock when it is formed. In the case of rocky material the parent isotope is present at the time the sediment is laid down or, for an igneous rock, it is the amount of isotope present when the nascent molten rock (lava) begins to cool. For plant or animal life, it is the amount of Carbon (C^{14}) present when the organism dies. There is a certain concentration of C^{14} in the air we breathe. This is incorporated into living cells and when the plant or animal dies, the C^{14} begins to decay to N^{14} then C^{13} and finally C^{12} (which is stable). The ratio of C^{14} to C^{12} can then give the age of the material, knowing the half-life of this reaction.

Knoll, A.H., et al. 2004, *A New Period for the Geological Time Scale*, Science, 305:621-622.

Swisher, C.C., et al. 1999, *Cretaceous Age for the Feathered Dinosaurs of Liaoning, China*, Nature, 400:58-64.

Op. cit. Lister, A.M., & Sher, A.V. 2001.

Leakey, M.G., et al. 1998, *New Specimens and Confirmation of an Early Age for Australopithecus anamnesis*, Nature 393:62-66.

Holden, C., 1997, *Archeology: Tooling Around—Dates Show Early Siberian Settlement*, Science, 275:1268-1270.

Tinkaus, E., et al., 2003, *An Early Modern Human from the Pester cu Oases, Romania*, PNAS, 100:11231-11236.

[163] Hominids are ancient ancestors of humans including apes.

years and by combining living tree ring counts with long-lived, but dead trees that were alive for a time when the living tree was first growing, carbon dating has been verified to 11,600 years. Because of the variation in yearly rainfall, tree ring patterns from tree to tree are the same for the same years and local and, thus, the pattern from dead and living trees will overlap and extend the period that dendrochronologic (tree ring) methods are useful.

Using these techniques, thousands of studies have been carried out in order to date a variety of fossils and rocks. This has included accurate dating of the onset of the Cambrian flowering of life,[164] the age of feathered dinosaurs,[165] dates of the woolly mammoth,[166] timing of early hominids,[167] antiquity of early human settlements,[168] occurrence of early modern humans,[169] chronology of Neanderthal burial sites,[170] and dating of cave paintings,[171] and many others such studies.

Although creationists have criticized some of these dating methods based on earlier errors that have been reported[172], the mountains of evidence, crosschecking of

---

[164] Knoll, A.H., et al. 2004, *A New Period for the Geological Time Scale*, Science, 305:621-622.

[165] Swisher, C.C., et al. 1999, *Cretaceous Age for the Feathered Dinosaurs of Liaoning, China*, Nature, 400:58-64.

[166] Op. cit. Lister, A.M., & Sher, A.V. 2001,

[167] Leakey, M.G., et al. 1998, *New Specimens and Confirmation of an Early Age for Australopithecus anamnesis*, Nature 393:62-66.

[168] Holden, C., 1997, *Archeology: Tooling Around—Dates Show Early Siberian Settlement*, Science, 275:1268-1270.

[169] Tinkaus, E., et al., 2003, *An Early Modern Human from the Pester cu Oases, Romania*, PNAS, 100:11231-11236.

[170] Valladas, H., et al., 1987, *Thermoluminescence Dates for the Neanderthal Burial Sites at Kebara in Israel*, Nature, 330:159-160.

[171] Valladas, H., et al., 2001, *Paleolithic Paintings: Evolution of Prehistoric Cave Art*, Nature, 413:479.

[172] Op. cit. Morris, H. M., 1985, pp. 161-2.

data and improved technology leaves no room for doubting their validity today.[173]

Molecular Biology

Molecular biology has been the most recent scientific advance in evolutionary research.[174] Genetic studies have not only defined the nature of humans and lower animals but they have also provided demographic data concerning geography, as well as, the timing of major migrations by *H. sapiens*.[175] Genetic studies have provided one more way of correlating data obtained from fossil finds, geological dating methods and linguistic studies.[176] These have also helped us understand what separates humans from lower species especially our nearest relatives, the chimpanzees.[177] The Y-chromosome has allowed the identification of time and place of our oldest male ancestor[178] and mitochondrial DNA provides the same information regarding our oldest female ancestor.[179] DNA studies of *H. sapiens* and *H. neanderthalensis* have settled the question of the relationship between humans and Neanderthals—finding that the two are not directly related and that Europeans are not descended from

[173] Godfrey, l. R., 1983, *Scientists Confront Creationism* (New York: W. W. Norton) pp. 37-40.

[174] Foley, R., 1998, The *Context of Human Genetic Evolution*, Genome Research, 8:339-347.

[175] Op. cit. Garber, J.J., 2008.

[176] Cavelli-Sfoza, L.L., et al., 1988, *Reconstruction of Human Evolution: Bringing Together Genetic, Archeological, and Linguistic Data*, PNAS, 85:6002-6006.

[177] Gibbons, A., 1998, *Which of Our Genes Makes Us Human?* Science, 281:1432-1434.

[178] Bertranpetit, J., 2000, *Genome, Diversity, and Origins: The Y-chromosome as a Storyteller*, PNAS, 97:6927-6929.

[179] Klicka, J., & Akin, R.M., 1998, *Pleistocene Speciation and the Mitochondrial DNA Clock*, Science, 282:1955-1959.

Neanderthals.[180] Most humans posses some Neanderthals genes; in the range of 4% of the human genome comes from Neanderthals indicating there was some interbreeding between the two species. My personal genome contains 2% Neanderthal genes. My wire3 has 4% Neanderthal genes. There is DNA evidence, however, for an association, even descent of humans from lower forms. This has been established by molecular studies.[181] The genome of *H. sapiens* is very close, for example, to that of the chimpanzee where 98% or more of their DNA is the same as ours. More and more animal and plant genomes have been elucidated, further establishing the genetic evolutionary processes present in all species of all biological domains.[182]

The Genographic Project has and continues to clarify our origins and migration patterns since *H. sapiens* left northeast Africa some 50,000 years ago.[183] These data have been chronicled in Spencer Wells' *Deep Ancestry* and his earlier book, *The Journey of Man*.[184] Wells describes the methodology used in the project and the information that has come out of it so far. In brief, by studying DNA in geographically isolated populations worldwide, it has been possible to find DNA patterns as they evolve over time. Mutation rates, though low, are predictable and from these data the timing of migratory movements can be determined. Since each geographical group develops a specific DNA sequence over a short period of time, about 200 years, it can be determined by comparison with other geographic populations where a given group came from and when this occurred. They have determined, for

[180] Ovchinnikov, I.V., et al., 2000, *Molecular Analysis of Neanderthal DNA from the Northern Caucasus*, Nature, 404:400-403.

[181] Op. cit. Gibbons, A., 1998.

[182] Biology Analysis Group, 2004, *A Draft Sequence for the Genome of the Domesticated Silkworm* ((*Bombyx more*), Science, 306:1937-1940.

[183] Wells, S., 2007, *Deep Ancestry: Inside the Genographic Project* (Washington, D.C.: National Geographic).

[184] Wells, S., 2002, *The Journey of Man* (New York: Random House).

example, that the vast majority of European males come from seven ancient 'fathers' and where these 'fathers' originally lived. Five 'racial' types have been identified. These five types developed, that is evolved, after leaving Africa. The five, as one might anticipate, are the Blacks, Whites, Native Americans, Asiatics and Australian aborigines. The genomic record is quite convincing and combined with other measures of evolution, leave no doubt that evolution is an established biological process which adequately explains all of the living organisms found on Earth, now and in the past. God may have devised this system but it is certain He need not be a hands-on deity that keeps all of creation going. Natural laws including the laws of evolution quite adequately maintain the Universe. As William Ockham (c. 1285--c. 1349) advised some 700 years ago, don't unnecessarily multiply explanations when one will do. The physical and biological laws we have quite adequately maintain the workings of our world.

This brief discussion will suffice for now in defining the role of genetics as one of the bases for the theory of evolution. More will be said regarding molecular biology later.

Chapter 11

The Origin of Life on Earth

We have seen the bases upon which evolutionary theory rests but just how did life begin on Earth in the first place? This is the next step we must take in our search for a solution to the Problem of Evil.

The perennial biological question has been, "How did life on Earth first begin?" It took over a billion years for life to emerge. Many of my doctor friends and classmates have balked at the idea of life arising out of some kind of ancient earthly soup. However, the experiments by Miller and Urey in 1953 simulated Earth's early environment with nothing more than water, hydrogen, ammonia, methane and electrical energy that produced complex organic compounds such as amino acids, the building blocks of proteins.[185] Since then scientists have learned more about the environmental and atmospheric conditions on Earth 3.5 billion years ago and no longer think that the conditions used by Miller and Urey were quite right. However, over time many scientists have performed experiments using more natural environmental conditions and employing alternate scenarios for these reactions believe they have found the secret to the origin of life here on Earth. Such experiments suggest that complex molecules could have formed in the conditions as found on Earth so many billions of years ago.

The earliest evidence for life on Earth comes from fossilized mats of cyanobacteria called stromatolites found in Australia. These early life forms are about 3.4 billion years old. Ancient as their origins are, these bacteria (which are still around today) are already biologically complex—they have cell walls protecting their protein producing DNA—so scientists think life must have begun much earlier, perhaps as early as 3.8 billion years ago. But despite knowing approximately when life first appeared on Earth, scientists are still far from answering how life actually developed. More will be said about this shortly. The answer to this question would not only fill one of the largest gaps in scientists' understanding of nature, but also would have important implications for the likelihood of finding life elsewhere in the Universe.

Today, there are several competing theories for how life arose on Earth. Some question whether life began on Earth at all, asserting instead that it came from a distant world or the heart of a fallen comet or asteroid as Fred Hoyle claims. He calls this panspermia.[186] Some even say life might have arisen here more than once.

Most scientists agree that life went through a period when RNA was the primary molecule, guiding life

---

[185] Miller, Stanley L., Harold C. Urey, 1959, *Organic Compound Synthesis on the Primitive Earth*, Science, 130 (3370): 245–51.

[186] Panspermia, Wikipedia.

through its nascent stages. According to this "RNA World" hypothesis, RNA was the initial molecule for primitive life and only took a backseat when DNA came on the scene. This complex molecule performs much more efficiently than RNA.

RNA is very similar to DNA, and today carries out numerous important functions in each of our cells, acting as a transitional-molecule between DNA and protein synthesis, functioning as an on-and-off switch for some genes.

However, the 'RNA World' hypothesis doesn't explain how RNA itself first arose. Like DNA, RNA is a complex molecule made of repeating units of thousands of smaller molecules called nucleotides that link together in very specific ways. While there are scientists who think RNA could have arisen spontaneously early on, others say the odds of this happening are astronomical.

The RNA World hypothesis got a big boost in 2009. Chemists led by John Sutherland at the University of Cambridge in the United Kingdom reported that they had discovered several relatively simple precursor compounds, namely acetylene and formaldehyde that could undergo a sequence of reactions which produced two of RNA's four nucleotide building blocks. This provided a plausible path to the production of RNA without the need for enzymes in Earth's primordial soup.[187] Critics, however, pointed out that acetylene and formaldehyde are still somewhat complex molecules themselves. According to Sutherland's critics this begs the question of where these early RNA precursors came from.

Subsequently, Sutherland and his colleagues set out to work backward from acetylene and formaldehyde to see if they could find a route to RNA from even more simple starting chemicals. They succeeded in doing so. In a later

[187] Pouder, J. W., Garland, b., and Sutherland, J. D., *Synthesis of activated pyrimidine ribonucleotides in prebiotically plausible conditions,* Nature, vol. 459, May 14, 2009.
[66] Rutherford, A., 2013, *Creation: How Science is Reinventing Life Itself,* Kindle e-book.

issue of Nature Chemistry, Sutherland's team reported that they created nucleic acid precursors starting with just hydrogen cyanide (HCN), hydrogen sulfide (H_2S), and ultraviolet (UV) light. The crash of meteors on early Earth likely generated the hydrogen cyanide and hydrogen sulfide, which may have set off the production of biomolecules needed to make the first cells.

Further, Sutherland showed that the conditions that produce nucleic acid precursors also created the starting materials needed to make natural amino acids and lipids. Amino acids are the building blocks of proteins. Instead of working step by step Sutherland and his colleagues mixed all the primordial ingredients together at once and obtained the beginning building blocks of ancient life. This suggests a single set of reactions could have given rise to life simultaneously. The origin of life seems not to be a stepwise process. Sutherland's approach was reminiscent of Miller and Urey's experiments of the 1950's. Lipids are known to spontaneously form cell walls and the amino acids and nucleosides came out of Sutherland's soup.[188] All these are components of living cells.

Sutherland's team argues that early Earth was a favorable setting for those reactions. HCN is abundant in comets, which rained down steadily for nearly the first several hundred million years of Earth's history. The impacts would also have produced enough energy to synthesize HCN from hydrogen, carbon, and nitrogen. Likewise, Sutherland notes, H_2S was thought to have been plentiful on early Earth, as was the UV radiation that could drive these reactions and the metal-containing minerals that could have catalyzed them; iron and nickel are abundant on Earth. Having said this, Sutherland cautions that the reactions that would have made each of the sets of building blocks are different enough from one another, requiring different metal catalysts, for example, that they likely would not have all occurred in the same location.

188

Rather, he says, slight variations in chemistry and energy may have favored the creation of one set of building blocks over another, such as amino acids or lipids, in different places. "Rainwater would then wash these compounds into a common pool," says Dave Deamer, an origin-of-life researcher at the University of California, Santa Cruz, who wasn't affiliated with Sutherland's research.

Could life have been kindled in that common pool? We may never know for sure, but the idea and the "plausible chemistry" behind it is worth careful consideration.

The Creationist's Rebuttal to Evolution: Religion as Science and Science as Religion

As noted before, creationists use the Bible, and the argument from Intelligent Design[189] as their warrants in support of creationism. In addition to these two proofs, they have raised questions about the validity of evolutionists' research. John MacArthur portrays 'naturalism'[190] as the belief system that supports evolution.[191] He sees 'naturalism' as essentially "anti-theistic" and based on a belief system not supported by scientific experimentation. For example, scientists assume that the laws governing the Universe are the same throughout the Universe but creationists claim this is only an assumption unproven scientifically. Evolutionary theory can, thus, be viewed as a 'secular religion' no different from traditional religious beliefs. Philip Johnson considers naturalism a metaphysical construct just as is religion,

---

[189] Intelligent Design implies that if one finds something that obviously has been designed, there must be a designer. Finding a watch means there must be a watchmaker. The Universe is a magnificently designed infinite structure, therefore, there must be a magnificent, infinite creator i.e. God.

[190] Some use naturalism interchangeably with materialism or atheistic materialism.

[191] Op. cit. MacArthur, J. 2001, p. 11.

though the latter has additional support from Scripture and faith, making it more solidly based than naturalism.[192] Johnson also separates naturalism from science because of its non-empirical, metaphysical character. MacArthur states that 'naturalism' is based on the "presupposition" that there are no supernatural forces at work in the Universe and that this "presupposition" is taken as a matter of faith by scientists. Thus, the theory of evolution, according to MacArthur uses as its warrant, a belief system unsupported by scientific data. MacArthur quotes Paul of Tarsus (Romans, 1:20-22) in describing 'naturalists':

"Professing to be wise, they became fools."

Furthermore, MacArthur speaks of the "spiritual barrenness of naturalism. He goes on to point out the dire consequences of 'naturalism', which, because it denies God, can only lead to immorality and the consequences of immorality, i.e. Hell. A depraved society necessarily follows upon deism or atheism.[193] This is one of the most emotional of all the traditionalists' arguments because in their view the very fabric and continuance of society are threatened by such an anti-theistic system.

Haught in *God and the New Atheism* also asserts that scientists require an unsupported belief system that differs little from religious faith.[194] Haught, however, does accept evolutionary theory. This is a theme basic to the creationist's objections to evolution because if science requires the unproved warrant that Nature is essentially uniform and its laws universal, then the scientific method does not differ from faith-based theology.

Naturalists do not necessarily deny the existence of God. Charles Darwin as a naturalist was a very spiritual person. The Catholic Church does not see evolution and

---

[192] Op. cit. Johnson, P. 2005.

[193] Ibid, p. 15.

[194] Haught, J. F., 2008, *God and the New Atheism* (Louisville, Kentucky: Westminster John Knox Press).

religion as mutually exclusive.[195] Deistic dogma holds to a scheme in which God created both the world and the forces or laws that carry evolution forward.

MacArthur's concerns regarding the association between naturalism and immorality, an issue often raised by religious writers, has not, to my knowledge, ever been shown to be statistically valid. Atheists appear to be as moral, if not more so, than the general population and since most are humanists they may be more attentive to and understanding of the needs of others than some members of fundamental religious groups. In fact, there is some evidence that fundamentalists tend to be more immoral than their atheistic friends. According to one Christian source atheists are more immoral.[196] On the other hand, if one looks at "Ask Atheists" atheists are not more immoral.[197] This latter source states that although 10% of Americans are atheists, only 2% of convicts are Atheists. Convicts, on the other hand, are said to be more often fundamentalists.

MacArthur insists that there is no essential conflict between a literal interpretation of Genesis and current scientific literature.[198] He asserts that the scientific studies, if interpreted properly, confirm the biblical view of creation. As a corollary of this, he condemns "theological liberals" who deny the literal truth of the Bible, because they distort science so as to undermine the word of God. MacArthur maintains that the "day" spoken of in Genesis is, indeed, one, 24-hour day and not some "long age" or epoch.

---

[195] In the 1950 encyclical *Humani generis*, Pope Pius XII confirmed that there is no intrinsic conflict between Christianity and the theory of evolution, provided that Christians believe that the individual soul is a direct creation by God and not the product of purely material forces.

[196] Evidence for God: http://www.godandscience.org/apologetics/atheists_more_immoral.html.

[197] Ask Atheists: http://www.asktheatheists.com/questions/7-are-atheists-immoral.

[198] Op. cit. Haught, J. F., 2008, p. 17.

MacArthur also believes that "all sorts of theological mischief" ensue when one rejects or compromises the literal truth of the Bible.[199] There must have been an Adam and Eve who sinned and were expelled from Paradise for if there were no Fall, there would be no need for redemption nor the God-man, Christ, the Redeemer who died on the cross for our sins. The whole basis of Christianity collapses without the sin of Adam and Eve. Several other basic religious tenets are also undermined if one denies a literal interpretation of the Bible. Divine revelation, divine providence, personal responsibility for our sins and the punishment of Hell all disappear as does personal morality and we are left once again with a corrupt society. The fundamentalists take this as a serious responsibility and are intent on saving the world from such a disaster. MacArthur, also, defends the Bible against attacks based on apparent contradictions found in it.[200]

In sum, MacArthur offers these arguments as a defense against "anti-theistic hypotheses". All the evolutionary claims amount to nothing more than unfounded, speculative hypotheses, not to be believed anymore than the philosophical speculations of the ancient Greeks. It is understandable that creationists wish to preserve the biblical version of creation. Their view of God and religion are at stake and these concepts are the major underpinnings for both their spiritual and to a large extend their emotional and intellectual lives. However, the scientific bases of evolution would seem very solid and not founded solely on the Bible and faith, as is the case with creationism. As one example, the idea that scientists assume rather than know that natural laws are uniform throughout the Universe is not true. With the current astronomical techniques we have, it is possible to look far into the Universe both temporally and physically. We can look back in time nearly to the Big Bang and, in fact, with

199   Ibid, p. 19.

200   Ehrman, Bart, 2009, *Misquoting Jesus*, Kindle ebook.

the physical evidence of the cosmic microwave background (CMB) as discovered by American radio astronomers Arno Penzias and Robert Wilson in 1964, we can look into space and back in time some 13 billion light years verifying that the same laws not only exist all over the Universe but have existed also in time since the beginning of the Universe.

Table X
Evolutionary Timeline
Time   Event
Million years ago (mya)
4600 mya: Earth formed.
3500-2800 mya: Prokaryotic unicellular organisms develop.
3500-2800 mya: Beginning of photosynthesis by blue-green algae putting oxygen into the atmosphere.
1500 mya: Eukaryotic unicellular organisms develop with cell nucleus.
1500-600 mya: Evolution of multicellular organisms.
580-545 mya: Ediacaran multicellular organisms evolve.
540 mya: Cambrian explosion of hard-bodied organisms.
500-450 mya: Appearance of fish; the first vertebrates.
430 mya: Waxy coated algae begin to live on land.
420 mya: Millipedes evolve as first land animals.
375 mya: Appearance of primitive sharks.
350-300 mya: Appearance of amphibians.
350 mya: Primitive insects appear.
350 mya: Primitive ferns evolve--first plants with roots.
300-200 mya: Reptiles first appear.
300 mya: Winged insects evolve.
280 mya: Beetles and weevils evolve.
250 mya: Permian period: major mass extinction.
230 mya: Roaches and termites evolve.

225 mya: Modern ferns evolve.
225 mya: Bees evolve.
200 mya: Pangaea starts to break apart. Continents form.
200 mya: Primitive crocodiles evolve.
200 mya: Appearance of first mammals.
145 mya: Archaeopteryx walks on the Earth. First dinosaurs.
136 mya: Primitive kangaroos evolve.
100 mya: Primitive cranes evolve.
90 mya: Modern sharks evolve.
65 mya: K-T Boundary; extinction of the dinosaurs and beginning of the dominance of mammals.
60 mya: Rats, mice, and squirrels evolve. Birds are only remnants of dinosaurs.
60 mya: Herons and storks evolve.
55 mya: Rabbits and hares evolve.
50 mya: Primitive monkeys evolve.
28 mya: Koalas[201] evolve.
20 mya: Parrots and pigeons evolve.
20-12 mya: The chimpanzee and other hominids evolve.
10-4 mya: Ramapithecus[202] evolves.
4 mya: Development of hominid bipedalism (walk on two feet).
4-1 mya: Australopithecines evolve.
3.5 mya: Prehistoric Lucy, *Australopithecus afarensis* walks the Earth.
2 mya: Widespread use of stone tools.
2-0.01 mya: Most recent ice age.
1.6-0.2 mya: *Homo erectus* evolves.
1-0.5 mya: *Homo erectus* tames fire.
0.5 mya: *Homo neanderthalensis* evolves.

0.2-0.03 mya: Archaic *Homo sapiens* evolves.
0.05 mya: *Homo sapiens* (modern humans) evolve. Leaves Africa.
0.055-0.012 mya: *Homo sapiens* enter Australia and North America. Neanderthals go extinct.
0.04-0.02 mya: *Homo sapiens* begin cave paintings.
0.025-0.01 mya: Most recent glaciation.
0.012 *Homo sapiens* domesticates cattle, sheep, goats and dogs. Agriculture begins.
0.01 mya: First permanent *Homo sapiens* settlements.
0.01 mya: *Homo sapiens* learn to use fire to cast copper, iron, silver, gold and make ceramic pottery.
0.006 mya: Writing is developed in Sumerian.

Table X above reviews the extensive empirical evidence that helps to verify the theory of evolution. These various fossil finds from all over the world and dating to the very beginning of life on Earth some 3.5 billion years ago are extensive and though there may be some variability in these data, it is very unlikely that evolution could be just a "belief system" as are religious and theological "belief systems". There is just too much empiric, truly scientific data.

Chapter 12
How Evolution Solves the Problem of Evil

In its simplest form evolutionary theory resolves the Problem of Evil by providing all species with challenges that force them to adapt and improve or go extinct. Without such challenges we would all still be bacteria.

---

[201] Kaolas: a bearlike arboreal Australian marsupial that has thick gray fur and feeds on eucalyptus leaves.

[202] *Ramapithicus:* an extinct anthropoid ape of the Miocene epoch, known from remains found in southwestern Asia, East Africa, and are ancestral to the orangutan.

Whether your God is theistic or deistic He has created an evolutionary world full of evil because suffering is necessary for us humans to become better, stronger, smarter, more resourceful and more moral. The Universe came into existence some 13.8 billion years ago. We know this now because astrophysical empirical studies have proven this to be the case. Earth and the Sun were formed 4.6 billion years ago. The Earth gradually cooled and life began to emerge on Earth 3.5 billion years ago and there was a flowering of flora and fauna 540 million years ago. Mammals emerged 50 million BCE and apes around the time the dinosaurs disappeared 64 million years ago. Hominids, including primates, our earliest ancestors, came on the scene six to eight million years ago having branched off from the apes. The hominids include the Australopithicines such as *Australopithecus afarensis* and all species of the genus, *Homo* including *Homo habilis, H. erectus,* and others. See table 10. These species, the homonyms, have been the most direct ancestors of us humans. All members of the genus *Homo* walked upright on two feet. *Homo sapiens* is the last living species of the genus *Homo.* Humans have been around for 200,000 to 160,000 years and became dominant 50,000 years ago. All of these developments speak to the evolutionary nature of the world and its creatures.

Life began with primitive bacteria; the so-called prokaryotes, that had no nucleus in its cell. Next in the evolutionary line came the eukaryotes that possessed a nucleus. This nucleus was home to all their DNA as is the case for humans today. In time multicellular organisms developed, then invertebrates such as insects, followed by vertebrates including sharks and fishes, amphibians that live in the sea as well as roaming on land. Soon there were reptiles of many sorts including alligators, iguanas, lizards, and snakes. The marsupials that hold their offspring in a pouch after birth are still seen in Australia and elsewhere. Then came mammals of many sort and finally humans.

Table?
Comparative table of *Homo* species[203]

Species	Temporal range Mya	Habitat	Adult height	Adult mass	Cranial capacity (cm³)	Fossil record	Discovery / publication of name
H. habilis	2.1 – 1.4[31]	Africa	150 cm (4 ft. 11 in)	33–55 kg (73–121 lbs.)	510–660	Many	1960/1964
H. erectus	1.9 – 0.07 [32]	Africa, Eurasia (Java, China, India, Caucasus)	180 cm (5 ft. 11 in)	60 kg (130 lb.)	850 (early) – 1,100 (late)	Many[33]	1891/1892
H. rudolfensis membership in *Homo* uncertain	1.9	Kenya			700	2 sites	1972/1986
H. gautengensis also classified as *H. habilis*	1.9 – 0.6	South Africa	100 cm (3 ft. 3 in)			3 individuals[34]	2010/2010
H. ergaster also classified as *H. erectus*	1.8 – 1.3[35]	Eastern and Southern Africa			700–850	Many	1975
H. antecessor also classified as *H. heidelbergensis*	1.2 – 0.8	Spain	175 cm (5 ft. 9 in)	90 kg (200 lbs.)	1,000	2 sites	1997
H. cepranensis a single fossil, *H. erectus*	0.9 – 0.35	Italy			1,000	1 skull cap	1994/2003
H. heidelbergensis	0.6 – 0.35	Europe, Africa, China	180 cm (5 ft. 11 in)	90 kg (200 lbs.)	1,100–1,400	Many	1908
H. neanderthalensis possibly a subspecies of *H. sapiens*	0.35 – 0.04[37]	Europe, Western Asia	170 cm (5 ft. 7 in)	55–70 kg (121–154 lbs.) (heavily built)	1,200–1,900	Many	(1829)/1864

203 Wikipedia: hominids.

H. rhodesiensis also classified as H. heidelbergensis	0.3 – 0.12	Zambia			1,300	Very few	1921
H. tsaichangensis possibly H. erectus	0.25 – 0.2	Taiwan				1 individual	pre-2008/2015
H. sapiens (modern humans)	0.2[38] – present	Worldwide	150 - 190 cm (4 ft. 7 in - 6 ft. 3 in)	50–100 kg (110–220 lbs.)	950–1,800	(extant)	—/1758
H. floresiensis classification uncertain	0.10 – 0.012	Indonesia	100 cm (3 ft. 3 in)	25 kg (55 lbs.)	400	7 individuals	2003/2004
Denisova hominin possible H. sapiens subspecies or hybrid	0.04	Russia				1 site	

Table ? Hominins.

All evolution was and is, a gradually progressive process. This is how God, if you will, devised the world. He made nature a world of woes so that all species beginning with the bacteria had to adapt to their environment in order to survive and, since the world is continuously changing, individuals and thus their several species had to get stronger and smarter than the other species they were battling, in order to stay alive. It is a world of ever improving individuals and species. Those that met this persistent challenge lived and those that did not, went extinct. So we humans as the dominant species made it because we were able to meet the evils of our environment. If you believe in a God, theistic, deistic or otherwise, this is why God made the world so difficult for us. If He hadn't we would not be her today. We would all still be unicellular bacteria.

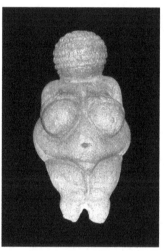

Figure 17. Venus of Willendorfd

We have been getting smarter and more sophisticated since then. We learned how to start fires; make simple tools such as axes; created ornaments including necklaces and bracelets; devised clothes and even developed carve art; and sculpted figures of women. Most of these figurines date from the Gravettian period (22,000–28,000 years ago), but examples exist from as early as 35,000 years ago (Venus of Hohle Fels,) and as late as the Venus of Monruz, from about 11,000 years ago.

These figurines were carved from soft stone (such as steatite, calcite or limestone), bone, ivory, or formed of clay and fired. The last are among the oldest ceramics known. In total, over a hundred such figurines are known; virtually all of modest size, between 4 cm and 25 cm (one eighth to one foot) in height. They are some of the earliest works of prehistoric art. There are figurines dating to 25,000 BCE. These statuettes have been titled according to where they were discovered. The most famous is the Venus of Willendorf. These many accomplishments of *Homo sapiens* give us some idea of the gradual growth of human characteristics and why *H. sapiens* became the dominant species on Earth. Humans have met, struggled with and overcome the many 'evils' they faced over the past hundreds of thousands of years, just as their predecessors have.

Neanderthals appeared around 500,000 BCE and comingled with humans in certain parts of the world, including present day Europe, until around 40,000 BCE, though some paleontologists believe they persisted until 25,000 BCE. It is uncertain as to why they died out and humans flourished.[204] Some authors believe that humans may have simply outsmarted them. Neanderthals, however, may have been physically stronger than humans and they had brains larger than humans: 1400 cm versus 1200 cm. Other authors suggest that a changing, colder climate made life difficult for the Neanderthals and they went extinct as a result. However, Neanderthals were stockier than

---

[204] Finlayson, Clive, 2015,*The Humans Who Went Extinct: Why Neanderthals Died Out and We Survived*, Kindle e-book.

humans, which should have made them more tolerant of cold.[205] The Neanderthals did bury their dead and there is some evidence they believed in an afterlife and thus were religious. Also, it is likely had developed language.[206]

Humankind's evolution has been indeed remarkable in many ways. As we have seen our world is full of evil but it seems we have been, over the centuries, gradually improving our lot. From what we know of prehistory, humans began as cave dwelling clans that numbered only a few dozen members per clan. The clan was our home and our security. Without the clan life was not possible. It made life, security, love and the hunting and gathering of food possible. But clans often fought each other for the territory necessary to produce and maintain life. Except for seeking wives from other clans and at times cooperating for the mutual benefit of our and other clans, things could get pretty dicey and we see such clan or tribal wars ongoing even today only on a larger scale. It seems as though humans continue to kill each other at an ever-increasing rate. -→Watching the news nightly it seems that religious, national and local wars continue throughout the world on a larger scale as in the Mid East or on a smaller scale in in the United States, France, or elsewhere. Steven Pinker in his, *The Better Angels of Our Nature: Why Violence Has Declined*, claims that since the Middle Ages violence has lessened over the centuries and he provides fairly solid evidence to support his view.[207] Nonetheless, we have maintained clannishness with larger groups but sticking to our clans whether family, local, national, racial or other clans. The clan is genetically hardwired within each of us.

---

[205] Stockier means less skin surface per body mass so they lose less heat than taller people with more skin surface per body mass in which case they radiate more body heat and tolerate warm weather better.

[206] Arsuaga, Juan Luis, 2015, *The Neanderthal's Necklace: In Search of the First Thinkers*, Kindle ebook.

[207] Pinker, S., 2011, *The Better Angels of Our Nature: Why Violence Has Declined*, Penguin Group, Kindle e-book.

Pain and the Problem of Evil

In spite of all these advances humans have managed to achieve, there remain many aspects of our lives that continue to impede what we consider a joyous, happy life. Pain is one of the nagging problems that we would like to rid ourselves of completely. As children a minor tumble would trigger a crying spell and vaccinations might initiate a flood of tears. A spanking, even if deserved, did the same. Pain is never welcome. As we grow older there are a host of pains that disturb a comfortable life. A broken bone, emotional turmoil, a bellyache or a nagging backache are all unwelcome discomforts.

In spite of these many painful interludes there is something to be said for pain: it alerts us to the need for pain relief. The majority of these pains tell us we need to do something to relieve the pain. As mentioned earlier, patients that have lost the sense of pain to a leg, may suffer numerous injuries to their ankle and foot that go unnoticed and over time lead to permanent damage to the extremity making it unsuited for walking. This is called a Charcot's ankle or foot. Pain tells us that it is time to avoid future injuries and to do something about the injury when it occurs. This is true for chest pain that may indicate a heart attack. Belly pain may mean cholecystitis (gallbladder inflammation and gallstones), a gastric ulcer or diverticulitis of the colon and many more ills that can be very serious and often need immediate attention. Many of these illnesses like appendicitis can lead to death if untreated. Personally I once had cholecystitis that was misdiagnosed resulting in rupture of the gallbladder and generalized infection of the abdomen and near death. Fortunately, everything came out OK.

Emotional pain indicates the need to adjust ones life in some way. Our relationships with a spouse, parents, kids, colleagues or friends may stir emotional 'pains' that tell us we need to adjust our thoughts or behaviors. Emotional

249

pain can be beneficial personally and in our relations with others. Depression can be so 'painful' that some seek suicide as an answer, though obviously there are very good treatments for depression that are lifesaving.

Pain as an evil can provide lifesaving stimuli to better health and a better life.

Sociobiology

Sociobiology is a concept that E. O. Wilson fostered in the twentieth century[208]. It deals with the evolutionary aspects of social behavior. Just as strength, intelligence, tools, fire to cook food, language etc. provide natural selective advantages for humans, so too social behaviors help people to have more children that live longer and thus perpetuate the species. Sociobiology has many critics who believe that genetically controlled sociology smacks of determinism and anti-feminism. However, it makes sense that evolution must have social aspects since the manner of our social interactions must have many effects on how well we do as individuals and as a species. The way we work, play, and emote with one another makes a difference in how well and how long we and our children survive. We need only look at ants and bees as E. O. Wilson did to see what a major effect socialization has on a species. Ants and bees have very complex social systems. Some of their members have no sexual interactions but through the 'work' they provide for the ant colony or beehive has a major impact on both the day to day functioning of the colony as well as the genetic constitution of the colony or hive. Some individual ants or bees actually give up their lives to maintain the species. This same might be said of the military that defend our homeland.

The same principles apply to the human species. What we do for ourselves and for others can impact the human community as a whole. Even if we bear no

---

[208] Wilson, E.O., 1975, *Sociobiology: The New Synthesis*, Kindle ebook.

children, we help the species persist and grow. Relatives including grandparents, aunts, uncles, friends of the family, and gay couples all play a social role in helping the species flourish. There is evidence that as humans lived longer, grandparents provided an ever-increasing role in maintaining our species.[209]

Just as humans have evolved in terms of art, clothing, ornaments, tools and other utilities, so too we have evolved socially. Social evolution is an essential aspect of human progress. Without socialization we would not be truly human. Socialization has been part of human nature for many eons beginning with the earliest hominids. But socialization is not limited to humans; it began with many ancient species. Societies are found in species from ants to zebras. To prosper and survive it is necessary for many species to develop a complex social structure that supports them as a group.

In 1975, Edward O. Wilson published his landmark book, *Sociobiology. The New Synthesis.*[210] Wilson was an evolutionist believing, along with Darwin, that the Universe is an ever-evolving system. Earth likewise is an ever-changing planet including its geology, flora and fauna. Wilson suggested that just as humans continue to evolve physically and intellectually, so too humans are evolving socially. Wilson first wrote about the social life of ants.[211] He then extended his studies to include a number of animal species. The ants were what he calls 'eusocial' meaning that they have but one female that bore all ant offspring. Many members of an ant society are sterile but provide support for the ant colony as a whole. All members of the colony contribute to the maintenance of the ant society. Much of

[209] Balter, Michael, *Why We're Different: Probing the Gap Between Apes and Humans*, Science 25 January 2008: 404-405.

[210] Ibid. Wilson, E. O., 1975.

[211] Hölldobler Bert & Wilson, Edward O., 2010, *The Leafcutter Ants: Civilization* Kindle e-book.

this support appears to be based on preservation of the ants' gene pool. Zebras on the other hand are not eusocial. Zebras live together in tight herds. Because of their black and white strips, when they run together and are attacked by lions, it is difficult for the lions to distinguish one zebra from another making it hard for a lion to choose which zebra to pounce on. I have seen the migration of thousands of animals through the Masai Mara national reserve in Kenya, Africa, which includes thousands of zebras and lions. Zebras seem to escape slaughter much better than deer do because of the confusion their stripes provide. So it is that various 'societies' provide benefit for their members. Likewise lions and wolves do better when preying on various animals by hunting in prides or packs. Different forms of societies offer benefits in a variety of ways. Wilson extended his study of societies ultimately to *Homo sapiens.* In *Sociobiology* he explains how social groups contribute to evolutionary natural selection.

Sociobiology has not been without its critics among them Stephen J. Gould, a Harvard colleague of Wilson's. At one point some opponents of sociobiology dumped cold water over Wilson at a conference he was attending, taunting him with chants of, "You are all wet! You are all wet!" Sociobiology has also been labeled, evolutionary psychology, a term to which Wilson does not object.

Wilson began by studying, ant colonies. Ants, wasps, termites and sixteen other insect species are eusocial. After determining the natural selective advantage these species obtained from their various social structures, Wilson moved on to the study of social elements that provide evolutionary advantages for humans. As with insects, humans helping humans seems to offer the potential for increased individual and consequently group survival. The numbers of additional human births and extended lives did provide evolutionary natural selective advantages.

John Alcock in, *Triumph of Sociobiology*, reviews
Wilson's work and offers a defense of sociobiology.[212] A
major criticism of sociobiology has been its perceived
genetic determinism that is said to be a major element
of sociobiology. Stephen J. Gould and others claim that
sociobiology supports a strict genetic determinism. Thus,
freewill is thereby limited and certain cultural mores
are etched in stone. Some feminists feel that sociobiology
would support an inferior social position for woman.
The anti-sociobiologists believe human nature is a blank
slate on which any cultural norms can be written thus
allowing for ever-improving social structure for all people
no matter what their socio-economic, gender, physical
strength or educational class. Rather than worsening
women's lot, sociobiology will improve it over time
because as women improve their status our species will
become stronger more adaptive to change thus making
for better and longer living humans. Women not only bear
our children but they are the primary nurturers and care
takers of the young. They provide a special role in society
that creates a stronger, more durable humanity. Alcock
denies that sociobiology means woman will suffer under
this genetically based system. He sees sociobiology as an
evolutionary process promoting natural selective changes
that make for a continually improving social structure,
a stronger species and an ever-improving human race.
Wilson claims this is how *Homo sapiens* became the world's
dominant species and Alcock believes that the debate
has been settled in favor of sociobiology. At bottom it
seems that evolutionary psychology (sociobiology) can
claim a solid scientific basis for its system. We do live
in an evolutionary world and most aspects of human
life seem solidly founded on Darwin's natural selection
and humankind's gradual genetic and cultural growth,
otherwise we would have faded from the scene long ago.

---

[212] Alcock, John, 2003, *Triumph of Sociobiology*, Kindle e-book.

It seems that our genes, culture, social behaviors and institutions have arisen out of random but not haphazard genetic happenings. Genes and adjustments to the environment have allowed us to hang around so long by promoting the birth of more babies that live longer and better. Though genes and environment may be random events our responses to genetic and environmental changes are not. Natural selection requires we either sink or swim.

Richard Dawkins has been helpful in supporting sociobiology although he doesn't always specify sociobiology as the concept he is defending. In *The Selfish Gene*,[213] Dawkins provides a well worked out defense of Darwinian natural selection.

The point in question here relates to random natural selective events, which are the essential feature of evolution. Because virtually all events that impact humans are random and not directed by a divine being, many of these events cause suffering or some kind of evil. But it is these evils that have helped us humans and all other species evolve to a higher level. Either we adapt to difficult environmental circumstances or we will go extinct. The fact is that there have been millions of species over the 3.5 billion years that life has been on Earth and over 90% of these species are now extinct. The world is always changing and all species must change, i.e. evolve to meet these changes or it is sayonara.

The Molecular Biology of Life

→The perennial biological question has been, "How did life on Earth first begin?" It took over a billion years for life to emerge. Many of my doctor friends and classmates

---

[213] Dawkins, Richard, 1990, *The Selfish Gene*, Kindle ebook. This is a well-done book that supports sociobiology although genes can't be selfish. This is an anthropomorphism that doesn't apply to unconscious human elements. It does reflect the notion of natural selection, however.

have balked at the idea of life arising out of some kind of ancient earthly soup. However, the experiments by Miller and Urey in 1953 simulated Earth's early environment with nothing more than water, hydrogen, ammonia, methane and electrical energy that produced complex organic compounds such as amino acids.[214] Since then scientists have learned more about the environmental and atmospheric conditions on Earth 3.5 billions years ago and no longer think that the conditions used by Miller and Urey were quite right. However, over time many scientists have performed experiments using more natural environmental conditions and alternate scenarios for these reactions. Such experiments suggest that complex molecules could have formed in the conditions as found on Earth so many billions of years ago.

The earliest evidence for life on Earth comes from fossilized mats of cyanobacteria called stromatolites in Australia that are about 3.4 billion years old. Ancient as their origins are, these bacteria, which are still around today, were already biologically complex—they have cell walls protecting their protein-producing DNA—and scientists think such life must have begun much earlier, perhaps as early as 3.8 billion years ago. But despite knowing approximately when life first appeared on Earth, scientists are still far from answering the question of how life actually developed The answer would not only fill one of the largest gaps in scientists' understanding of nature, but would have important implications for the likelihood of finding life elsewhere in the Universe.

Today, there are several competing theories for how life arose on Earth. Some question whether life began on Earth at all, asserting instead that life came from some distant

---

[214] Miller, Stanley L., Urey, Harold C. 1959, "Organic Compound Synthesis on the Primitive Earth", Science, 130 (3370): 245–51.

world on a comet or asteroid, as Fred Hoyle claims.[215] Some even say life might have arisen here more than once.

Most scientists agree that life went through a period when RNA[216] was the primary molecule, guiding life through its nascent stages. According to this "RNA World" hypothesis, RNA was the initial molecule for primitive life and only took a backseat when DNA[217] came on the scene. This complex molecule performs much more efficiently than RNA.

RNA is similar to DNA, and today carries out numerous important functions in each of our body's trillions of cells, acting as a transitional-molecule between DNA and proteins. DNA provides the pattern for proteins and RNA carries the information to the ribosomes that make the proteins. The proteins are the 'worker bees' of our body and keep our body going. RNA also functions as an on-and-off switch for some of our genes. This is all very complex but generally works well in keeping our body functioning well. DNA is where mutations take place a make evolution by natural selection possible.

However, the 'RNA World' hypothesis doesn't explain how RNA itself first developed. Like DNA, RNA is a complex molecule made of repeating units of thousands of smaller molecules called nucleotides that link together in very specific ways. While there are scientists who think RNA could have arisen spontaneously early on Earth, others say the odds of this happening are astronomical.

The RNA World hypothesis got a big boost in 2009. Chemists led by John Sutherland at the University of Cambridge in the United Kingdom reported that they had discovered several relatively simple precursor compounds, namely acetylene and formaldehyde that could undergo a sequence of reactions which produced two of RNA's four

---

[215] Hoyle, Fred, & Wickramasinghe, Chandra, 1984, *Evolution from Space*, Kindle ebook.

[216] RNA: ribonucleic acid.

[217] DNA: deoxyribonucleic acid.

nucleotide building blocks. This provided a plausible path to the production of RNA without the need for enzymes in Earth's primordial soup.[218] Critics, though, pointed out that acetylene and formaldehyde are still somewhat complex molecules themselves. According to Sutherland's critics this begged the question of where these early RNA precursors came from.

Subsequently, Sutherland and his colleagues set out to work backward from acetylene and formaldehyde to see if they could find a route to RNA from even less complex starting materials. They succeeded in doing so. In a later issue of Nature Chemistry, Sutherland's team reported that they created nucleic acid precursors starting with just hydrogen cyanide (HCN), hydrogen sulfide (H_2S), and ultraviolet (UV) light. The crash of meteors on early Earth likely generated the hydrogen cyanide and hydrogen sulfide, which may have set off the production of biomolecules needed to make the first cells.

Further, Sutherland showed that the conditions that produce nucleic acid precursors also create the starting materials needed to make natural amino acids and lipids. Instead of working step by step he and his colleagues mixed the primordial ingredients together all at once and obtained the beginning building blocks of ancient life. This suggests a single set of reactions could have given rise to life. The origin of life seems not to be a stepwise process. Sutherland's approach is reminiscent of Miller and Urey's experiments from the 1950's. In addition, lipids are known to spontaneously form cell walls that enclose the amino acids and nucleosides found in Sutherland's soup.[219]

Sutherland's team argues that early Earth was a favorable setting for these reactions. HCN is abundant

---

[218] Pouder, J. W., Garland, B., and Sutherland, J. D. Synthesis of Activated Pyrimidine Ribonucleotides in Prebiotically Plausible Conditions, Nature, vol. 459, May 14, 2009.

[219] Rutherford, A., 2013, *Creation: How Science is Reinventing Life Itself,* Kindle ebook.

in comets, which rained down steadily for nearly the first several hundred million years of Earth's history.[220] The impacts would also have produced enough energy to synthesize HCN from hydrogen, carbon, and nitrogen. Likewise, Sutherland notes, H_2S is thought to have been abundant on Earth, as was the UV radiation that could drive these reactions. Metal-containing minerals that catalyzed these reactions would also have been abundant. Iron and nickel are the primary minerals found on Earth.

Having said this, Sutherland cautions that the reactions that would have made the building blocks of life are different enough from one another that they likely would not have all occurred in the same location on Earth. Rather, he says, slight variations in chemistry and energy may have favored the creation of one set of building blocks, such as amino acids or lipids, in different places. "Rainwater would then wash these [disparate] compounds into a common pool," says Dave Deamer, an origin-of-life researcher at the University of California, Santa Cruz, who wasn't affiliated with Sutherland's research.

Could life have been kindled in that common pool? We may never know for sure, but the idea and the "plausible chemistry" behind these reactions is worth careful thought.

So Here We Are

The fact that humans abide and survive on Earth is self-evident. That we and our ancestors have been around for several million years is well established, although all the details of the road we took to get here are not entirely worked out, nonetheless, modern science has laid out a convincing road map for how we have made our way so far. We know with a high degree of certitude how life started, what a struggle it has been for life to even get going— taking a billion years to do so—and what a complicated

---

[220] Ibid.

unpaved, bumpy road it has been. Starting with very simple one-celled organisms that consisted of only amino acids, nucleosides, RNA and a simple lipid covering to hold all these chemicals together. From these simple beginnings we have evolved into a rather complex organism with trillions of cells and many sophisticated functions There was no DNA and no nucleus to house the RNA. In time DNA evolved because it allowed the cell to grow, divide and replicate more efficiently and thus produce more cells better and faster. Life had begun and it begun to evolve upwardly. The first life was relatively simple but it was able to stay alive in its environment. Soon, however, primitive life began to demonstrate its ability to cope with its ever-changing environment. As it is said: "The one constant in the world is change." Life is continuously faced with change and change means challenges. Challenges are often viewed as evils. The other truism about life is that living beings must continually adapt to this ever-changing environment. If an organism fails to do so, it will fail to survive. Without adaptation to the 'evils', extinction is life's final end. As noted earlier, over 90% of all species that have lived on Earth are now extinct. Life is an endless battle. Because the world is always evolving, we too must always evolve.

Now we come back to the Problem of Evil. Change comes in many forms. We are first embryos, then babies, children, teenagers, adults, middle aged, elderly and finally we die. Theists believe we go to Heaven after death if we have been generally moral during our life on Earth. Of all these stages of life the last is the only one that is not certain. It is a matter of faith not science as to whether we have a life after death.

Just as each individual evolves throughout life, *H. sapiens* evolves as a species. Though the Bible tells us that God created all things in six days, with humans coming into being on the sixth day and all this accomplished simply by the word of God. God spoke the words and there was Adam and Eve with no preliminary HCN, H_2S, nucleosides or nucleotides, no UV light or lightening. The first humans just popped into existence. This is all simple but specious. The world is much more complicated than the Bible makes it out to be. One has to remember that the OT was written 2000 to 3000 years ago and the NT 2000 to 1500 years ago with many revisions and copying errors. Changes were often made based on the theological views of the scribes who were doing the copying. Even more important, the science of the day was little more than rationalizations based on anecdotal observations lacking any semblance of modern empiricism. Things have changed monumentally in the past 500 years since Copernicus figured out the Sun was the center of our Solar System and the Universe came out of the Big Bang 13.8 billion years ago. The Greek atomists posited an infinite number of variously shaped miniscule atoms whose shapes determined the characteristics of the substances they formed. Now we have protons, neutrons, electrons, quarks, Higgs bosons, neutrinos and many more physical particles.

The way we look at God has also changed. God, too, is more complex. In Antiquity the Sun, Moon and planets were all considered divine. The planets are, in fact, all named after ancient gods. The gods were polytheistic and very anthropomorphic. They were bigger and better than we humans but just as emotional, frivolous, oversexed and given to anger, jealousy and murderous behavior as we humans are. Some of these personality traits are found in the OT God and maintained in medieval and present day theology.

As modern physics emerged with Isaac Newton, God became more mechanical and deterministic. The World looked like one huge series of billiard balls. Even Einstein said famously in the early twentieth century, said, "God doesn't play dice." But then along came quantum physics a discipline that Einstein helped to create and Einstein had to eat his words. Werner Heisenberg in 1927 discovered that if an observer of a given particle determined its position, its momentum (mass X velocity) is unknown. We can't know both position and momentum. If you know one you can't know the other. In other words, we cannot know everything about a particle at one and the same time. There are always physical unknowns. Then it was discovered that certain objects only come into existence when someone looked for them. It was also observed that there were physical particles that would come into existence for no apparent reason and similarly go out of existence for no evident reason. The entire Universe became probabilistic. There were no absolute certainties in the Universe. There were only statistical probabilities that certain things may happen at any given time or place. One could only predict that there was a percentage chance that a given event would happen at any given time or place. We now are faced with a world without absolutes. With Newton the world was totally deterministic and now Heisenberg and others tell us the world is one big crapshoot. This is very unsettling for many of us.

Now we have Darwin's concept of evolution by natural selection. The world, including us humans, had not come into existence by a few divine words. Every living thing has developed by the random interactions of primordial elements and chemicals. Living beings turn out to be combinations of lipids, RNA, DNA and a host of other cellular elements coming together randomly. If these random combinations over time allow an organism to manage in their continuously changing environment, then their species will hang around for a time, sometimes for millions of years. Yes, the world is much more complex and so is the way it and we evolve.

Evolution is a reality. There is no doubt about this. It is a scientifically established fact. But why is there evolution and what does it all mean? I believe there is a God or if you will, a 'higher power' but I don't believe in a theistic God. I would go with a deistic God that started the Universe and its rule and regulations—its laws—but what is God and how does He, She or It fit into this evolutionary world of ours. This is the ultimate $64,000 question. Does the world have a beginning and if so how does the theistic God or any other type of God fit into the origin and organization of our Universe?

We do not know if the world is a created or uncreated entity. If it is created, how did this come about? Who or what cause the Big Bang? The age-old answer to this question has been God. Just how did God manage this monumental moment? As we have seen, according to the traditional Biblical account God just spoke a word and the Universe suddenly came into existence. But the world as demonstrated is very complex and it didn't just pop into being. It and we evolved from more primitive states taking billions of years to do so. In fact, we are still being created and we are still evolving. If you side with a secular view of evolution, matter is mysterious and the more we study it the more mysterious it seems. Mater, as we know it today, can even explain what for centuries we have labeled our spiritual side or soul. This is a monistic view of Nature that avoids the "mind-body" dichotomy that has frustrated so many philosopher and theologians for centuries. On the other hand, the dualists, the philosophers and theologians that maintain there are two worlds, one material and one spiritual and these two realms or magistaria, as Stephen J. Gould labels them, are forever separate but in some way united as Descartes claims.

We, it seems, live in a "cause and effect" world. Every action or event has its cause. So the world must have had a cause. Thus, we have the God of the Bible. Aristotle believed the 'stuff' of the world was uncreated but was organized by an "uncaused cause'. The ancient Greeks generally believed in a cosmos that began as an uncaused 'soup' that was finally organized by a maternal deity, Gaea or Mother Earth. With the emergence of monotheism, God was the creator of everything though the Christian Trinity is said to be one God composted of three divine, consubstantial persons, God the Father, Christ and the Holy Spirit. The Christian Trinity is claimed not to be polytheistic.

Because we seem to live in a 'cause and effect' world it is hard for us to accept or conceive of an uncreated cosmogony. Whether created or uncreated, for the moment we are unable to imagine such world. We may never find the answer to the why of the Universe even though we seem to know much of the when and how of our vast Universe.

Having said this, we now must return to the Problem of Evil. We live in an evolving cosmos. It is always evolving and this means continuous change and this in turn means that we, and every living thing on Earth must change or go extinct. For us humans, change is not always pleasant. There are events that have occurred on Earth that have been pleasant and seemingly helpful and some not so helpful it seems. There have been multiple ice ages with intervening interglacial periods. The glacial and interglacial periods last thousands of years. We have been in an interglacial or warming period for about 12,000 years. When it is warmer we humans can spread out over the Earth and when colder we are limited to warmer regions that are closer to the equator. When it is colder life is more difficult and when warmer life is easier. We suffer more when the environment is colder. Food is harder to obtain and hunting may be more difficult. When warmer agriculture is easier. There may be wetter and dryer periods that affect our lives. There are thousands of such environmental events that make life easier or harder. These may be considered evil happenings. Why God made the world so changeable and therefore so difficult is part of the Problem of Evil. Evolution as a fact of life can only be explained as a progressive process that is integral to us as an ever improving species. If the world were strictly stable so too would all living beings. We and all other species would still be a primordial soup or at best one celled bacteria. It is likely there would be only bacteria, but no invertebrates, vertebrates, mammals or humans. we and all living things would have never come into existence. God of whatever sort had to make a world full of challenges, suffering, and evil or I would not be here typing away at my computer. Thus, unless we believe that a static, stationary earthly soup is good enough, then there must be change, suffering and evil.

This solution to the Problem of Evil doesn't solve all the philosophical, theological or scientific problems we face every day but it does at least offer us a better world in the future. Maybe this is what God and we really want. In the end, this all depends on how we, as individuals, view the world around us.

This solution does allow room for a God of any type. Whether it is the deistic God that makes the rules and then lets the world go on its merry way, or the theistic God that is involved in all aspects of the world and our lives, this solution to the Problem of Evil works because God is responsible for what we call evil. However, is really a stimulus for us to improve and ultimately live a better life. These may be thought of as sufferings, discomforts, or inconveniences but these 'evils' are all good because they challenge us and through the vehicle of evolution make us better beings. I don't know what it is like being a bacterium but I prefer being a not so perfect human being that faces challenges each day.

One aspect of this evolutionary solution to the Problem of Evil relates to the sociobiology. [221] Sociobiology as you recall is an evolved genetic and cultural predisposition to helping our fellow human beings gets better as a member of *Homo sapiens*. God has made us not only evolutionary creatures allowing us to do most of the battling with our constantly changing environment but it seems He wants us to help out our family, friends and neighbors in their struggles as well. David Hume (1711 –1776) speaks of

---

[221] http://beliefcloset.com/wp-content/uploads/2010/05/Virtues-The-Master-List.pdf

Printed in the United States
By Bookmasters